Engaging Neighbors and Nations

Engaging Neighbors and Nations

Factors Shaping Local Church Involvement in Mission

TIM SILBERMAN

Foreword by Michael W. Goheen

☙PICKWICK *Publications* · Eugene, Oregon

ENGAGING NEIGHBORS AND NATIONS
Factors Shaping Local Church Involvement in Mission

Copyright © 2024 Tim Silberman. All rights reserved. Except for brief quotations in critical publications or reviews, no part of this book may be reproduced in any manner without prior written permission from the publisher. Write: Permissions, Wipf and Stock Publishers, 199 W. 8th Ave., Suite 3, Eugene, OR 97401.

Pickwick Publications
An Imprint of Wipf and Stock Publishers
199 W. 8th Ave., Suite 3
Eugene, OR 97401

www.wipfandstock.com

PAPERBACK ISBN: 978-1-5326-9770-8
HARDCOVER ISBN: 978-1-5326-9771-5
EBOOK ISBN: 978-1-5326-9772-2

Cataloguing-in-Publication data:

Names: Silberman, Tim, author. | Goheen, Michael W., foreword.

Title: Engaging neighbors and nations : Factors shaping local church involvement in mission / Tim Silberman ; foreword by Michael W. Goheen.

Description: Eugene, OR: Pickwick Publications, 2024. | Includes bibliographical references and index.

Identifiers: ISBN 978-1-5326-9770-8 (paperback). | ISBN 978-1-5326-9771-5 (hardcover). | ISBN 978-1-5326-9772-2 (ebook).

Subjects: LCSH: Missions. | Missions—Theory. | Church. | Social exchange theory. | Social capital theory.

Classification: BV601.8 S55 2024 (print). | BV601.8 (epub).

03/25/24

All Scripture quotations, unless otherwise indicated, are taken from the Holy Bible, New International Version®, NIV®. Copyright ©1973, 1978, 1984, 2011 by Biblica, Inc.™ Used by permission of Zondervan. All rights reserved worldwide. www.zondervan.com. The "NIV" and "New International Version" are trademarks registered in the United States Patent and Trademark Office by Biblica, Inc.™

For Peggy

Contents

List of Tables and Figures | ix
Foreword by Michael W. Goheen | xi
Acknowledgments | xv
Abbreviations | xvii

1   Evangelical Church Involvement in Mission | 1
2   Literature Review | 20
3   Patterns of Church Mission Involvement | 65
4   Ecclesiology of Local Churches | 87
5   Missiology of Local Churches | 111
6   Church Mission Practices and Organizational Analysis | 139
7   Relational Networks and Social Capital | 178
8   Participatory, Delegatory, and Bifurcated Mission | 226
9   Implications for Local Churches and Mission | 250

Appendix 1: Survey Tool | 261
Appendix 2: Semi-structured Interview Guide | 268
Appendix 3: Qualitative Analysis Codes | 270
Bibliography | 273

Tables and Figures

TABLES

Table 1. Number of Churches Studied and Percentage of Each Sample, by Denomination | 66

Table 2. Number of Supported Organizations, People, and Missionary Units Stratified by Church Attendance | 69

Table 3. Financial Support for Mission Overseas and within Australia Stratified by Church Attendance | 70

Table 4. Average Number of Local Mission Activities per Church Stratified by Church Attendance | 71

Table 5. Local Church Involvement in Australian Based Mission Stratified by Level of Involvement in Local Mission | 72

Table 6. Local Church Involvement in Overseas Mission Stratified by Level of Involvement in Local Mission | 73

Table 7. Local Church Involvement in Overseas Mission Stratified by Level of Involvement in Overseas Mission | 74

Table 8. Local Church Involvement in Australian Based Mission Stratified by Level of Involvement in Local Mission | 74

Table 9. Denominational Representation in Each Category of Involvement in Local and Overseas Mission | 77

Table 10. Denominational Representation in Each of the Extreme Combined Categories of Mission Involvement | 77

Table 11. Profiles of Local Church Mission Involvement Based on Survey and Interviews | 79

FIGURES

Figure 1. Self-Identification of Evangelical Churches | 67

Figure 2. Number of Evangelical Churches by Attendance with Income Evident | 68

Figure 3. High Overseas Mission Church Involvement in Local Mission and High Local Mission Church Involvement in Overseas Mission | 76

Figure 4. Relationship between Culture and Climate | 143

Figure 5. Relationship between Missional Culture, Practices, and Climate for Mission | 144

Figure 6. Relationship between Missional Beliefs and Climate for Mission | 170

Figure 7. Espoused and Enacted Priorities Differ Due to Differing Beliefs | 173

Figure 8. Misalignment between Espoused Priorities and Missional Beliefs | 174

Figure 9. Two-by-Two Matrix of Church Mission Engagement | 227

Figure 10. The Positive Feedback of a Unified Participatory Missiology | 231

Foreword

The word "mission" is not a biblical word. But like other theological terms—Trinity and providence, for example—the word mission is designed to identify, express, and protect an important theme in the biblical story. The word "mission" was first used by Jesuits in the sixteenth century to describe their cross-cultural endeavors. It became popular among Protestants in the nineteenth and twentieth centuries when cross-cultural mission became the new orthodoxy.

At that time "mission" was tied to the colonial paradigm. While something biblically important was captured, there were a number of problems with the colonial understanding of mission. Mission was understood geographically. The world was divided into the Christian West (colonializing countries), that was the home base for missions, and the non-Christian non-West (colonies) that was the mission field. Mission ran along colonial lines from Europe to the global South and East.

Parachurch mission agencies initiated and gave oversight to the task of missions in the non-Western world reducing local congregations in the West to their pastoral role. Mission and church were separated. There were two different and parallel institutional bodies with one committed to the missionary enterprise and the other supporting it. The result was churches without mission and missionary organizations that were not churches. The churches in the West were reduced to their pastoral role to care for believers and became introverted. Mission organizations carried on their work outside of ecclesial structures. And then as churches were planted and grew up in the global South and East there remained a division between the older and more mature churches of the West and the younger less mature churches of the non-West. The Western churches took the lead for mission and the non-Western churches were aquariums where the freshly caught "fish" were placed for safekeeping. Thus, non-Western churches were also stripped of mission and reduced to their pastoral role.

A further problem resulted in the West. If missions was done in the non-West there was no need for mission in the West. The West was already Christian and there was only a need for the evangelism of individuals. Critical or prophetic challenge to cultural idolatry was eclipsed. The myth of a "Christian culture" or a "neutral culture" prevailed. The church took its place comfortably as part of the broader culture.

We can be thankful that the colonial mission initiative protected something of the Scripture's teaching. The horizon of the church's mission is indeed the "ends of the earth" (Pss 22:27; 67:7; 72:8; Isa 45:22; 49:6; 52:10; Acts 1:8; 13:47) and "all nations" (Gen 18:18; Ps 72:17; Isa 66:18; Jer 3:17; Dan 7:14; Matt 24:14; 28:19; Luke 24:47; Rev 15:4). Before the twentieth century, the majority of places where there was no witness to the gospel was found in the global South and East. Nevertheless, there were a host of biblical and theological problems with the paradigm that carried this biblical insight.

The colonial paradigm of mission began to break down in the twentieth century as colonialism collapsed, as the Western church declined in numbers and vitality, as the non-Western church matured and grew in numbers and vitality, and as it became clear, with the catastrophic events of the twentieth century, that Western culture was far from Christian.

Toward the middle part of the twentieth century a new paradigm began to develop in which mission was understood as part of, not Western colonialism, but the biblical story. The mission of the triune God, as it unfolded in the narrative of Scripture, was the new framework for understanding mission. The biblical story manifested a missionary trajectory as it moved from one man and one nation to all nations, from one place to the ends of the earth. The people of God have a missional role to play in that story. This means that the church is missional by its very nature called to witness to Christ in life, word, and deed. Indeed, in this time between the resurrection and return of Christ, the biblical story has come to its fulfilling moment; the blessing promised to all nations in the Abrahamic promise is now being realized as the church is sent to all nations to gather in the end-time harvest (Gen 12:2–3; Gal 3:6–9).

This new paradigm of mission requires new reflection on the past. How is the church to be involved in mission today in its own local neighborhood? What does mission in Western culture look like? Is missions to distant places still part of our task? If so, what is it and what does it look like in a new era? Is there a role for mission organizations? If so, how should they relate to local congregations? Who should take initiative for mission in distant places? What is the relationship between local mission and mission far away? Is everything done in non-Western settings "mission" or is there a specific task that establishes a witness in unevangelized places where there is none? Should local mission or global missions take priority or is that a false dichotomy? How do we think about our resources as we consider missional priorities? What does partnership look like—between churches in the West and non-West, between churches and mission organizations, between mission organizations, between churches in each geographical location? And the questions go on.

Tim Silberman begins to tackle some of these questions in this book in the context of local congregations in Sydney, Australia. One of the key findings of Tim's research is that churches that are involved in mission in distant places are more involved in mission in their local neighborhoods. In my experience I have found that churches tend to prioritize either local or global. In fact, there are a raft of missional church books that have appeared in the last twenty-five years that ignore cross-cultural missions. And there are other books on cross-cultural mission that remain entrenched in the older paradigm reducing missions to what takes place overseas.

Theologically, I believe Tim's thesis is important. The horizon of the "ends of the earth" should stimulate local congregations to be involved in making known the good news of Jesus the Christ in their own backyard *and* to all nations. There is no competition: global mission will nurture and strengthen local mission and vice-versa.

There is so much more to think through if we are to faithfully align ourselves with God's missionary purpose. Tim's book will start us down that path. But we dare not draw back! Mission is not an activity of the *bene esse* (well-being) of the church but an essential characteristic of the very *esse* (being) of the church. A congregation that does not have a missionary identity is not a church in the New Testament sense at all. So, we must wrestle with our new situation, our past traditions, and our past structures. But most of all we must return to the Scriptures and prayerfully listen to what God would have us be and do and say today.

I pray that Tim's book will lead more congregations, not just in Australia but also in North America and elsewhere, to reflect prayerfully on what it means to participate in God's mission in our own backyards and to the ends of the earth.

MICHAEL W. GOHEEN
Professor of Missional Theology and Director of Theological Education, Missional Training Center, Phoenix, Arizona, USA

Acknowledgments

A project like this can only be completed with the input, support, and encouragement of many people. I am forever grateful to everyone who has shared their experiences, provided valuable feedback, and cheered me on to completion. A heartfelt thanks goes to all my colleagues at SMBC who have supported me since the beginning of this research. I have benefitted greatly from your wisdom, input, and patience at every stage. Derek Brotherson, Ed Grudier, and Jonathan and Barbara Geddes have been especially helpful as they accommodated my absences and helped me persevere. A special mention must go to Richard Hibbert who passed into glory before this project was complete. Through his mentoring, leadership, friendship, and care, Richard helped me to become the missiologist I am today.

I am also deeply thankful to the numerous people who shared their time, wisdom, and experience at various points along the journey. Bruce Dipple planted and formed my commitment to the place of local churches in global mission. I hope that my work can continue to stimulate churches and mission agencies as he has been doing for decades. Carole Cusack was a wonderful guide through the research process. Her wide experience, scholarly perspectives, constructive feedback, and constant encouragement kept me on the rails. Darrell Jackson was always available and willing to guide me as I entered the world of research. His suggestions, reflections, discussions, and detailed input helped to shape my project throughout. I know that my future students will benefit from the model of scholarly care and leadership Carole and Darrell gave me. Richard Shumack's and Evelyn Hibbert's willingness to read drafts and give incisive and constructive feedback was invaluable.

Throughout a journey like this, it is usually those closest to you that bear the greatest burden, so I want to thank my family and friends. My parents, Bob and Denise Silberman, and my siblings, David and Heidi, and Michelle have helped me in innumerable ways. Your encouragement, support, and prayers have sustained me throughout. My parents-in-law, Ian and Kathy Spring, and all the Spring clan have also been a constant source of support and care. A very special thank you goes to my children, Hannah, Chloe, and Jonathan. They have endured my absence and distraction at numerous times, and I look forward to being fully present and walking with each of them as they grow, learn, and love the world God has placed them in. Finally, deep thanks to my precious wife, Peggy. Her willingness to support me at every step is humbling. Her love, patience, joy, and endless confidence in me has sustained me in the ups and the downs, and her keen editorial eye has improved this book immeasurably. I could never have completed this without her, and it is to her that it is dedicated.

T. S.
December 2023

Abbreviations

ABFM	Australian Baptist Foreign Mission
ABS	Australian Bureau of Statistics
ABM	Australian Board of Missions
ACT	Australian Capital Territory
AEC	All Evangelical Churches
AFES	Australian Fellowship of Evangelical Students
AIM	Australian Indigenous Ministries
APWM	Australian Presbyterian World Mission
ASV	American Standard Version
BMS	Baptist Missionary Society
CEMES	Canadian Evangelical Missions Engagement Study
CMS	Church Missionary Society
CSB	Christian Standard Bible
CSFs	Critical Success Factors
ECM	European Christian Mission
ESL	English as a Second Language
ESV	English Standard Version
HWCs	High Worker Churches
IMC	International Missionary Council
LGE	Less Globally Engaged
LWCs	Low Worker Churches
MGE	More Globally Engaged
MTS	Ministry Training Strategy
NCLS	National Church Life Survey
NIV11	New International Version (2011)

NKJV		New King James Version
NRSV		New Revised Standard Version
NSW		New South Wales
OMF		Overseas Missionary Fellowship
SET		Social Exchange Theory
SMBC		Sydney Missionary and Bible College
STM		Short-Term Mission
UK		United Kingdom
US		United States
WCC		World Council of Churches

1

Evangelical Church Involvement in Mission

Ever since the day of Pentecost, local gatherings of Christians have been involved in communicating the Christian faith to non-believers (Acts 2:42–47). The priorities of these Christian gatherings have varied through the ages but over the last fifty years the role of the local church as an agent of mission has received significantly more attention.[1] Through the twentieth century, multiple missionary conferences, ecumenical gatherings, and Vatican II have discussed the nature and purpose of the church and its relationship to mission.[2] Influenced by these conversations, in 1974 evangelist Billy Graham and Anglican minister John Stott called together 2,700 evangelicals from 150 nations for a congress on world evangelization.[3] This gathering produced the Lausanne Covenant which affirmed the central role of the local church in evangelization, and concluded that "all churches should therefore be asking God and themselves what they should be doing to reach their own area and to

---

1. The definition of mission is widely discussed and contested in the literature. This study will not engage deeply with this discussion but uses the term to describe activities that have the goal of communicating the Christian faith to non-Christians. This communication may happen in any location and may take many forms. The ways the term is used by participants in this research is explored in chapter 5. Michael Stroope provides a comprehensive historical overview of the term's use. See Stroope, *Transcending Mission*.

2. Bosch, *Transforming Mission*, 368–89.

3. Graham, Stott, and other leaders in the evangelical movement had been brought together through involvement in the World Evangelical Fellowship—later World Evangelical Alliance—which was founded in 1951. See Dowsett, "Lausanne Movement," 402–3.

send missionaries to other parts of the world."[4] This conviction has been reaffirmed in subsequent evangelical gatherings, manifestos, and commitments,[5] though there is great diversity among evangelical churches in how these priorities are expressed.

Evangelicals have long been known for their commitment to mission. David Bebbington's oft-quoted historical analysis identified a quadrilateral of evangelical qualities: biblicism, crucicentrism, conversionism, and activism.[6] While the former three highlight the basis, core convictions, and experientialism of the movement, activism is defined as "the expression of the gospel in effort."[7] This refers to the commitment of evangelicals to intentionally engage non-believers through the preaching of the gospel and social action in the hope that they also become Christians. Despite significant denominational and ecclesiological diversity across the movement, this commitment to mission has been a consistent feature of evangelical churches.[8] Australian evangelicalism reflects this same commitment to mission and has been described by historians Stuart Piggin and Robert D. Linder as "gospel-focused, mission-minded, biblical experientialism."[9] They note that, throughout Australian history, "to be evangelical was to have a passion for missions, for the gospel or 'evangel' had to be taken to all nations."[10]

This passion for missional engagement is evidenced today by the vast array of evangelical books, programs, conferences, and para-church organizations addressing the task of mission both locally and around the world. Yet, this multitude of missional resources also hints at the diversity of ways in which this conviction is expressed. Evangelical local churches invariably espouse a commitment to mission, but their actions differ significantly from church to church. One church may be actively engaged in mission to people in its neighborhood, while another is primarily

---

4. Lausanne Movement, "Lausanne Covenant," par. 6 and 8.

5. Lausanne Movement, "Manila Manifesto," par. 8; Lausanne, "Cape Town," part II/E.

6. Bebbington, *Evangelicalism*, 3. Other defining characteristics may include trans-denominational, christocentric, and committed to "orthodoxy, orthopraxy and orthopathy." See Warner, *Reinventing*; Stackhouse, "Evangelicalism," 259–73; Noll et al., *Evangelicals*.

7. Bebbington, *Evangelicalism*, 3.

8. Stackhouse, *Evangelical Ecclesiology*; Kärkkäinen, *Introduction*.

9. Piggin and Linder, *Fountain*, 26.

10. Piggin and Linder, *Fountain*, 26.

focused on sending missionaries to other nations.[11] A local church's mission activities may be central to its identity and engaging every one of its members, or limited in nature, scope, or geography such that few people consider it. It is this diversity of mission involvement that concerns this study. What is the nature, extent, and cause of this diversity among evangelical churches in Australia today?

SHIFTS IN LOCAL CHURCH INVOLVEMENT IN MISSION

The twentieth century saw a profound transformation in the theology and practice of mission which has influenced evangelical church practice. David Bosch described it as a "crisis in mission" in which "the *foundation*, the *motive and aims*, and the *nature* of mission" were reconsidered and reformulated.[12] A core dimension of this reformulation concerned the relationship between the local church and mission. With the remarkable growth of Christianity in the majority world,[13] the realization that mission was not the sole responsibility of Western Christians became clear. Roland Allen argued that each church established by the apostle Paul had been autonomous and responsible for mission activities and as the twentieth century progressed, this pattern was affirmed in both the Roman Catholic and Protestant world.[14] Missionary engagement was no longer limited to distant lands, and the local church, rather than ecclesiastical or parachurch structures, was to have a central role in the task. As Bosch observed,

> The fundamental change in favor of the local churches, everywhere, as the agent of mission both in its own environment and further afield, cannot be gainsaid and constitutes a decisive advance over positions that had been in vogue for many centuries.[15]

---

11. The terms "missionary" and "mission worker" are used interchangeably through this study to refer to anyone who has left their home for an indefinite period, typically four years or more, to participate in gospel ministry. See Plueddemann, *Leading*, 13.

12. Bosch, *Transforming Mission*, 4–6.

13. Africa, Asia, and Latin America have collectively been described using various terms. The "non-western world", "developing world", "global south", "third world", or "two-thirds world" all have significant limitations. The term "majority world" was identified as the preferred term at an international gathering of evangelicals in 2004 and is consistent with the size and growing influence of the Christians in these continents. See Claydon, *New Vision*, 118.

14. Allen, *Missionary Methods*, 111–25; Bosch, *Transforming Mission*, 379–80.

15. Bosch, *Transforming Mission*, 381.

Lesslie Newbigin reflected this conviction as he called for churches to have a "missionary *dimension*" woven into every aspect of their life together, as well as a "missionary *intention*" which involved sending people out "for the specific purpose of taking the gospel to unreached peoples."[16] Yet, local churches have responded to this changing tide in a variety of ways. While increasingly accepting their role in the missionary endeavor, they have had to negotiate the relationship between local mission activities and their involvement with mission overseas.

In their efforts to encourage Australian local church participation in mission, local authors have expressed a variety of opinions on the patterns of involvement that are needed. Michael Frost and Alan Hirsch's influential book, *The Shaping of Things to Come*, emphasizes the need for churches to engage with their communities as "genuine cross-cultural missionaries."[17] The previous restriction of mission language to describe sending people overseas is critiqued and they bemoan the separation between the local church and the mission agency, arguing that every Christian must take on a missionary identity in their own context.[18] Colin Marshall and Tony Payne, in a book widely embraced by Australian evangelicals, similarly challenge the narrow emphasis on mission as sending people overseas. They argue that Jesus' commission in Matt 28:18–20 "is not fundamentally about mission out there somewhere else in another country" but about equipping every Christian to make disciples where they are.[19] For these and other evangelical leaders in Australia, the missionary dimension of the Christian faith must first and foremost be evident at home. By contrast, several leaders in the Australian evangelical mission community feel that the task of distant mission is being neglected by local churches. Regarding the state of Presbyterian churches in Australia, mission leader Kevin Murray observes that "overall there has been a decline in interest in overseas mission."[20] Churches of Christ pastor and former National Director of OMF, Allan Webb similarly suggests that "too many churches are in maintenance mode—missions is perceived of as a local event rather than a global cause."[21] And as Bruce Dipple observes, "many churches have become so preoccupied with

---

16. Newbigin, "Cross-Currents," 149–50.
17. Frost and Hirsch, *Shaping*, 10.
18. Frost and Hirsch, *Shaping*, 103.
19. Marshall and Payne, *Trellis*, 13.
20. Murray, "Overseas Mission," 255.
21. Webb, *Your Church*, 28.

reaching out to their immediate locality, that they have let slip the global perspective found in Scripture."[22] This trend towards greater emphasis on local mission has resulted in some evangelical churches engaging heavily in their local context while neglecting the opportunities for wider participation in mission.

A recent informal survey of Australian evangelical mission agencies suggests that there has been a decline in the number of overseas mission workers being sent and supported by conservative evangelical churches. Twenty-one evangelical mission agencies[23] were asked to report the number of missionary units[24] that were serving through their organization in 2010 and in 2020. This survey indicated that there had been a 9 percent decline in the total number of missionaries being sent from Australia (558 units in 2010; 510 in 2020), and a 5 percent decline in the number of missionaries being sent from New South Wales (NSW) and the Australian Capital Territory (ACT) (244 units in 2010 to 231 in 2020). According to the National Church Life Survey (NCLS), during this period regular church attendance has been stable.[25] This supports the perspectives of Murray, Webb, and Dipple suggesting that shifting patterns of mission involvement of evangelical local churches have taken place. Many churches are actively engaged in mission activities locally and at a distance, but patterns of participation are changing.

This study explores the nature, extent, and cause of these different patterns of involvement among evangelical churches in Sydney and surrounds as it arises out of my own work and church experience. I am an Australian evangelical Christian who has attended Anglican, Baptist, Churches of Christ, and Presbyterian churches in various parts of Sydney and surrounds in the last twenty-five years. Since 2007, I have been one of the teaching faculty of Sydney Missionary and Bible College (SMBC), an interdenominational evangelical tertiary institution which prepares

---

22. Dipple, *Becoming Global*, 12.

23. The agencies surveyed were Africa Inland Mission, Australian Indigenous Ministries, APWM, CMS, Crossview, European Christian Mission, Global Interaction, Global Recordings Network, International Teams, Interserve, Mission Aviation Fellowship, OM, OMF, Peoples International, Pioneers of Australia, Power to Change, SIM, WEC, World Team, and Wycliffe.

24. A missionary unit is a family, couple, or individual serving as a cross-cultural missionary either overseas or in Australia.

25. The NCLS recorded a marked decline in regular church attendance in Australia from 1991 to 2011, but it has since plateaued. See Powell, "Part 1."

people for Christian ministry in Australia and overseas.[26] There are a range of evangelical churches in Australia,[27] however, Piggin and Linder describe a "trifurcation in the evangelical movement [in Australia] into conservative, progressive, and Charismatic/Pentecostal streams by the beginning of the twenty-first century."[28] My institution and church experience is most closely aligned with the conservative stream which is particularly strong in New South Wales due to the size and influence of the conservative Sydney Anglican Diocese.[29] The churches under examination in this study are from various denominations yet are predominantly aligned with this conservative stream. For ease of expression, they are referred to as Sydney evangelical churches.

RESEARCH QUESTIONS

The central research question explored in this study is: What are the factors shaping the different patterns of mission involvement in Sydney evangelical churches?

This is answered by exploring the following sub-questions:

- How do Sydney evangelical churches vary in their patterns of local and distant mission involvement?
- Are there any observable connections between participation in local and distant mission in these churches?
- Are there theological or missiological differences that may explain the varying patterns of local church participation in local and distant mission in these churches?
- Are there organizational or sociological differences that may explain the varying patterns of local church participation in local and distant mission in these churches?

For the purposes of this study, mission involvement refers to intentional Christian practices which have the goal of enabling non-Christians

---

26. For a history of SMBC, see Brammall, *Out of Darkness*.

27. These include Anglican, Baptist, Brethren, Churches of Christ, Congregationalist, Methodist, Salvation Army, Pentecostal, Presbyterian, and many independent evangelical churches.

28. Piggin and Linder, *Attending*, 503.

29. For a review of the history, vitality and conservatism of the Sydney Anglican Diocese, see Judd and Cable, *Sydney Anglicans*.

to hear, see, understand, and respond to Christian beliefs about God and his offer of salvation. Local mission takes place in a church's immediate context, through people who attend the church, with the expectation that those who become Christians as a result may join the church. Distant mission is predominantly cross-cultural and takes place overseas or in other regions of Australia through the agency of people who do not regularly attend the church.

METHODOLOGICAL APPROACH

This study explores the factors shaping the missional practices of Sydney evangelical churches and is therefore concerned with the behavior of social units. Local churches are the primary units of analysis, and, like all social units, they are complex, open systems shaped by both internal factors and interactions with their surroundings.[30] A church congregation, as defined by Ammerman, is a "locally situated, multi-generational, voluntary group of people who see themselves as distinct and engage jointly in religious activities."[31] Though the members of each local church have their own histories, values, beliefs, and perspectives, they have a shared identity as members of a specific local church and can therefore be analyzed as social units.

To both describe and explain the patterns of local church involvement in mission, this study employs an explanatory sequential mixed-method grounded theory approach.[32] Grounded theory was first described by Barney Glaser and Anselm Strauss as a means of generating theory through the systematic analysis of empirical data.[33] Drawing on Glaser's background in quantitative research at Columbia University and Strauss's experience with qualitative approaches in the "Chicago tradition," they sought to develop a research method that would give greater empirical strength to social scientists.[34] Strauss later joined with Juliet Corbin to further develop the approach and its application to qualitative research.[35] Though Glaser criticized these developments for "forcing"

---

30. For an understanding of systems theory and its application to a local church, see Bertalanffy, "History," 407–26; Luhmann, *Introduction*; Fuller, "Evaluating."
31. Ammerman, "Congregations," 562.
32. Johnson et al., "Grounded Theory," 66.
33. Glaser and Strauss, *Discovery of Grounded Theory*.
34. Glaser and Strauss, *Discovery of Grounded Theory*, vii–viii.
35. Strauss and Corbin, *Basics of Qualitative Research*.

the data, Strauss and Corbin's approach has been widely employed.[36] In describing their method, Strauss and Corbin explicitly note the influence of pragmatism and symbolic interactionism as developed in the writings of John Dewey, George Mead, and Herbert Blumer.[37] The third edition of their manual for developing grounded theory lists sixteen assumptions that shape the method they propose.[38] These assumptions recognize the powerful influence of culture and society on shaping a person's view of reality. A social context creates meaning as its members interact with the symbols of language and culture that surround them. To understand the beliefs, values, and actions of a social unit, a researcher must endeavor to see the world from the perspective of the actors.[39] The grounded theory method provides a set of tools to aid in this process.

The belief that grounded theory researchers can achieve this goal and faithfully attain the standpoint of their subjects has been challenged for its naivety. Corbin and Strauss state that the researcher must be able "to step back and critically analyze situations, to recognize and avoid bias, to obtain valid and reliable data, and to think abstractly."[40] Anthony Bryant questions the suggestion that a researcher can set aside their preconceptions like this, arguing that "unfortunately human cognition just does not work in this manner."[41] The perspective and experience of the researcher has a profound impact upon their capacity to interpret the data. Furthermore, the data collected is shaped by the contexts from which it arises and the experiences, values, and intentions of the subjects. As John Law states, "methods help us to analyze reality, but at the same time, they, in part, produce the data that are to be analyzed."[42] Glaser and Strauss showed some awareness of this limitation in their discussion of theoretical sensitivity, yet their confidence that it may be overcome may not be well founded. As Kathy Charmaz summarizes her constructionist position, "we are part of the world we study, the data we collect, and the analyses we produce."[43] This has been accepted by many proponents of

---

36. Glaser, *Basics of Grounded Theory*; Charmaz, *Constructing Grounded Theory*, 11–12.

37. Strauss and Corbin, *Basics of Qualitative Research*, 24–25.

38. Corbin and Strauss, *Basics of Qualitative Research*, 5–8.

39. Crotty, *Foundations of Social Research*, 74–76.

40. Strauss and Corbin, *Basics of Qualitative Research*, 18.

41. Bryant, *Grounded Theory*, 22.

42. Law, *After Method*, 143.

43. Charmaz, *Constructing Grounded Theory*, 17.

grounded theory, including Juliet Corbin,[44] and has led to a proliferation in the ways in which the method is applied. Grounded theory is now a "constellation of methods"[45] from which the researcher must select their approach, aware of the assumptions and limitations that they bring.[46]

This epistemological acceptance of constructionism does not necessitate a subjectivist or relativist ontology. Constructionism recognizes the many ways in which knowledge of an object will be shaped by the knower, but it need not deny the reality of the object itself. Crotty highlights this truth through appeal to the phenomenological concept of "intentionality" which asserts that "when the mind becomes conscious of something, when it 'knows' something, it reaches out to, and into, that object."[47] This knowledge is therefore dependent upon and constrained by its engagement with the object. The meaning applied to the object is constructed through the dialectic between the object's intrinsic qualities and the perspective of the knower. The knower's understanding is limited, yet the ontological reality of the object remains.

To complete social research, a researcher identifies a social unit as their object of study and the knowledge they construct will be influenced by the extent to which they share the culture and language of that group. While a purely etic perspective may be better able to analyze the data "objectively," an emic perspective provides shared frameworks and language to grasp the social knowledge being communicated more fully. As Engler explains, semantic theory affirms the value of this enculturated engagement, "semantic atomism locates meaning at the level of individual words (the meaning is *in* it); semantic holism locates meaning at a broader level, ranging from an indefinite network of linked units to an entire language."[48] A researcher who shares the cultural perspective of the participants will be able to effectively employ the holistic semantic frame to interpret the data. The knowledge thereby constructed will be more strongly constrained by the object of study. Though this may constrain the range of perspectives the researcher employs to interpret the data, it

---

44. Corbin and Strauss, *Basics of Qualitative Research*, 8–12.

45. Charmaz, *Constructing Grounded Theory*, 14.

46. Adele Clarke reviews the development of grounded theory and the various streams that have evolved. Her own method of "situational analysis" draws on postmodern epistemologies that were not consistent with the epistemological convictions underpinning this project. See Clarke, "Situating Grounded Theory," 3–48.

47. Crotty, *Foundations of Social Research*, 44.

48. Engler, "Grounded Theory," 266.

provides a foundation upon which the knowledge stands and a conceptual language with which to share it.[49] In this case the study of Sydney evangelical churches by a researcher who attends a similar church and works at a related educational institution will inevitably result in findings being shaped by the evangelical presuppositions and perspectives. But the analysis will also reflect a deep understanding of the relevant issues and will speak in the voice of the most interested parties: those who lead and attend evangelical churches.

METHODS

To both describe and explain the patterns of local church involvement in mission among Sydney evangelical churches, this project collected quantitative data through a questionnaire of church leaders and qualitative data through semi-structured interviews with church leaders and members. The inclusion of both quantitative and qualitative data in this research is consistent with mixed method grounded theory as described by Johnson, McGowan, and Turner.[50] Though grounded theory is typically applied to qualitative data, Glaser and Strauss affirmed the use of both quantitative and qualitative data in theory generation.[51] When utilizing both forms of data, Johnson, McGowan, and Turner advocate a "convergent parallel" approach which gives equal status to both sources such that theory is generated through "dialectical pluralism."[52] Yet other methods are equally valid. An "explanatory sequential" method begins with quantitative research and uses qualitative research to explain the results more fully, while an "exploratory sequential" approach begins with qualitative research which is then followed by a quantitative phase to test the theories developed.[53] A recent review of research employing mixed method grounded theory methods in the health sciences, education, and social sciences found that most studies employed a convergent design, but explanatory and exploratory methods each accounted for 13 percent of the sample.[54] This combination of data is thus a valuable approach to theory generation.

49. Corbin and Strauss, *Basics of Qualitative Research*, 10–11.

50. Johnson et al., "Grounded Theory," 66.

51. Glaser and Strauss, *Discovery of Grounded Theory*, 17–18; Strauss and Corbin, *Basics of Qualitative Research*, 18–19.

52. Johnson et al., "Grounded Theory," 73; Creswell, *Research Design*, 14.

53. Creswell, *Research Design*, 14–17.

54. Guetterman et al., "Contemporary Approaches," 179–95.

This research employed an explanatory sequential mixed method grounded theory approach through the survey of evangelical church practices across a wider geographical area followed by semi-structured interviews of members and leaders from selected Sydney evangelical churches included in the survey. The survey utilized closed questions to provide a quantitative picture of church patterns of involvement in mission activities. This revealed what local evangelical churches were doing regarding local and distant mission and how involvement in the two arenas related to each other. The interviews then explored the practices, structures, and beliefs that shaped these patterns, thereby investigating how and why churches were engaged in mission in these ways. The qualitative and quantitative data was integrated through a "connecting" method whereby the interview participants were approached based on their church's patterns of mission involvement according to the survey.[55] This combination of quantitative and qualitative data provided both a broad understanding of church involvement and a deep insight into the reasons for these patterns of practice.

ANALYSIS

Though there are many ways to approach a grounded theory project, Melanie Birks and Jane Mills have summarized nine key features common to grounded theory methods which this study sought to employ.[56] "Initial coding and categorization of data"[57] was achieved through transcription of the interviews and coding utilizing NVivo software. "Concurrent data collection and analysis"[58] took place as interviews were performed between March 28, 2019 and October 9, 2019 while data analysis was taking place. "Memo writing"[59] was a regular practice of recording analytical notes and developing theory through the process of analysis. "Constant comparative analysis"[60] was utilized throughout this process by bringing

  55. Fetters et al., "Achieving Integration," 2134–56.
  56. Birks and Mills, *Grounded Theory*, 10–14; See also Glaser and Strauss, *Discovery of Grounded Theory*; Strauss and Corbin, *Basics of Qualitative Research*; Corbin and Strauss, *Basics of Qualitative Research*; Charmaz, *Constructing Grounded Theory*, 15; Bryant, *Grounded Theory*, 27–33.
  57. Birks and Mills, *Grounded Theory*, 10.
  58. Birks and Mills, *Grounded Theory*, 11.
  59. Birks and Mills, *Grounded Theory*, 11.
  60. Birks and Mills, *Grounded Theory*, 11–12.

together the developing theory with the new data as it was collected. "Intermediate coding, identification of a core category, advanced coding, and theoretical integration"[61] was performed by the researcher throughout using the NVivo software platform. Purposive sampling was employed by inviting interviewees from the churches that were selected based on the quantitative results. An ideal grounded theory approach would then employ a process of "theoretical sampling"[62] whereby further sources of data were sought after initial analysis to find the sources appropriate to the developing theory. Unfortunately, due to the limited time frame and resources of the project, this was not possible and concept saturation cannot be guaranteed. This limitation does constrain this study's findings; however, the attention to all other facets of a grounded theory approach ensured that the understanding of church practice was firmly grounded in the available data.

As core categories became evident through the process of analysis and interviews, literature from diverse disciplines was engaged to enhance theoretical sensitivity and theoretical integration. "Theoretical sensitivity" is a core concept in the practice of grounded theory that refers to the quality of the researcher which enables them to develop theories from the data that are consistent with existing analytical frameworks.[63] Ten years after the first publication of *The Discovery of Grounded Theory*, Barney Glaser used this term as the title of his rearticulation of the grounded theory method to highlight its importance.[64] Charmaz defines theoretical sensitivity as "the ability to understand and define phenomena in abstract terms and to demonstrate abstract relationships between studied phenomena."[65] The place of literature reviews in developing theoretical sensitivity has been a point of discussion. Glaser and Strauss originally encouraged researchers to "ignore the literature of theory and fact on the area of study" so that theory might be purely grounded in the data.[66] The impracticality of this approach led to a softening by Strauss and Corbin who recognized the literature, professional experience, and personal experience as sources of theoretical sensitivity. They therefore recommend careful attention to grounded theory methods and "an attitude of

---

61. Birks and Mills, *Grounded Theory*, 12–13.
62. Birks and Mills, *Grounded Theory*, 11.
63. Birks and Mills, *Grounded Theory*, 12.
64. Glaser, *Theoretical Sensitivity*.
65. Charmaz, *Constructing Grounded Theory*, 161.
66. Glaser and Strauss, *Discovery of Grounded Theory*, 37.

skepticism" to minimize the impact of presuppositions.[67] Similarly, Bryant advocates a "review of the literature" at the beginning of the project followed by a "return to the literature" at the end.[68] This allows for the necessary theoretical sensitivity while retaining the primacy of the data analysis to further develop the grounded theory.

In this study, the researcher had been reading and researching in the topic area for many years prior to data collection. A review of relevant theological and missiological literature was performed at the beginning of the project and as quantitative data was collected and analyzed the literature was further engaged. Analysis of the qualitative data identified core categories that led to wider engagement with literature in the fields of organizational studies, social exchange theory, and social capital theory. The insights from this literature were integrated with analysis of the data to enhance theoretical sensitivity. As these analytical frameworks were not explored in the initial literature review, they are introduced and discussed with the core findings in later chapters. In all these ways this study displays the core criteria of a grounded theory approach employing a cross-sectional design that utilizes both quantitative and qualitative data to generate theory regarding the factors influencing evangelical local church involvement in mission activities.

POPULATION AND SAMPLING

The units of analysis for this research were local churches in NSW and ACT in Australia with increased attention on a selection of churches in Sydney. Though individuals who attend churches may be involved in mission activities in a variety of ways, the focus of the study was on the mission involvement of the local churches as collective entities. In the first phase of the research, a wide sample of churches was surveyed using an online questionnaire. Purposive sampling was employed for the selection of this initial sample to ensure that evangelical churches from a variety of denominations with diverse patterns of involvement in local and distant mission were included. This involved contacting the leaders of fifteen large evangelical mission organizations with offices in NSW and asking them to supply the names of churches that they believed to have either

---

67. Strauss and Corbin, *Basics of Qualitative Research*, 41–47.
68. Bryant, *Grounded Theory*, 30.

high or low levels of involvement in mission.[69] These organizations were chosen because of their membership in Missions Interlink, the Australian Evangelical Alliance's global mission network. Three of these organizations have close affiliations with the Anglican, Baptist, and Presbyterian denominations, and they supplied the names of most of the churches surveyed. This likely skewed the sample towards churches in the conservative evangelical stream that may be described as Sydney evangelicals.

A total of 254 churches were named and their contact details were collected from public listings on church and denominational websites. Church leaders were initially contacted via telephone, the nature of the research was explained, and they were invited to take part in the survey. The 242 people who expressed a willingness to participate were sent an email with a link to the questionnaire for completion online. Questionnaires were usually completed by clergy, but in some cases the primary respondent was a lay leader with responsibility for the church's mission activities. A 91 percent response rate was achieved, with 220 responses received. The questionnaire responses were analyzed, and churches were ranked according to their level of local mission activity and involvement with distant mission. As there was a clear relationship between size and level of activity, churches were ranked for reported level of participation while controlling for church size. The 25 percent of churches displaying the highest level of local mission activity (HLM) and the 25 percent of churches showing the lowest level of local mission activity (LLM) were identified. Similarly, the 25 percent of churches displaying the highest level of involvement in distant mission (HDM) and the 25 percent of churches showing the lowest level of involvement in distant mission (LDM) were identified. These categories were then used to determine the churches that would be approached for interviews by identifying those displaying high levels of local involvement and either high or low levels of distant involvement.

Of the 220 respondents, 140 indicated a willingness to participate in the interview phase of the study. From these, ten churches displaying high levels of local mission activity were selected. Six displayed high levels of distant mission involvement and four displayed low levels of distant

---

69. The organizations were Africa Inland Mission, Australian Presbyterian World Mission, Church Missionary Society, Crossview, European Christian Mission, Global Interaction, Global Recordings Network, Interserve, Operation Mobilization, OMF, People International, Pioneers, SIM, WEC, and Wycliffe Bible Translators.

mission involvement, according to their questionnaire responses.[70] Respondents were contacted and invited to participate in an individual semi-structured interview and to invite two other members of the church to also be interviewed. From each church there was one member of clergy, one church member with a notable commitment to mission, and another generally active member of the church interviewed: a total of thirty people.

Nine of the interviewees, four of whom were church leaders, were known to the researcher prior to the project being undertaken due to the researcher's employment at an evangelical theological college in Sydney. All interviewees knew the college and understood the researcher's role prior to being interviewed. This association may have influenced the interviewees' assumptions and expectations of the researcher. By seeing him as an insider to Sydney evangelical church culture, interviewees were able to assume a shared set of beliefs and presuppositions. One church leader indicated this shared perspective when speaking about the church's view of mission by noting, "I'm sure we have a similar definition."[71] This shared culture would have given interviewees confidence that the researcher could understand their church context and experiences. However, the interviewees' awareness of the researcher's role and experience may also have influenced their portrayal of church practices.[72] Some may have been motivated to present a more positive view of their church to gain affirmation by an expert outsider and reinforce their own perspective. Those who had pre-existing misgivings about their church's involvement in mission may have presented a more negative perspective. This is unavoidable with the collection of interview data and is a reality that is realized with a constructivist approach which was taken into consideration during analysis. Interviewing three members of each church helped to moderate any extreme perspectives among interviewees.

This method of limited purposive sampling does not strictly meet the criteria of theoretical sampling as suggested for a grounded theory

---

70. One other respondent was contacted but declined the invitation to participate in this second phase of the research.

71. Interview with CH3_SP, August 8, 2019. Throughout this work interviews are notated to preserve the anonymity of the participant. The interviewee's church is designated by the initial code (i.e., CH1, CH2, etc.). The role that the participant fulfilled in the church is indicated by the suffix: SP represents the pastor or member of staff, MC represents a person on the mission committee or active in the church's mission activities, and CM represents an active congregation member.

72. Charmaz, *Constructing Grounded Theory*, 91–103; Polkinghorne, "Validity Issues," 471–86.

approach. The goal of theoretical sampling is to attain concept saturation which ensures that all relevant data has been collected. Charmaz states that "theoretical sampling occupies a crucial place in grounded theory"; however, she also notes that this is not always possible in research performed under the auspices of an institution.[73] Theoretical sampling is usually achieved by allowing the grounded categories that arise through data analysis to guide the selection of additional data sources. The time frame, available resources, and institutional limitations of this project made it difficult to employ true theoretical sampling. Yet, Engler suggests that this does not invalidate the study's classification as grounded theory.[74] Theoretical sampling ultimately relates to the relevance of the data collected to the emerging categories. The churches approached for interviews were selected based on the survey analysis and the questions developed as the analysis of earlier interviews progressed. Though allowing the developing theory to guide selection of interviewees through the process may have provided a more comprehensive understanding of the issues, the core categories displayed high levels of saturation through the analysis.

DATA COLLECTION AND PROCESSING

The data collection methods of this study were informed by the Australian Government's *National Statement on Ethical Conduct in Human Research*.[75] These guidelines uphold the core values of "respect, research merit and integrity, justice, and beneficence."[76] All research participants were adult members of local churches who willingly participated in the completion of an online questionnaire, an in-person semi-structured interview, or both. To protect the privacy of all participants, both individuals and churches included in the study have been de-identified and every effort has been made to avoid including details about the churches that were not relevant to the findings.

The questionnaire was designed to provide an insight into the identity, size, wealth, and activity of the local churches represented by the respondents. Questionnaires with twenty-four questions were distributed

73. Charmaz, *Constructing Grounded Theory*, 209–24.
74. Engler, "Grounded Theory," 259.
75. National Health and Medical Research Council (NHMRC), *National Statement*. The project was approved by the University of Sydney Human Research Ethics Committee prior to the collection of any data.
76. NHNRC, *National Statement*, section 1.

and collated online and only the question pertaining to informed consent was mandatory.[77] The use of checkbox and numerical responses sought to minimize the inconvenience to respondents and facilitate completion. Questions were modelled on items in the Australian National Church Life Survey (NCLS) *2016 Operations Survey* and *2016 Leader Survey* with some adjustments to wording where necessary to suit the population and focus of the research.[78] Section 1 (questions 1–3) asked about church identity, attendance, and income. Section 2 (questions 4–11) asked about local mission activities within the local community and support of mission work in Australia. Section 3 (questions 12–23) asked about mission activity outside of Australia. Questions about the church's support for mission workers used and defined the term "missionary units" to avoid the confusion that may arise from counting an individual, a couple, or a family of mission workers. Questions were modelled on the NCLS questionnaires because they have already been widely used in an Australian church context and have been found to be reliable and valid. Though direct comparison to NCLS was not possible where questions had been changed, the format and style was retained wherever possible because of their known acceptance.

The first question invited respondents to select one or more adjectives that they would use to describe their church. The options were "evangelical, missional, charismatic, reformed, pentecostal, and emerging/emergent."[79] The self-identification of evangelical was used to determine whether churches were included in the core data sample for the study. This methodology is consistent with the *World Christian Encyclopedia* which defines evangelicals as "a subdivision mainly of Protestants consisting of all affiliated church members *calling themselves Evangelicals*."[80] Though the questionnaire specifically asked the respondent how *they* would describe the church, given that most questionnaires were completed by clergy, it is reasonable to conclude that this reflects the beliefs and practices of the church as a social unit. Questions related to attendance, income, and expenditure gave checkbox options which allowed respondents to indicate the range in which their church fell.[81]

77. See Appendix 1.

78. NCLS Research, *Operations Survey*; NCLS Research, *Leader Survey (LS1)*; NCLS Research, *Leader Survey (LS2)*.

79. See Appendix 1, Question 1.

80. Barrett et al., *World Christian Encyclopedia*, 28; emphasis added.

81. See Appendix 1, Questions 2, 3, 11, and 21. This approach could have been

Pseudonymous codes were assigned to each questionnaire response to allow for analysis without knowledge of the respondent's identity. A comprehensive descriptive analysis was completed for all variables and those displaying notable patterns of variance were further examined for evidence of explanatory factors. Due to the nature of the scales and the size of the sample, no advanced or inferential analysis was performed.

Interviews were semi-structured to allow for elaboration and exploration of issues raised by the participant. An interview guide was prepared with questions related to church nature and purpose, practicalities of mission involvement, motivations, priorities, people, and ideals, though questions were developed as the study progressed.[82] Interviews lasted between forty and eighty minutes and audio recordings were taken. Where possible, any church policies or documents mentioned by interviewees were collected and included in the analysis. Interviews were transcribed and NVivo was used for coding and analysis. Initial coding was performed on all qualitative data, followed by focused and axial coding to identify the core categories of interest.[83] These categories were shaped through interaction with the relevant literature and constant comparison with the data. This iterative process facilitated the development of theories that were grounded in the qualitative data and informed by the core categories of ecclesiology, missiology, church mission practices, and church relational networks. Organizational theory, social exchange theory, and social capital theory provided appropriate analytical frameworks for the latter two categories.

OUTLINE

This chapter has introduced the research topic and described the research methodology and methods employed in this study. In chapter 2, a review of the relevant ecclesiological and missiological literature explores the prevailing theological, practical, and empirical perspectives on evangelical local church involvement in mission.

Chapter 3 presents the findings of the survey with particular attention to the relationship between local church involvement in mission activities

---

improved by asking respondents to provide approximate numbers for attendance, income, and expenditure.

82. See Appendix 2.
83. See Appendix 3.

locally and those at a distance. The qualities of the ten churches selected for interviews are discussed and the profiles of the less globally engaged (LGE) and more globally engaged (MGE) churches are presented.

Chapter 4 discusses the ecclesiological convictions evident among interviewees with particular attention to the nature and purpose of the church. Ecclesiological metaphors are considered and the similarities and differences in purposes between interviewees from less globally engaged churches and more globally engaged churches are discussed.

Chapter 5 explores the missiological convictions of interviewees noting the many similarities in perspectives on the nature, location, agents, and motivation for mission across the churches. Some differences in emphasis on distant mission and the agency of God are noted.

Chapter 6 considers the mission practices described by interviewees and examines them using the tools of organizational analysis. The approaches of organizational culture and climate are considered, and their complementary qualities identified. Church mission practices are described with reference to prayer, finances, equipping for mission, local mission activities, and missional leadership. The impact of these practices on church climate for mission is explored and the influence of cultural integration discussed.

Chapter 7 analyzes the relational networks described by interviewees highlighting their significance among church mission practices. Social exchange theory and social capital theory are employed to appreciate the influence of these relationships on church involvement in mission. Social capital is particularly noted for its value in understanding the relational and cognitive consequences of the relational networks in more globally engaged churches.

Chapter 8 integrates the findings of the previous analyses and proposes a spectrum of church engagement. This spectrum is used to describe a church's approach to both local and distant mission thus creating a two-by-two matrix of mission engagement. The missional beliefs shaping these different patterns of mission engagement are discussed and the theological and sociological influences on these beliefs are also considered. The final chapter summarizes the findings and explores opportunities for further research and possible implications for evangelical churches and mission organizations.

2

Literature Review

To understand the range of factors that may be influencing local church practice, this chapter reviews the relevant literature in three parts. Theological perspectives impinging upon contemporary Australian evangelical church involvement in mission are discussed with particular attention to shifts in ecclesiology and missiology in the last fifty years. This is followed by an examination of the various practical approaches to church mission involvement that have influenced Sydney evangelical churches. Finally, a review of empirical research into evangelical church involvement in mission from around the world highlights key issues that have previously been identified.

THEOLOGICAL PERSPECTIVES ON LOCAL CHURCH INVOLVEMENT IN MISSION

Among the fundamental influences on evangelical local church involvement in mission are the biblical and theological convictions shaping practice. Evangelical ecclesiology and missiology have undergone profound change through the twentieth and twenty-first centuries. To understand the influence of these theological shifts on Sydney evangelical churches, consideration of several key perspectives is required. In particular, the ecumenical movement, Lausanne gatherings, and missional church conversations have been engaged by Sydney evangelicals in a variety of ways. Understanding these different streams helps to interpret their impact on Sydney evangelical churches.

The Rise of Ecumenism

David Bosch, in his magisterial review of mission, argues that the dominant biblical text employed by evangelicals to drive the missionary endeavor from the beginning of the twentieth century was Matt 28:18–20.[1] Highlighted by William Carey in his *Enquiry into the Obligations of Christians to Use Means for the Conversion of the Heathen*, this "Great Commission" became the ground upon which Protestant participation in mission was encouraged. John R. Mott and other leaders of the 1910 Edinburgh World Missionary Conference appealed to this verse as they sought to unite global missionary efforts.[2] This was a time of great optimism as the "evangelization of the world in this generation" through obedience to Christ's commission was considered a realistic possibility.[3] Though this enthusiasm was dampened by the world wars in continental Europe, missionaries continued to be sent from the United States and Britain. Spurred on by the Reformation principle of *sola scriptura* and the right to private judgment, evangelicals formed a range of voluntary societies many of which were concerned with world mission.[4] These societies provided structures for individuals to voluntarily participate in mission with little involvement from their local churches.

This pattern was notably less evident in the ecumenical movement where theological and missiological shifts progressively redefined the relationship between the church and mission. As Bosch argues, "the traditional interpretation of mission was gradually modified in the course of the twentieth century."[5] This shift in the theology of mission both stimulated and was stimulated by changes in ecclesiological thinking.[6] The 1910 World Missionary Conference led to the formation of the International Missionary Council (IMC) which wrestled deeply with the relationship between the church and mission. Was mission limited to the actions of the church? What of the younger churches in the majority world? What is God's role in mission? At the 1952 IMC meeting in Willingen, Germany, it was argued that the church was neither the source nor the goal of mission but rather was sent by God into the world for

---

1. Bosch, *Transforming Mission*, 340–41.
2. Mott, *Decisive Hour*.
3. Bosch, *Transforming Mission*, 334–39.
4. Bosch, *Transforming Mission*, 327–34.
5. Bosch, *Transforming Mission*, 2.
6. Moltmann, *Church*, 7.

the purposes of mission.[7] This was consistent with the theology of Karl Barth, whose theocentric perspective marginalized the agency of humanity.[8] Rather than mission being a way for people to glorify God, Barth believed all missionary endeavors were fundamentally expressions of God's grace.[9] As Bosch later affirmed, "mission is not primarily an activity of the church, but an attribute of God. God is a missionary God."[10] In the post-conference report, missiologist Karl Hartenstein used the Latin phrase *missio Dei* (mission of God) to communicate this concept which was later popularized by Georg Vicedom.[11]

From a *missio Dei* perspective, the church is not the source of mission, but mission must be recognized as fundamental to its essence. The church of a missionary God is inevitably a missionary church. As Barth stated, "The [church] community is as such a missionary community or it is not the Christian community."[12] Or, as Vatican II later declared, "The Church on earth is by its very nature missionary."[13] This perspective on the place of the church in God's purposes stimulated a search for a robust biblical foundation for a missional ecclesiology. Paul Minear, appointed by the Faith and Order Commission of the World Council of Churches (WCC), examined the New Testament images of the church,[14] and Johannes Blauw, commissioned by the IMC, reviewed the biblical foundations for the mission of the church.[15] These works added to the growing body of literature supporting the view that the church has a missionary role and responsibility which is derivative of and dependent on God.[16] Bosch highlights the significance of this *missio Dei* perspective

---

7. Bosch, *Transforming Mission*, 370.

8. John Flett argues that the theology articulated at Willingen was a poor reflection of Barth's theology and therefore lacked the theological rigor needed for a robust missionary ecclesiology. Flett, *Witness*, 78–80.

9. "In the abstract, it is a complete untruth to say that we have the power to thank and serve the glory of God. It does not belong to the essence of the creature to have or to be the power or ability to glorify God." Barth, *CD* II/1:671.

10. Bosch, *Transforming Mission*, 390. Similarly, Christopher Wright, "mission was not made for the church; the church was made for mission—God's mission." Wright, *Mission of God's People*, 62.

11. Vicedom, *Mission of God*.

12. Barth, *CD* III/4:505.

13. Vatican II, "Ad Gentes," 814.

14. Minear, *Images*.

15. Blauw, *Missionary Nature*.

16. Paradoxically, the *missio Dei* perspective also served to marginalize the church's role in mission among those who saw it as referring to the work of God to bring about

as he states, "It is inconceivable that we could again revert to a narrow, ecclesiocentric view of mission."[17]

The incorporation of mission into the broader work of the church was further emphasized when, in 1961, the IMC was absorbed into the WCC to become the Commission for World Mission and Evangelism. This reflected the growing convictions that mission was the responsibility of the church, and the church was now present in all the nations of the earth. As Stephen Neill summarized, "the age of missions is at an end; the age of mission has begun."[18] In 1971 John Gatu, General Secretary of the Presbyterian Church in East Africa, called for a "moratorium on missionaries" arguing that foreign missionaries and funds were inhibiting the growth of the indigenous African church.[19] This view was affirmed by many in the ecumenical movement on the assumption that local churches could now reach out to their local communities in every corner of the earth.[20] Mission was seen as the responsibility of the church, but there was minimal perceived need for overseas missionaries because the task could be fulfilled in every nation by churches addressing the social needs in their local communities.

The Lausanne Movement

With these changes, many evangelicals felt that Stephen Neill's statement, "When everything is mission, nothing is mission" was being fulfilled and the missionary focus of taking the gospel message to all nations was being lost.[21] This strengthened their motivation to gather in Lausanne, Switzerland, in 1974, for the First International Congress on World Evangelization. The Lausanne Covenant, which resulted from this gathering, set forth the evangelical understanding of mission and evangelism for that time. Reflecting parts of the theology of the ecumenical movement, it affirmed that the church is sent into the world by God to fulfill its mission as his

---

his redemptive purposes through the events of secular history. See Bosch, *Transforming Mission*, 390–93.

17. Bosch, *Transforming Mission*, 393.
18. Neill, *History*, 572.
19. Wagner, "Colour," 165–76; Reese, "John Gatu," 245–56. The *International Review of Mission* gave the entire April 1975 issue to discuss the suggested moratorium.
20. Bosch, *Transforming Mission*, 378–79.
21. Neill, *Creative Tension*, 81; Engen, *Mission*, 145–56.

servants and witnesses.[22] Almost echoing the words of Barth, the covenant states that, "a church that is not a missionary church is contradicting itself and quenching the Spirit."[23] It also recognizes the presence of churches in all nations declaring that "world evangelization requires the whole church to take the whole gospel to the whole world."[24] Nevertheless, noting that "more than 2,700 million people, which is more than two-thirds of all humanity, have yet to be evangelized" the ongoing need for churches to send missionaries to other places was affirmed.[25] The Covenant demands that "all churches should therefore be asking God and themselves what they should be doing both to reach their own area and to send missionaries to other parts of the world."[26] It also affirms that, "evangelism is primary" in the church's mission in all contexts.[27] This commitment to sending missionaries and emphasizing the verbal proclamation of the gospel were key points of difference from the ecumenical affirmations.

Later Lausanne Movement meetings produced similar documents which affirmed the original covenant and its statements regarding the church. The Manila Manifesto declares that "God has committed to the whole church and every member of it the task of making Christ known throughout the world."[28] It expounds the implications for local churches noting that "the local church bears a primary responsibility for the spread of the gospel."[29] Also noting that, "a church which sends out missionaries must not neglect its own locality, and a church which evangelizes its neighborhood must not ignore the rest of the world."[30] The third Lausanne International Congress was held in 2010 and produced the Cape Town Commitment. This document affirms the earlier documents stating that "the Church's participation in God's mission continues,"[31] although the emphasis on the local church highlighted in the Manila Manifesto was not evident. "Local churches in the Global South"[32] were encouraged

22. Lausanne Movement, "Lausanne Covenant," par. 1.
23. Lausanne Movement, "Lausanne Covenant," par. 14.
24. Lausanne Movement, "Lausanne Covenant," par. 6.
25. Lausanne Movement, "Lausanne Covenant," par. 9.
26. Lausanne Movement, "Lausanne Covenant," par. 8.
27. Lausanne Movement, "Lausanne Covenant," par. 6.
28. Lausanne Movement, "Manila Manifesto," affirmation 12.
29. Lausanne Movement, "Manila Manifesto," section 8.
30. Lausanne Movement, "Manila Manifesto," section 8.
31. Lausanne Movement, "Cape Town Commitment," Preamble.
32. Lausanne Movement, "Cape Town Commitment," section IID.

to engage unreached people groups, but otherwise it was the actions of the worldwide church that were primarily in focus. This emphasis on the global church as the agent of mission reflects the theology of the Cape Town Commitment's lead author, Christopher J. H. Wright.[33] Wright is a key evangelical voice on the theology of mission whose 580-page tome, *The Mission of God: Unlocking the Bible's Grand Narrative*, employs a missional hermeneutic to explore the nature and scope of mission in the Bible. He discusses at length the mission of the church, yet primarily emphasizes the universal church as the agent of mission. There is only one reference to the local church which he defines as "the organism effectively and strategically placed for God's mission in any given community."[34] This highlights the local missional responsibilities of the local church while suggesting that the global missionary task is the responsibility of the wider Christian population.

Though the movement has not influenced all corners of the evangelical world, Lausanne's theology impacted Sydney evangelical churches through several key local Christian leaders. Jack Dain, Assistant Bishop of the Anglican Diocese of Sydney and Federal Secretary of CMS Australia, was the Executive Chairman of the 1974 Congress.[35] David Claydon, who chaired the group which produced the Lausanne Covenant, was later appointed to be the Federal Secretary of CMS Australia (1988–2002) and the International Director of the Lausanne Movement (2002–4).[36] Glenn Davies, who served as Archbishop of the Sydney diocese (2013–21), attended both the second (1989) and third (2010) Lausanne Congresses and served on the Lausanne board of directors. These men and others brought many of the values and insights from these gatherings to Sydney evangelical churches. The movement therefore had significant influence on the approach to church and mission engagement in these churches.[37]

The Missional Church Movement

Another notable influence on Sydney evangelical theology on church engagement in mission has been the missional church conversation. This

---

33. Lausanne Movement, "Cape Town Commitment," Foreword.
34. Wright, *Mission of God*, 322.
35. Piggin and Linder, *Attending*, 361.
36. Paterson, *Never Alone*, 168, 212, 216.
37. Chilton, "Evangelicals," 299–349.

traces its history to the insights of another highly influential voice in the ecumenical movement, Lesslie Newbigin (1909–98). Newbigin was a British missionary to India who served as the General Secretary of the IMC during the time when it became part of the WCC (1959–65).[38] In *The Open Secret*, Newbigin articulates a theology of mission that showed the relevance of the *missio Dei* for the local church. He argues that the *missio Dei* was seen most clearly when Jesus Christ was sent by God the Father to announce and manifest the reign of God and then together they sent the Holy Spirit into the world. The church is now sent by the Son and empowered by the Spirit to participate in this mission of the triune God. As the church proclaims and lives out the implications of its relationship with God it functions as a "hermeneutic of the gospel" which enables the unbelieving world to see and understand the ministry and message of Jesus.[39] Newbigin describes the church as a "sign, instrument, and foretaste of the reign of God" in the world.[40] To support this view he appeals to the *ekklēsia* (ἐκκλησία) language of the New Testament. He argues that just as the *ekklēsia* of Greco-Roman society was called together to address matters that impacted the whole community, so the *ekklēsia* of God is gathered to live out the implications of a message that impacts the whole world.[41] The church's task is to communicate to all, through word and deed, that "Jesus is Lord." Through its intimate relationship with Christ, the church becomes the focal point for God's mission as the reign of God is embodied and proclaimed.[42]

Though Newbigin served as a missionary in India and was active in the WCC, his "most noteworthy historical accomplishment" was arguably his challenge to apply the insights of missiology to churches in a Western context.[43] In *Foolishness to the Greeks*, Newbigin considers "what would be involved in a genuinely missionary encounter between the gospel and the culture that is shared by the peoples of Europe and North America."[44] This question stimulated the formation of the Gospel in Our Culture Network in North America which published the highly influential book, *Missional Church: A Vision for the Sending of the Church*

38. Wainwright, *Lesslie Newbigin*, v.
39. Newbigin, *Foolishness*, 227.
40. Newbigin, *Gospel*, 13, 50, 110.
41. Newbigin, *Gospel*, 16–17.
42. Goheen, "'As the Father,'" 115–62.
43. Goheen, "Liberating," 360.
44. Newbigin, *Foolishness to the Greeks*, 1.

*in North America.*⁴⁵ This book seeks to explore the practical implications of the church being the "instrument and witness" of the gospel in the world.⁴⁶ It examines the post-modern cultural shift in North America and critiques the "functional Christendom" of the church which had resulted in it being marginalized and divided.⁴⁷ The authors explicitly affirm the theology of Newbigin noting that mission is not a task given to the church but is core to its identity. This missional identity is to be expressed by being a genuine community in its relationships, by compassionately serving the world around it, and by announcing the reign of God in the world.⁴⁸

The publication of *Missional Church* stimulated a far-reaching and diverse conversation about the place of the church in God's mission in Western contexts. A 2004 occasional paper produced by a Lausanne forum on "The Local Church in Mission" demonstrated the clear influence of the missional church conversation as it called churches to be "mission congregations" that eschewed the "Constantinian model" of church.⁴⁹ Though Lausanne was one way that these concepts influenced Sydney evangelical churches, more significant was local Baptist leader and educator Michael Frost who has been an active proponent of missional thinking in the city. Together with Alan Hirsch, he challenged the "attractional, dualistic and hierarchical" approach of the institutional churches, arguing that they are captive to the Christendom model of church inherited from Constantine.⁵⁰ They argued that the church must rather be missional, incarnational, committed to whole-of-life spirituality, and employing flat leadership structures that recognize the diverse gifts of Christian people.⁵¹ Darren Cronshaw and others have explored the expression of this kind of missional thinking in Australian churches noting a number of churches utilizing this approach.⁵² Though many of these would be more closely aligned with the progressive stream of evangelicalism, missional church perspectives have had wide influence. Tim

---

45. Guder, *Missional Church*; Goheen, "Father," 371–414.

46. Guder, *Missional Church*, 5.

47. Guder, *Missional Church*, 46.

48. Guder, *Missional Church*, 77–109.

49. Lausanne Movement, "Local Church."

50. Frost and Hirsch, *Shaping of Things*, 21–29.

51. Frost and Hirsch, *Shaping of Things*, 48–49.

52. Cronshaw and Devenish, "Continuing Conversion," 78–96; Cronshaw and Taylor, "Congregation," 206–28; Groza, "Seldom Acknowledged," 163–81.

Chester and Steve Timmis affirm these same beliefs about the changes in Western culture and the need for a comprehensive approach to local mission in ways that resonate more strongly with conservative evangelical churches. Their emphasis on "being both gospel-centered and community-centered" was appreciated for its use of familiar language.[53] Timothy Keller also engages with and appropriates many key missional church principles in *Center Church* using reformed theological categories.[54] These perspectives on the missional church have thereby had a significant ongoing influence on Sydney evangelical churches.

Although the missional church conversation has highlighted the role of the local church in local mission, it has been critiqued for its lack of attention to distant mission.[55] Michael Goheen notes that, "in the burgeoning missional church movement little is said about taking the gospel to places where it is unknown. Mission has swallowed up missions."[56] Evangelical scholar Ed Stetzer observes the same tendency and suggests that the missional church's rediscovery of mission for the local church led some people to lose sight of the global need for mission.[57] By contrast, Tim Chester avers that missional churches in the United Kingdom are actively involved in distant mission.[58] Whether or not this is the case in Australia needs to be considered. There are many Sydney evangelical churches that have been shaped by the missional conversation, yet the impact of this on local church involvement in distant mission has not previously been explored.

Sydney Anglican Ecclesiology and Mission

Arguably the most significant missiological issue to arise from the 1974 Lausanne Congress pertained to the relationship between evangelism and

---

53. Chester and Timmis, *Total Church*, 18; Payne et al., "Talking about Total Church."

54. Keller, *Center Church*, 258–61.

55. Goheen, *Light to the Nations*, 219.

56. Goheen, *Introducing*, 404. Goheen is here following Newbigin's definition of missions as, "particular enterprises within the total mission which have the primary intention of bringing into existence a Christian presence in a milieu where previously there was no such presence or where such presence was ineffective." Newbigin, "Cross-Currents," 149.

57. Stetzer, "Five Reasons."

58. Chester, "Missional Church."

social concern in the mission of the church.[59] The Lausanne Covenant affirmed the need for Christian social responsibility with the support of several Australian evangelicals and the opposition of others. Jack Dain and David Claydon actively supported the inclusion but John Chapman, a highly influential evangelist in the Sydney Anglican Diocese, and Paul Barnett, who later became the Anglican Bishop of North Sydney, were vocally opposed.[60] They saw it as a confusion of the gospel message which undermined the central task of evangelism.[61] In doing this, Chapman and Barnett were reflecting the theological conservatism of Sydney Anglicanism which reacted to the fact that "Lausanne . . . expressed the aspirations of more progressive evangelicals."[62] This conservativism has considerable implications for church and mission as it was championed by D. Broughton Knox (1916–94) and Donald Robinson (1922–2018) who served together as the Principal and Vice-Principal respectively of the Sydney Anglican training institution, Moore Theological College.[63]

The primary source of Knox and Robinson's enduring influence was their shaping of theological method. Donald Robinson was a linguist and exegete who was committed to semantics and careful biblical interpretation.[64] He saw Scripture as the progressive story of God's redemptive purposes culminating in the death and resurrection of Jesus and looking forward to Jesus' return and the consummation of all things. Specific biblical concepts were interpreted through the lens of this metanarrative and with reference to the present stage of redemptive history. Knox's method displayed similar commitment to exegesis, though as a systematic theologian his exegetical insights led to wider reflections on matters of doctrine. Knox and Robinson rarely collaborated on publications, but the influence of their friendship is evident throughout their work, and their theological perspectives are often considered together.[65]

The topic on which they are best known for collaborating is the doctrine of the church. Their views in this area are so notable that they have

---

59. Stanley, *Global Diffusion*, 151–79.

60. Chilton, "Evangelicals," 326–28.

61. Chilton, "Evangelicals," 339–40.

62. Piggin and Linder, *Attending*, 363.

63. Kuhn, *Ecclesiology*, 132.

64. Robinson, "'Church' Revisited," 6.

65. Kuhn, *Ecclesiology*; Judd and Cable, *Sydney Anglicans*, 287–90; Cameron, *Enigmatic Life*, 192–93.

become known as the Knox-Robinson Ecclesiology (KRE).[66] Stephen Judd and Kenneth Cable have described their position as "a revision of the traditional concept of the nature of the church."[67] A significant impetus to Knox and Robinson's development of their ecclesial perspectives was the unifying efforts of the ecumenical movement.[68] From the middle of the twentieth century, the WCC was seeking to facilitate a visible unity among all Christians across the world so as to "enable the churches to render their common witness to the world."[69] Yet, as early as 1954 Donald Robinson was expressing disagreement with "the exaggerated and misleading doctrines of "Christian unity" promulgated by many World Council leaders."[70] Knox and Robinson were not convinced that the kind of global church unity the WCC was promoting was consistent with the teaching of Scripture. Rather, they believed that only the local congregation could legitimately be described as the church on earth.

The KRE essentially holds that, in the New Testament, church either refers to a physical local gathering of Christians on earth or the heavenly gathering of all believers around Christ. Consequently, a denomination, a building, an institution, or even a community of people could not legitimately be called a church. This conclusion was built upon linguistic study of the *ekklēsia* word-group which Robinson argued always referred to a literal gathering of people.[71] Theologically, Knox and Robinson saw the heavenly gathering as the pre-eminent church in the New Testament (Eph 1:22–23; Heb 12:23), while the local churches were understood to be earthly manifestations of the heavenly reality.[72] Knox argues that there are churches on earth, but when the Bible refers to "the church" it is the heavenly church that is in view.[73] On earth, church should be considered something that Christians *do*, rather than something that Christians *are*. Robinson concludes, "although we often speak of these congregations collectively as the New Testament church or the early church, no New

---

66. Kuhn has argued that the foundational contribution of Donald Robinson suggests it could more aptly be named the "Robinson-Knox ecclesiology." Kuhn, *Ecclesiology*, 208; Jensen, *Sydney Anglicanism*, 75–89.
67. Judd and Cable, *Sydney Anglicans*, 289.
68. Robinson, "'Church' Revisited," 8–11.
69. Visser't Hooft, *Genesis and Formation*, 92.
70. Robinson, "WCC Assembly," 4.
71. Robinson, "'Church' Revisited," 4–5.
72. Knox, "De-Mythologizing," 23.
73. Knox, "De-Mythologizing," 27.

Testament writer uses *ekklēsia* in this collective way."[74] The language of church should not be used to describe people who do not physically gather, so there can be no such thing as the "universal church" or even the "church of Australia."[75] Furthermore, the gathering becomes the primary expression of church such that the church effectively ceases to exist on earth between meetings. As Robinson states, "it is not too much to say that the church on earth does not exist, or is not visible, except in the actual assembly of believers."[76]

Another surprising implication of this ecclesiological position is the separation that it brings between church and mission.[77] The primary purpose of the church gathering, according to the KRE, is to meet with Christ.[78] Church is a place of worship and fellowship with other believers who come to edify each other through the word of Christ. This profoundly impacts the relationship between the church and non-Christians. In a paper addressing these issues, Robinson states,

> The purpose of the ecclesia is that God's children, ordinarily scattered in the world, might strengthen one another's hands in the sharing of ministries to their mutual edification, and be renewed and inspired for godly living in their ordinary avocations. But the church as such has no *face to* the world, and is therefore not a direct agent in evangelism.[79]

Or, as many Moore Theological College students remember Robinson stating more bluntly, "the church has no mission." Graham Cole sought to address this concern by suggesting that while the *ekklēsia* may have no mission, Christians participate in mission as "the people of God."[80] However, Robert Doyle, a lecturer at Moore Theological College and close ally of Knox and Robinson, refutes this suggestion arguing that God is the

---

74. Robinson, "Church," 222–29. While this may seem like an atypical ecclesiology, the inclusion of Robinson's article in the *New Bible Dictionary's* first (1962), second (1985) and third edition (1996) indicates the breadth of its reach.

75. Robinson, "Church of God," 230–53.

76. Robinson, "Church of God," 236.

77. For a fuller exploration of the place of mission in the KRE, see Silberman, "Un-Missional Church," 61–76.

78. Robinson, "Liturgical Patterns," 321.

79. Robinson, "Doctrine of the Church," 109. Emphasis original.

80. Cole, "Doctrine," 3–17.

one who sends missionaries, and the church participates only through "prayer and praise."[81]

The suggestion that mission is not one of the purposes of the church has continued to be disputed by Sydney Anglicans. In 1992, the Moore Theological College annual School of Theology was on *Exploring the Missionary Church*.[82] Mark Thompson's paper specifically addresses Robinson's view that the church has "no face to the world."[83] He argues that on the basis of the diverse corporate metaphors used for Christians in the Bible, the character of God, and the various ways that Christians are called to be active in the world, "the church has a face to the world and the essence of its mission is the intelligible communication of the gospel of Christ to those who are lost."[84] Similarly, Peter Jensen states that the local church has "a gospel which demands that we reach out in evangelism."[85] These papers reveal a belief among many faculty at Moore Theological College that there is a place for evangelism in the life of the church, though it is not considered the church's primary purpose. The Diocesan Doctrine Commission asserted a similar view in a report titled *A Theology of Christian Assembly*.[86] The report emphasizes the view that the Christian assembly is first and foremost "a consequence of God's purpose and work."[87] In considering whether evangelism is part of the purpose of the assembly, the report states that "the Christian assembly itself is characteristically the fruit of evangelism, not its agent."[88] The Christian gathering is, however, seen to serve the missionary task in three ways. Firstly, "by building outward-looking mission-minded Christians," secondly, through the partnership of assembly members in "gospel work" with other Christians, and finally, by sending out "some of their members" to engage in mission elsewhere.[89] Mission was therefore

---

81. Doyle, "Response," 25.
82. Webb, *Exploring*.
83. Thompson, "Local Church," 1–26.
84. Thompson, "Local Church," 23.
85. Jensen, "Architecture of a Missionary," 108.
86. This had been requested by the 2007 Synod, to inform future efforts to "shape authentic, biblical and Anglican orders of service suitable for the contemporary church." See Sydney Diocesan Doctrine Commission, *Theology*.
87. Sydney Diocesan Doctrine Commission, *Theology*, 28.
88. Sydney Diocesan Doctrine Commission, *Theology*, 30.
89. Sydney Diocesan Doctrine Commission, *Theology*, 30.

considered an important part of the Christian life, but it was removed from the responsibility of the local church.

Arguably one of the most influential voices in Sydney Anglicanism in the last thirty years has been that of Philip Jensen. Brother to Archbishop Peter Jensen, Jensen's involvement in university ministry, publishing, and the foundation of the Ministry Training Strategy has profoundly influenced the theology and ministry philosophy of hundreds of Sydney evangelical clergy.[90] In an article entitled, "What Is Church For?"[91] Jensen rehearses the arguments of the KRE and reflects its core convictions by describing the church as the goal of Jesus' salvific work. He acknowledges that evangelism would happen in the gathering when non-Christians are present, but "building the church is the aim of evangelism (wherever it happens), not the other way around."[92] He continues,

> Perhaps we can begin to see why asking "what church is for" is to ask the wrong question. Jesus' intention is to build his church, his gathering. And the glorious gathering of Jesus is not an instrument to achieve something else; it is the goal, or object of Jesus' work. It is the thing that Jesus is building.[93]

It is therefore clear that the KRE continues to influence thinking about the purpose of the church in Sydney Anglican circles. The consistent theme is that the local church is foremost an event that *primarily* exists for fellowship with God and with other believers. Christians are to be personally involved in mission, and church gatherings should equip them to be mission-minded, but the church as a corporate entity has limited responsibility for mission, particularly mission beyond its local community. The difference between this position and that championed by the Lausanne movement is stark, yet both have influenced local church practice among Sydney evangelicals. This dispute about the place of mission in the local church has primarily influenced Anglican churches, however the dominance of this denomination among Sydney evangelicals has influenced practice in a range of churches. Though other denominations have generally accepted the importance of local church involvement in mission, the expression of this conviction has varied from church to church.

---

90. MTS is the Ministry Training Strategy, a two-year ministry apprenticeship that many people do before attending theological college. See https://mts.com.au.
91. Jensen, "What Is Church For?"
92. Jensen, "What Is Church for?"
93. Jensen, "What Is Church for?"

The Nature of Mission

The definition of mission is another arena in which the theological conservatism of Sydney evangelicalism impinges upon the involvement of local churches in mission, and it too has been emphasized at Moore Theological College. At his inaugural address as the Head of the Department of Mission at Moore Theological College, Michael Raiter defined mission using the tools of biblical theology and exegesis.[94] He reviewed the use of the sending word group in the New Testament and concluded, "when used in a technical sense, *pempein* and *apostellein* refer to the ministry of the verbal proclamation of the gospel to the end that mature churches are planted and established . . . anything that does not have as its defining characteristic gospel proclamation . . . is not mission."[95] Similarly, Peter O'Brien, Moore Theological College Vice-Principal (1985–2000), co-authored a biblical theology of mission with Andreas Köstenberger in which they trace the theme of mission through the whole of the Bible.[96] Though they do not explicitly define mission, they investigate the theme by considering Bible passages that relate "to the proclamation of God's name and of his saving purposes in Christ to the unbelieving world."[97] This understanding of mission is a correction of the definition of mission promoted by John Stott as "everything the church is sent into the world to do"[98] which was seen to be a departure from the traditional evangelical understanding of mission.[99] Works of compassion are considered valuable and important for Christians to do, but the mission of God's people can "more or less, be equated with evangelism."[100] The godly lives of Christians will "adorn and commend the message,"[101] but without proclamation there is no mission.

One dissenting Sydney evangelical voice in this conversation is Anglican minister and author, John Dickson. Dickson asserts that gospel proclamation is primarily the responsibility of specifically gifted evangelists, while all other Christians should "promote the gospel" through

---

94. Raiter, "Sent for This Purpose."
95. Raiter, "Sent for This Purpose," 123.
96. Köstenberger and O'Brien, *Salvation*.
97. Köstenberger and O'Brien, *Salvation*, 21–22.
98. Stott, *Christian Mission*, 30.
99. Woodhouse, "Evangelism," 3–26.
100. Mascord, "Equipping," 125.
101. Jensen, "2001 Presidential Address."

their daily life and worship.[102] Notably, Dickson defined mission as "the range of activities by which members of a religious community desirous of the conversion of outsiders seek to promote their religion to non-adherents."[103] Given the teleological nature of his definition, it is not surprising that his conclusions about mission included a wider range of activities. These views have been both affirmed and disputed by Sydney Anglican leaders and are influential in Sydney evangelical churches.[104]

This emphasis on proclamation does not mean that Sydney Anglicans are opposed to Christians being involved in social action. Believers have a duty to show compassion and love to one's neighbors both inside and outside the church; it is just not considered part of mission.[105] Evangelism and social action are important and may well happen together but they must be understood as two distinct activities and proclamation must be central.[106] David Williams recently explored the relationship between care for the poor and Sydney Anglican perspectives on the church and mission.[107] He concluded that acts of social concern are best understood by Sydney Anglicans as expressions of "holistic discipleship" and "holistic churches," but they are not part of mission.[108]

Theological Perspectives: Interim Conclusions

Evangelicalism in the twentieth and twenty-first centuries has seen significant shifts in ecclesiological and missiological thinking. The ecumenical movement initiated a reconsideration of the nature of mission and the relationship between God, the church, and mission. These conversations stimulated an evangelical response which affirmed the centrality of God in the mission endeavor and discussed the implications for local churches. Inspired by the work of Lesslie Newbigin, the missional church movement embraced the *missio Dei* and affirmed mission as the hallmark of the local congregation. While these conversations have had a notable influence on evangelical churches in Australia, the theology of church

---

102. Dickson, *Mission-Commitment*, 131–32.
103. Dickson, *Mission-Commitment*, 10.
104. Forsyth, "Promoting the Gospel"; Perkins, "Danger of Living."
105. Thompson, "Does the Local Church?," 23.
106. Chester, "Social Involvement (Part I)"; Chester and Payne, "Social Involvement (Part II)"; Raiter, "Social Involvement (Part III)."
107. Williams, "Relocating Holism."
108. Williams, "Relocating Holism," 98–101.

and mission that has arisen among many Sydney evangelical churches has emphasized local mission activities focused on the growth of the local church while minimizing the need for local church involvement in social ministries and distant mission. The relationship between these dimensions of church practice is therefore a key issue to be explored.

PRACTICAL APPROACHES TO CHURCH INVOLVEMENT IN MISSION

Just as different theological perspectives have influenced Sydney evangelical church involvement in mission, so too have the various practical approaches. These approaches emphasize different dimensions of church involvement according to the theological convictions and cultural context of their proponents. Much of the current conversation addresses the needs in North America or the United Kingdom (UK) and does not directly apply to the Australian situation. There have been a small number of resources developed specifically for Australian churches, though the influence of distant paradigms and the theological diversity among the authors has produced a wide range of emphases.

Churches and Agencies

One of the earliest approaches to missional engagement among evangelicals arose with the proliferation of mission societies in the late eighteenth century. It was a time of profound global change as explorers, traders, and colonizers extended European influence around the world and evangelical leaders like William Carey began to mobilize Christians for the cause of global mission. In his *Enquiry into the Obligation of Christians to Use Means for the Conversion of the Heathen,* Carey drew on Jesus' command in Matthew 28 and the global statistics of those who had never heard the gospel to conclude that "all these things are loud calls to Christians, and especially to ministers, to exert themselves to the utmost in their several spheres of action."[109] The *means* by which they could do this, Carey proposed, was by forming voluntary societies that would bring together those that were committed to this goal.[110] In the years that followed many mission organizations were founded to facilitate the movement of

---

109. Carey, *Enquiry*, 66.
110. Carey, *Enquiry*, 82–83; Walls, *Missionary Movement*, 244–47.

missionaries into the world. In 1793, William Carey was sent to India by the "Particular Baptist Society for the Propagation of the Gospel among the Heathen" and in the following years the London Missionary Society (1795), the Church Missionary Society (1799), and the American Board of Commissioners for Foreign Missions (1810) did likewise. These organizations were mostly denominationally aligned yet administratively separate from the church hierarchies and functioned as para-church organizations. Churches and church leaders were exhorted to support foreign missions, but it was through local engagement of lay people that the societies grew. Andrew Walls argues that mission organizations were pragmatic responses to the incapacity of church structures to fulfill the missionary task and in the process of mobilizing people for mission engagement they "subverted the old church structures."[111] Walls describes this as a "fortunate subversion,"[112] but it created a disconnection between churches and overseas mission which has continued.

In the aftermath of the Second Evangelical Awakening, a growing commitment to global mission in America and the UK resulted in the formation of numerous interdenominational missionary organizations.[113] J. Hudson Taylor is often identified as the pioneer of this development as his concern for the interior regions of China led him to establish the China Inland Mission in 1865.[114] Taylor was not only motivated by geographical differences, he also wanted to see missionaries raised up from working-class backgrounds, he promoted deep cultural engagement and contextualization, and he required missionaries to never solicit financial support.[115] However, it was his commitment to field based leadership that had the greatest impact on church involvement in mission.[116] Taylor was adamant that decisions were no longer to be made by the home base or sending churches but in the context of mission engagement. In the years that followed many similar faith missions were established including the Christian and Missionary Alliance (1887), the African Inland Mission (1895), and the Sudan Interior Mission (1893).[117] These societies

---

111. Walls, *Missionary Movement*, 249.
112. Walls, *Missionary Movement*, 241.
113. Neill, *History of Christian Missions*, 323–24.
114. Tennent, *Invitation*, 263; Winter, "Three Mission Eras," 271–72.
115. Neill, *History of Christian Missions*, 333–34; Winter, "Three Mission Eras," 271.
116. Neill, *History of Christian Missions*, 334.
117. Arthur, *Mission Agencies in Crisis*, 35.

employed similar methods which engaged enthusiastic believers outside the structures of the church.

Despite this administrative distance, many mission leaders spoke of the importance of local churches in the task of world evangelization. At the 1900 Ecumenical Missionary Conference in New York, evangelist George Pentecost highlighted the central role of the local church pastor.

> To the pastor belongs the privilege and the responsibility of solving the missionary problem. Until the pastors of our churches wake to the truth of this proposition, and the foreign work of the Church becomes a passion in their hearts and consciences ... the chariot wheels of foreign missions will drive heavily ... If there are churches that give not and pray not for foreign missions, it is because they have pastors who are false and recreant to the command of Christ.[118]

Reflecting on this conference, pastor Andrew Murray similarly bemoaned the failure of many local church leaders to recognize that "missions is the supreme end of the church!"[119] These men believed that local churches were vital to the missionary task, yet a lack of engagement was evident. In 1910, the Edinburgh World Missionary conference brought missionaries from all over the world together to identify how they might achieve, "the evangelization of the nations in this generation."[120] John R. Mott, who presided over the gathering, later asserted that "it is on the home Church that the foreign work depends for its inspiration, guidance, and support."[121] This growing concern about the involvement of churches in the work of global missions suggests that the subversion of the church was bringing negative consequences.

Following World War II, the number of interdenominational faith missions continued to increase. Missiologist Ralph Winter counted 145 new mission organizations in the US between 1945 and 1971, as well as a growing trend among church leaders to emphasize the importance of the indigenous church and church-to-church partnerships while minimizing the role of the mission structures. In response, he argued that para-church mission structures were essential to the task of mission. He contended that God had ordained two separate redemptive structures

---

118. Pentecost, "Pastor," 125–26, 130.
119. Murray, *Key to the Missionary Problem*, 162.
120. Tennent, *Invitation to World Missions*, 278.
121. Mott, *Decisive Hour*, 150.

for the purpose of his mission; the "church" and the "mission band."[122] Utilizing sociological constructs, he described the church as a modality and the mission band a sodality; that is "a structured fellowship in which membership involves an adult second decision beyond modality membership."[123] Winter appealed to church history to argue that, since the time of the apostles, sodalities have been essential to the growth and spread of the Christian faith. In the Catholic church it was the monastic orders that reached into new regions, while "the vehicle that allowed the Protestant movement to become vital was the structural development of the sodality."[124] Winter valued both church and mission structures and considered them equally part of the universal church.[125] His desire was to see mission structures established in majority world contexts and for the church and mission structures to work together. However, these categories further legitimized the separation of church and mission structures.

Several voices have refuted Winter's assertion that these two structures are intended by God. From a Latin American context, Orlando Costas argues that the relationship between church and mission was too complex to replicate mission structures throughout the majority world. He describes mission organizations as a "historical particularity" that may be God's "judgment upon the church" or at least his "permissive rather than his perfect will."[126] Costas suggests that the Pietistic roots of the modern mission movement gave it a weak ecclesiology.[127] In his view, "the biblico-theological model of the church does not allow for a missionary structure apart from the church,"[128] because it undermines the church's apostolic function. Mission structures exist because churches have not participated in mission as they should. Bruce Camp similarly questions the theological validity of Winter's two structure argument while noting that many missiologists and mission leaders supported and extended it.[129] Though Camp does not deny the many ways in which mission structures have served to extend the reach of Christian mission, he denies the suggestion that they are theological necessities. Through a

---

122. Winter, "Two Structures."
123. Winter, "Two Structures," 127.
124. Winter, "Two Structures," 132.
125. Winter, "Protestant Mission Societies," 143–45.
126. Costas, *Church*, 168.
127. Costas, *Church*, 158–59.
128. Costas, *Church*, 169.
129. Camp, "Theological Examination," 198–200.

careful analysis of the Bible passages used by Winter and others to justify their position, he concludes that a local church "ought to minister locally *and* globally, mono-culturally *and* cross-culturally."[130] Mission agencies have a valuable role in the missionary task, but the church should be considered the primary actor.

Despite these dissenting voices, Winter's two-structure perspective has continued to have influence. The Lausanne occasional paper on the role of the local church in mission affirms the importance of mission sodalities, while encouraging churches to be active in developing their own "go-structures,"[131] or, in other words, to establish more mission sodalities. This emphasis on the autonomy of mission organizations encourages a separation between mission and church. In 2005, this separation was acknowledged by a gathering of Australian mission leaders representing more than twenty evangelical mission agencies. As members of the Australian Evangelical Alliance's Missions Commission, known as Missions Interlink,[132] they acknowledged,

> There have been many instances in which mission agencies have assumed a role in regard to the approval, equipping, sending, and pastoral care of missionaries that biblically belongs to the home church . . . We express our sincere regret for the tendency of many mission agencies in past years to ignore or supplant the rights of churches in regard to mission efforts.[133]

This declaration reflects a commitment among Australian mission agency leaders to "affirm the churches' primary responsibility in mission ministry."[134] However, as one Sydney Anglican minister notes, there is a tendency among local churches to outsource key ministries, like global mission, to denominational and para-church organizations.[135] Even where agencies acknowledge the responsibility of the local church, the willingness of local churches to accept the task may be lacking.

---

130. Camp, "Theological Examination," 207.
131. Lausanne Movement, "Local Church in Mission," section 2.14.
132. See https://missionsinterlink.org.au.
133. Missions Interlink, "Croydon Declaration," para. 3–4.
134. Missions Interlink, "Croydon Declaration," para. 2.
135. Kellahan, "Outsourcing Church."

The Church Growth Movement

Another significant influence on evangelical church thinking about mission through the nineteen seventies and eighties was the church growth movement. This movement grew out of the work of Donald McGavran who, in the middle of the twentieth century, suggested that the greatest need in global mission was to help the "younger churches" embrace the opportunities for growth in their contexts.[136] McGavran's recommendations drew on the biblical, sociological, and anthropological frameworks he had explored in his earlier work, *The Bridges of God*, to argue that Christianity spreads freely through family and relational networks. Mission strategy should therefore utilize these networks by focusing on homogeneous groups of people and contextualizing evangelism to their culture. These insights built upon many of the views of earlier missiologists, such as Henry Venn, Rufus Anderson, and Roland Allen.[137] In 1970, McGavran's *Understanding Church Growth* articulated what he had observed through field studies in many contexts to be the core principles that facilitate church growth.[138] The revised edition, released in 1980, expanded the book significantly and also applied the ideas to church growth in America, encouraging an emphasis on quantitative as well as qualitative growth.[139] Measurable results were prioritized, and goals were to be set and pursued. McGavran's ideas were widely embraced and taught through the Fuller Theological Seminary School of World Mission in Pasadena, California, where he served as the founding dean.[140] Together with Win Arn, he also established the Institute for American Church Growth and wrote *How to Grow a Church*.[141] Through the nineteen seventies and eighties, Win Arn visited Australia on several occasions and church growth principles gained increasing influence.

One influential Australian student of church growth principles was Sydney Anglican minister Dudley Foord. Foord studied at

---

136. McGavran, *How Churches Grow*, 10–17.

137. Allen, *Missionary Methods*; Allen, *Spontaneous Expansion*.

138. McGavran, *Understanding Church Growth*.

139. McGavran, *Understanding Church Growth*, 2nd ed.

140. Wagner, "Church Growth Movement," 199.

141. McGavran and Arn, *How to Grow a Church*. C. Peter Wagner also worked closely with McGavran and published a number of books developing the Church Growth approach. See Wagner, *Your Spiritual Gifts*; Wagner, *Your Church Can Grow*; Wagner, *Leading Your Church*.

Fuller Seminary and applied what he learnt at Christ Church Anglican, St. Ives.[142] Though he preferred to emphasize church health rather than church growth, Foord's ministry saw St. Ives become one of the largest churches in Sydney at the time.[143] His influence throughout the Sydney region through university student ministry and involvement with interdenominational evangelical conventions saw church growth principles spread widely. Other evangelical denominations also embraced the church growth movement and, in 1975, Churches of Christ pastor Gordon Moyes published *How to Grow an Australian Church* which applied the principles of McGavran and Arn's work to the Australian context. Moyes had successfully grown a church in Melbourne, Victoria, and later led the Wesley Central Mission in Sydney to become the largest church in Australia at that time.[144] Sydney evangelicals have varied in their opinion on church growth principles. While Donald Robinson, Anglican Archbishop from 1982 to 1993, challenged the pragmatism of the movement, his successor, Harry Goodhew, was more supportive and widely encouraged similar strategies in Anglican churches.[145]

Wider reflections on the church growth movement have flowed in various directions. Latin American Missiologists labelled the movement "managerial missiology," suggesting that it sought to make missions manageable by "reduc[ing] reality to an understandable picture."[146] While acknowledging that this may be more evident in McGavran's disciples than in his own work, the fundamental assumptions of the approach were challenged. American Baptist Rick Warren was a great admirer of McGavran but, like Foord, argued that churches would grow by focusing on church health.[147] He instructs church leaders to pursue the five purposes of "mission, magnification, membership, maturity, and ministry."[148] According to Warren, the task of mission includes reaching those in the local community, training church members in evangelism, sending people on short-term mission, and sending and supporting long-term missionaries.[149] Warren has had significant influence in Australia through being a

142. Piggin and Linder, *Attending*, 379.
143. Piggin and Linder, *Attending*, 379.
144. Piggin and Linder, *Attending*, 425.
145. Piggin and Linder, Attending, 425–26.
146. Escobar, "Movement Divided," 11.
147. Warren, *Purpose Driven Church*, 17.
148. Warren, *Purpose Driven* Church, 102–7.
149. Warren, *Purpose Driven* Church, 148.

speaker at Sydney Hillsong Conference in 2006 and 2015,[150] and a variety of churches from different denominations have implemented his principles.[151] More recently, a modified version of Warren's five purpose model of ministry has been promoted among conservative evangelical churches through the Geneva Push and Reach Australia training networks.[152]

Australian Approaches to Local Church Mission

Even those evangelicals that rejected the pragmatism of the church growth movement were spurred on in their local mission efforts. John Chapman led the charge in the Sydney Anglican churches as his training and books equipped people for evangelism. In *Know and Tell the Gospel*, Chapman outlines the gospel message and instructs every Christian in how they can be involved in mission through personal evangelism. Chapman's teaching was consistent with the Knox-Robinson ecclesiology and understanding of mission as the proclamation of the message of Jesus by individual Christians. The local church was encouraged to hold occasional evangelistic events, but its primary role was to provide encouragement and training for church members in "lifestyle evangelism."[153] Though Chapman was eager to see people well equipped for evangelistic preaching, he believed that "evangelism is not a congregational activity, but an individual one."[154] Moore Theological College lecturer Peter Bolt placed a similar emphasis on personal evangelism as he encouraged churches and other Christian ministries to be *Mission Minded*. He states "mission is clearly the priority for individual Christians, and for groups of Christians, for it is the priority of our Lord and our God."[155] From Bolt's perspective, a mission minded church should categorize all its activities as facilitating either "evangelism, edification, or support to ministry."[156] These are the ways to be "engaged in Christ's Mission,"[157] yet Bolt notes

150. Hillsong is the largest Pentecostal church in Australia. In 2015, over 23,000 people from nineteen denominations attended the annual Hillsong conference. Hillsong Church, *Annual Report 2015*, 38.
151. Halcrow, "Sydney Churches Accelerate."
152. Lynch, "Dissecting the '5Ms.'"
153. Chapman, *Know and Tell*, 106–7.
154. Chapman, *Know and Tell*, 93.
155. Bolt, *Mission Minded*, 8.
156. Bolt, *Mission Minded*, 11–17.
157. Bolt, *Mission Minded*, 11.

that "support to ministry," which encompassed participation in distant mission, was not true ministry.[158] Being committed to mission in these Sydney evangelical churches is primarily fulfilled through encouraging and participating in personal evangelism locally.

This separation between participation in Christian mission and involvement in activities that support mission is even more evident in Colin Marshall and Tony Payne's widely read *The Trellis and the Vine* and *The Vine Project*. These resources assert that the primary ministry of the church is to teach people to be disciples of Jesus who will in turn make other disciples of Jesus. They appeal to Jesus' final words in Matthew's Gospel as the ground of their approach, but note that, "the commission is not fundamentally about mission out there somewhere else in another country. *It's a commission that makes disciple-making the normal agenda and priority of every church and every Christian disciple.*"[159] Church ministries should be structured to equip all Christians for involvement in local mission, with an awareness that some trained people may leave the church for mission elsewhere. Marshall and Payne appear to promote this sending of people out for the purposes of mission when they state, "we must be exporters of trained people instead of hoarders of trained people."[160] However, the training is heavily focused on near culture disciple making with no discussion of preparing people for distant cross-cultural mission.

Despite this heavy emphasis on local mission engagement, there is awareness among some Sydney evangelicals of the local church's role in identifying and supporting people for involvement in distant mission. Moore Theological College lecturer Keith Mascord argues that the need to send people out was a key implication of the belief that God gifts individuals for the task of evangelism.[161] He argues that the local church has a responsibility to recognize, equip, and support those people who have been equipped by God specifically for mission locally and overseas. Peter O'Brien provides a biblical foundation for this partnership through his study of the "fellowship" (κοινωνία) language in Paul's letter to the Philippians.[162] Though he denies that it provides a specific model for

---

158. Bolt acknowledges that his may be an "unbiblical distinction," yet practically it is seen to bring clarity to the task. Bolt, *Mission Minded*, 49.

159. Marshall and Payne, *Trellis*, 13. Emphasis original.

160. Marshall and Payne, *Trellis*, 83.

161. Mascord, "Equipping," 139–41.

162. O'Brien, "Fellowship," 9–18.

missionary care, he identifies clear principles for financial and prayer support that he believes should inform the practice of a local church. This echoes Broughton Knox's earlier emphasis on the place of fellowship in the life of the local congregation.[163] Knox noted that by supporting people in their evangelistic ministry outside the church, Christians have fellowship with them, "even though they are not themselves part of the evangelistic team."[164] Churches can therefore partner in mission elsewhere, though Doyle clarifies this relationship by emphasizing that it is not the church but "God who sends the missionaries."[165] The implication being that structures and organizations outside of the local church, like Winter's sodalities, will provide the primary sending structures for distant mission. Individuals and local churches may support these structures, but the primary emphasis for local church involvement in mission is through equipping its members for personal evangelism. A church may host evangelistic events, but mission is ultimately the responsibility of individual Christians. Some of these Christians may be sent by God to participate in mission at a distance and the local church may support them, but this is not core to the mission of the local church.

The Church as Sender

In stark contrast to this perspective is the view that it is the local church that is primarily responsible for sending the missionary. Missiologists and mission leaders are the most vocal proponents of this view, though it is certainly not a new perspective. Interestingly, despite their later opposition to the idea, this was previously the view of Knox and Robinson who stated that "the church itself is God's missionary society."[166] Yet it was much later that Paul Beals outlined *A Church-Based Missions Strategy* which argued that the local church must fulfil the missionary responsibilities of the universal church by enlisting, preparing, commissioning, sending, and supporting missionaries to evangelize the world.[167] This requires committed pastors, church policies, and partnership with

---

163. Knox, "Biblical Concept," 59–82.
164. Knox, "Biblical Concept," 66.
165. Doyle, "Response," 25.
166. Knox and Robinson, "Missionary Society," 2. There is no author listed for this editorial. However, Knox's personal collection on which he noted the joint authorship is held in Moore College library.
167. Beals, *People for His Name*. The first edition of this book was published in 1985.

mission agencies and theological institutions, however the local church is considered the primary sending body. Neal Pirolo presented a similar perspective in his popular book *Serving as Senders*.[168] Pirolo's intended audience is individual Christians who will take up the responsibility to send overseas missionaries by providing moral, logistical, financial, prayer, communication, and re-entry support. Though he does not emphasize the role of the local church, he encourages integrating missions into every dimension of church practice.[169] While Beals and Pirolo both wrote from a North American perspective, Michael Griffiths applies similar principles to churches in the UK.[170] Griffiths highlights the central role of the local church and church leaders in the sending of missionaries and presents several exemplary churches as models. Though these books may not have had a wide readership in Australia, they shaped the approach of Australian mission organization leaders who affirmed "the churches' primary responsibility in mission ministry."[171]

Since then, a small number of Australians have also written about the ways in which local churches might support overseas missionaries. Pastor and mission leader Allan Webb, suggests that *Your Church Can Make a World of Difference* by being actively involved in raising up and sending people out to serve around the globe.[172] Webb emphasizes the place of prayer and financial support of missionaries and outlines the qualities of a sending church with particular reference to his own experience leading Swanston Street Church of Christ in Melbourne.[173] In 2011, Bruce Dipple, Director of the School of Cross-Cultural Mission at SMBC, released *Becoming Global* to encourage the involvement of local churches in global mission. Dipple outlines the biblical foundations for the central role of the local church in sending missionaries and discusses ways to develop a culture of mission involvement. He draws on his experiences as a theological educator, mission organization director, and Baptist pastor to suggest ways to both educate and engage church members in global mission. These two books speak directly to Australian church involvement in mission, yet their impact on Sydney churches has been limited. In the last decade there have also been several popular level books published from an

168. Pirolo, *Serving as Senders*.
169. Pirolo, *Serving as Senders Today*, 36–38.
170. Griffiths, *Task Unfinished*.
171. Missions Interlink, *Croydon Declaration*.
172. Webb, *Your Church*, 15–16.
173. Webb, *Your Church*, 123–44.

American perspective addressing the issue of local church involvement in mission, but they have also had limited impact on Australian churches.[174]

Practical Approaches: Interim Conclusions

Though the theological emphasis on the role of the local church in mission has grown significantly since the middle of the twentieth century, the practical ways in which that involvement is understood varies greatly across the literature. For much of the twentieth century, mission was considered a distant activity and mission organizations were the primary sending structures. Local churches supported this work, though they were not encouraged to be directly involved. Ralph Winter provided a theological justification for this pattern by arguing for the biblical necessity of mission sodalities. At the same time, the ecumenical and Lausanne movements were focusing more attention on the role of local churches in the mission endeavor. Missiological insights were applied to the practices of the local church and the central place of the local church in mission was highlighted. Through the church growth movement, and later the missional church movement, the role of local churches in mission has been further discussed. Local churches are primarily responsible for mission, both theologically and practically, though there is a greater emphasis on local mission than distant mission. Drawing on these foundations, a small number of authors in the US, UK, and Australia have emphasized the central role of the local church in both local and distant mission. Though this body of literature has grown in recent years, particularly in the US, its influence among Sydney evangelicals appears to have been limited. By contrast, a stream of Australian literature emphasizing the role of the individual Christian in the task of mission, rather than the church, has been more widely accepted. Often reflecting the convictions of the Knox-Robinson ecclesiology, these authors stress the role of the church in equipping people for involvement in local mission activities focused on growing the local church, but distant mission receives little attention. It is evident that these differing practical expressions of church involvement in mission are influenced by ecclesiological, missiological, and pragmatic concerns, though the primary motivation is not clear from the literature.

174. These include Bradley, *Sending Church Defined*; Beirn and Murray, *Well Sent*; Crider et al., *Tradecraft*; Greear, *Gaining by Losing*; Hoover, *Mapping Church Missions*; Johnson, *Missions*; Trinity Church and Wilson, *Mind the Gaps*; Wilson and Wilson, *Pipeline*.

EMPIRICAL RESEARCH ON CHURCH INVOLVEMENT IN MISSION

With this understanding of the theological and practical discussions, it is necessary to consider the empirical research available on evangelical local church involvement in mission. There are several examples of research into churches in North America, South Africa, Singapore, and Europe; however, differences in church size, resources, and culture limit the relevance of their findings to the Australian context. In Australia, the most comprehensive source of empirical data on church practices is the National Church Life Survey (NCLS). This data is drawn from all Christian traditions and represents about a quarter of all churches in Australia, yet the factors shaping local church mission practice have not been a primary concern of the survey.

One local church mission practice that has been more widely considered in empirical research is the sending of short-term mission teams. Short-term mission (STM) refers to domestic or international trips of less than one year duration, although most trips last less than two weeks.[175] STM grew significantly towards the end of the twentieth century and in the first decade of the twenty-first century it was estimated that 1.6 million US Christians went on short-term trips each year.[176] In Australia, the 2016 NCLS revealed that 23 percent of churches had helped to organize a trip in the previous two years.[177] The impact of these trips on the broader patterns of global mission involvement has been widely considered with both critics and advocates abounding. Those in favor of STM often emphasize the positive impact that it can have upon the participants, though the long-term benefits have been questioned.[178] Recent research has focused on the opportunities these trips provide to develop partnerships between churches in the Western world and those in the majority world.[179] STM needs to be considered as one element of the mission involvement of local churches, yet the longer term patterns of engagement is of greater interest to this study.

---

175. Priest, "Introduction," ii–iii.

176. Wuthnow, *Boundless Faith*, 23; Priest, "Introduction," ii; Horton, "Long-Term Impact," 17.

177. Sterland and Hancock, *Mission Trips*, 1; For comparison, "In 2012, 27% of US congregations reported STM travel." Adler and Ruiz, "Immigrant Effect," 336.

178. Ver Beek, "Lessons," 475–97.

179. Brown, "Friendship," 209–37; Horton, "Long-Term Impact," 26; Hunter, "Short Time," 1–16.

Model Church Research

Several publications have sought to describe the factors that shape effective local church involvement in global mission by observing the practices of model churches. Writing from a South African context, Verster and Hancke describe what they consider to be the "Critical Success Factors (CSFs)" that are key to stimulating church involvement in mission.[180] Drawing on a limited number of Bible texts and other literature, the authors describe ten CSFs which emphasize the need for dynamic and intentional leadership, the involvement of most church members in the mission activities, and a widespread acceptance of the church's responsibility for world mission.[181] A qualitative study of five model churches then sought to validate these factors.[182] While the logic of these factors may be sound, the limitations of the study's methodology makes the validity of the findings questionable. Similar church practices are recommended by Tom Telford drawing on his experience as a church missions consultant in the United States.[183] The core principles Telford describes are strong biblical foundations for mission, commitment to missionary care and financial support, integration of mission into all aspects of church life, developing mutual partnerships with mission agencies, developing national leadership in other countries, and empowering lay members for leadership of mission initiatives. Though presented as a series of case studies, this book is essentially a summary of Telford's own principles for church mission involvement illustrated with specific examples. Furthermore, the fact that most of these churches have a Sunday attendance between two thousand and five thousand people limits the generalizability of these practices to average Australian churches of one hundred to one hundred and fifty attenders.

A third example of this model church approach is found in David Horner's self-described "unscientific survey" of mission practices in American evangelical churches.[184] Drawing from a qualitative survey of 107 churches believed to have a strong "missions culture," Horner describes ten best practices under three category headings: "building a vision for missions, adopting a strategy for missions, and sustaining the

---

180. Verster and Hancke, "Common," 103.
181. Verster and Hancke, "Common," 111–17.
182. Verster and Hancke, "Common," 109.
183. Telford and Shaw, *Today's All-Star*.
184. Horner, *When Missions*, 140.

support for missions."¹⁸⁵ The practices include clear leadership structures, focused missions events, giving attention to missions in sermons and services, arranging mission trips, partnering with indigenous church leaders, identifying and evaluating missionary candidates, maintaining relationships with missionaries, and encouraging generous giving.¹⁸⁶ This research provides a valuable insight into the practices that American church leaders believe shape their involvement in mission activities. However, the lack of comparison with less engaged churches and the differences in church size and culture between Australia and the United States limit the generalizability of these findings to churches in Sydney.

Landscape of North American Church Involvement

A small number of studies have more empirically assessed the broader patterns of North American local church involvement in mission. In 2007, Priest, Wilson, and Johnson completed a comprehensive survey of the mission practices of US megachurches.¹⁸⁷ The survey was limited to churches with a regular attendance over two thousand, and included responses from 405 churches with a median attendance of 3,100.¹⁸⁸ On average, these churches gave over 10 percent of their annual expenditure to global missions, but over a third of the churches gave less than 5 percent.¹⁸⁹ The median number of career missionaries supported was sixteen, but the mean was thirty-one suggesting a small number of churches supported very large numbers of people. While 61 percent affirmed the importance of partnering with career missionaries, the number of long-term missionaries being supported was not proportional to differences in attendance, income, or total global mission expenditure.¹⁹⁰ The authors describe this as a "softening of support for full-time missionaries" which they postulate was a possible factor in the declining number of long-term workers being sent from the US.¹⁹¹ What was notable in these churches was participation in short-term mission. Over 99 percent of these

185. Horner, *When Missions*, 137–40.
186. Horner, *When Missions*, 151–206.
187. Priest et al., "US Megachurches," 97–104.
188. Priest et al., "US Megachurches," 97.
189. The question asked about "support of ministries and needs outside the United States." See Priest et al., "US Megachurches," 97.
190. Priest et al., "US Megachurches," 98.
191. Priest et al., "US Megachurches," 98.

churches had attendees involved in STM trips in the previous twelve months.[192] The financial support of these trips was significant, but it was noted that the trips benefitted the participants more than those they visited. The authors observed that this "paradigm of mission channels mission funding in ways that serve the interests of the North American sending church as well as (sometimes more than) the interests of those being served."[193] Though this research highlights some of the shifting patterns of church mission involvement, the megachurches in this study differ from Australian evangelical churches in size, capacity, and culture. Furthermore, despite the vast differences in levels of support for distant mission, the factors causing these differences between churches were not explored.

A more broad-based survey of Christian perspectives on mission was The Canadian Evangelical Missions Engagement Study (CEMES) completed in 2017 by the Canadian Missions Research Forum and The Evangelical Fellowship of Canada.[194] Drawing from interviews with fifty-six evangelical leaders and lay people and a survey of over 3,400 respondents, including 1,410 evangelical pastors and 2,059 laity, this study explored evangelical views of missions in Canada.[195] The survey found that 85 percent of pastors and 63 percent of lay members believed that the local church has "primary responsibility for the Great Commission."[196] This includes "challenging young people to consider long-term, career missions" and helping people to discern if they are called to be a missionary.[197] Over half of all pastors (58 percent) stated that missions was promoted from the pulpit at least once a month and nearly nine out of ten respondents had personally connected with a missionary in the last twelve months.[198] Over a third of pastors reported that a long-term missionary had been sent out from their church in the last five years and, on average, congregations spent 13.5 percent of their budget on missions.[199] This commitment to missions was also expressed through involvement in short-term mission with 67 percent of pastors and 22 percent of laity

---

192. Priest et al., "US Megachurches," 98.
193. Priest et al., "US Megachurches," 100.
194. Hiemstra, "Methodology."
195. Hiemstra, "Methodology," 4.
196. Hiemstra, "Long-Term," 3.
197. Hiemstra, "Long-Term," 3.
198. Hiemstra, "Missions Promotion," 3.
199. Hiemstra, "Long-Term," 3; Hiemstra, "Mission Priorities," 3.

having participated in the previous decade.[200] Despite this widespread enthusiasm for mission involvement there were some notable features. Forty-four percent of pastors and 29 percent of lay respondents indicated that "it is better to send money to indigenous missionaries than to send long-term, career missionaries from Canada."[201] Furthermore, the amount of time given to missions in worship services was noted to be limited due to the demand of other priorities. This research suggests that mission involvement is highly regarded among evangelicals in Canada, though there is great variety in the way this is expressed.

This survey provides valuable insights into the perspectives on mission among Canadian evangelicals, but the conclusions that can be drawn about local church practice are limited. Significant efforts were made to ensure the respondents were representative of the evangelical population in Canada and responses were weighted according to region, tradition, age, and gender.[202] This is a reliable and valuable "snapshot of how and why Canadian evangelicals engage with missions."[203] However, apart from conclusions about the impact of church size on mission involvement, the research does not compare different church approaches. Interviewees noted the importance of "congregational interest" in determining the ministries that churches support, but no other church factors were discussed. General approaches to mission among Canadian evangelicals were assessed but the causes of variation in local church mission participation cannot be ascertained.

Using a similar approach to this Canadian study, Missio Nexus surveyed American church mission leaders in 2016 and 2019, exploring the levels of church mission involvement across evangelical churches.[204] On average, these churches were larger than Australian churches and they partnered with a higher number of missionaries.[205] The levels of financial support for missions varied widely with annual missions

200. Hiemstra, "Short-Term," 3–4.
201. Hiemstra, "Long-Term," 3.
202. Hiemstra, "Methodology," 6–7.
203. Hiemstra, "Methodology," 3.

204. VanHuis, *2016 Mission*; VanHuis, *Church Missions*. Missio Nexus is a US based association of mission organizations and churches committed to global mission. See https://missionexus.org/who-we-are/.

205. VanHuis, *2016 Mission*; VanHuis, *Church Missions*. In 2016, 42 percent of the churches surveyed had regular attendance over one thousand people and in 2019 it was 50 percent. Approximately a third of these churches supported ten or less missionaries with some churches supporting more than one hundred long-term missionaries.

budgets ranging from $1,200 to $2.5 million.[206] On average these churches spent 19 percent of their budget on missions.[207] The churches surveyed were predominantly sending long-term missionaries in partnership with mission agencies or denominational structures (in 2016, 64 percent; in 2019, 84 percent), with a small number of people sent directly by the churches.[208] The mission strategies employed were primarily focused on evangelism and discipleship, and unreached people groups, with only marginal involvement in social justice and humanitarian aid activities.[209] More than half of all the churches believed they were promoting mission internally "moderately or extremely well," and over 60 percent were engaging with missionaries on the field "moderately or extremely well."[210] Similarly to the Canadian research, this survey provides a valuable snapshot of the levels of involvement in mission in North American churches. These findings show that there is significant diversity in the ways that local evangelical churches participate, although the lack of comparison between those that are highly engaged and those that are not means that the causes of this diversity are not known.

Causes of Diversity in Church Involvement

One of the largest empirical studies of church involvement in global mission was led by sociologist Robert Wuthnow in 2005.[211] The Global Issues Survey was completed by 2,231 American church members and three hundred people were interviewed, including clergy, lay leaders, church members, and mission agency leaders across the United States.[212] Wuthnow's findings sought to demonstrate the vitality of American Christianity and the extent of its global influence in the age of globalization. In particular, he challenged the views of Philip Jenkins, Andrew Walls, Samuel Escobar, and others who promoted what he termed, the "global Christianity paradigm."[213] He saw their discussion around the demo-

---

206. VanHuis, *2016 Mission*, 65.
207. VanHuis, *Church Missions*, 74.
208. VanHuis, *2016 Mission*, 55; VanHuis, *Church Missions*, 49.
209. VanHuis, *2016 Mission*, 52; VanHuis, *Church Missions*, 10–11.
210. VanHuis, *Church Missions*, 50–51.
211. Wuthnow, *Boundless Faith*.
212. Wuthnow, *Boundless Faith*, 251–58.
213. Wuthnow, *Boundless Faith*, 32–61.

graphic shift of Christianity to the non-western world as implying that the American church was increasingly irrelevant on the world stage and American Christians should therefore focus on their own neighborhood and partner with non-Western migrant Christians to revitalize the waning Western church. To repudiate this narrative, Wuthnow explored the ways in which American Christianity influenced the rest of the world with an emphasis on the multidimensional aspects of globalization, the proliferation of transnational ties, the role of Christians in shaping American foreign policy, and the "global role of congregations."[214] Wuthnow's work has been critiqued for his analysis of the global Christian paradigm and his overly optimistic view of the role of American Christianity in the world scene.[215] However, he provides an incomparable insight into US evangelical church involvement in international mission and the factors that stimulate participation. It is this last aspect of the work that is of greatest relevance to this study.

Drawing on his survey findings, Wuthnow discusses the ways that local churches engage in transnational ministry including "humanitarian assistance, partnering with international agencies and local congregations in other countries, working with refugees, sponsoring missionaries, and on occasion becoming involved in peacemaking and human rights issues."[216] Of all these activities, it was sponsoring long-term missionaries that was most strongly supported by members of evangelical churches. Eighty-four percent of evangelicals said their church had sponsored a missionary in the last twelve months, compared to 73 percent of mainline Protestants and 69 percent of Catholics, while 75 percent of evangelicals said that their church "emphasizes supporting missionaries a lot."[217] Evangelicals were also more likely than others to state that "their congregation should emphasise the work of Christians and Christian organizations in other countries a lot."[218] Wuthnow observed that some churches were considerably more involved than others and discussed the causes for this difference. He notes the frequency with which leaders of highly involved churches presented the theological reasons for participation, such as the biblical commissions, yet argues that "organizational

---

214. Wuthnow, *Boundless Faith*, 140–87.
215. Shaw, "Robert Wuthnow," 179–84.
216. Wuthnow, *Boundless Faith*, 141.
217. Wuthnow, *Boundless Faith*, 148–49.
218. Wuthnow, *Boundless Faith*, 151.

factors are critical."²¹⁹ Through multiple regression analyses, Wuthnow concludes that the most transnationally engaged churches were those that sponsored a missionary, invited missionaries to speak, had a mission committee, and sponsored people to go on short-term mission trips.²²⁰ By contrast, taking up a hunger relief offering, helping refugees, or having staff dedicated to overseas outreach was less predictive. He also notes that congregations were increasingly using personal contacts to develop strong relationships which facilitated these transnational connections. This emphasis on organizational practices and relationships in shaping local church involvement in mission must be considered as the practices of Sydney evangelical churches are explored.

In a smaller culturally defined study, Jeanne Wu sought to examine the mission involvement of Chinese churches in the United States with particular attention to the practice of short-term mission.²²¹ Through a quantitative study of 317 churches, Wu analyzed the ways that Chinese churches conducted STM trips and how these patterns correlated with other dimensions of the churches' mission involvement. Her findings indicate that US Chinese churches show high levels of involvement in mission with 59 percent of churches sending a short-term mission team in the previous twelve months.²²² The majority of these churches sent teams to countries with a predominance of ethnic Chinese people. Some churches sent teams to work amongst both Chinese and non-Chinese people, but less than 10 percent only went to non-Chinese people. Wu concludes that this is not simply ethnocentrism, but that most Chinese churches are practicing "mission through diaspora" to reach the many ethnic Chinese people scattered around the world.²²³ Though the study did not comprehensively examine the differences between churches, it was noted that the churches with the most developed mission programs were the ones focused on mission among unreached or Muslim people. These churches gave more money to global mission, sent more STMs, supported more long-term missionaries, and were observed to be "more mature and healthier churches."²²⁴ In Wu's analysis, local churches that expressed a commitment to mission among those with less knowledge of

219. Wuthnow, *Boundless Faith*, 163.
220. Wuthnow, *Boundless Faith*, 163–64, 292.
221. Wu, *Mission through Diaspora*.
222. Wu, *Mission through Diaspora*, ch. 5.
223. Wu, *Mission through Diaspora*, ch. 6.
224. Wu, *Mission through Diaspora*, ch. 6.

Christianity were more highly engaged in mission. This reflects a missiological conviction that complements the organizational and theological factors noted by Wuthnow.

In addition to the research into American churches there have been several research projects exploring the involvement of Singaporean churches in mission. According to the 2001 edition of the World Christian Encyclopedia, there were five hundred Christian missionaries sent from Singapore in 2000, equivalent to 1,241 for every one million Christians.[225] This earned Singapore the nickname the "Antioch of Asia" referencing the first church in the New Testament to send missionaries (Acts 13:1–3).[226] Yet, while the church has continued to grow, the number of missionaries has stagnated such that in 2020 there were 560 missionaries or 464 for every one million Christians. This relative decline has stimulated several investigations into the involvement of local churches in mission. Mark Syn employed a qualitative case-study approach to examine the relationship between churches and mission agencies in Singapore. Viewing the evangelical church-agency nexus as a system, he drew from fifty-eight interviews with people involved in church and mission leadership.[227] Affirming the decline in the sending of long-term mission workers he notes an increase in participation in short-term mission and in churches sending workers independent of mission agencies. To regain prior levels of long-term sending, Syn argues that churches and agencies need to develop deeper mutual partnerships in which they recognize each other's expertise and work together to send mission workers.[228] A similar proposal was offered by Ivan Liew who investigated the relationships between a single church and three mission agencies in Singapore.[229] Liew's "Relational Model of Church-Agency Partnerships" recognizes the complementary qualities of churches and mission agencies and recommends ways in which they might work together.[230] These studies by Syn, Liew, Wuthnow, and Wu underline the impact that organizational factors have on local church participation in mission; however, unlike the US studies, they also emphasize the role of mission organizations. This again

---

225. By comparison, in 2001 Australia had sent 5,500 missionaries, or 437 for every million Christians.

226. Syn, *On Being*.

227. Syn, "Extended Model," 73–75.

228. Syn, "Extended Model," 252–59; Syn, *On Being*, 259–75.

229. Liew, "Partnerships."

230. Liew, "Partnerships," 152–61.

highlights the value of considering theological, missiological, and organizational factors with an awareness that the cultural context will impact the influence of different factors.

This global diversity was particularly evident in the international investigation into mission promotion and recruitment commissioned by the World Evangelical Alliance Mission Commission.[231] Based on semi-structured interviews with people involved in mission from nine different nations, this study sought to understand the factors that accelerate and retard mission involvement.[232] Questions about the nature and location of mission reveal some significant global differences within evangelicalism. While some people held to a traditional understanding of mission as primarily concerned with spiritual needs in transnational and cross-cultural contexts, most respondents had a broader perspective that included a range of social ministries, to all kinds of people, locally and at a distance.[233] The traditional view was more popular among North American interviewees, while people from Oceania often distinguished between "global mission" and "missional" activities, with the latter being predominantly local and socially concerned.[234] There was a note of concern among some respondents that this growing "missional" emphasis was obscuring the spiritual needs in other places. Yet, this here—there distinction was much greater in Oceania than it was in the UK and non-western countries.[235]

As the research explored the factors that stimulate and inhibit people's involvement in mission, the practices of local churches were not the primary concern; nevertheless, the role of local churches featured heavily. The survey found that, aside from the impact of a "missionary call," relationships were the most noteworthy factor influencing people's personal participation in mission.[236] This included relationships with family members, individuals, missionaries, mission organization staff, and church ministers. Many interviewees noted that local church ministers who were passionate about mission had a profound effect on their church

---

231. Matenga and Gold, *Mission in Motion*.
232. Matenga and Gold, *Mission in Motion*, 25.
233. Matenga and Gold, *Mission in Motion*, 31–60.
234. Matenga and Gold, *Mission in Motion*, 45–52.
235. Matenga and Gold, *Mission in Motion*, 47. Though the interviewees in Oceania were in New Zealand rather than Australia the regional similarities make this factor worthy of consideration.
236. Matenga and Gold, *Mission in Motion*, 119–33.

members. This influence may even extend beyond their congregation as ministers with a vision for mission can stimulate other ministers to do the same.[237] As the authors conclude, "a minister's enthusiasm can go a long way toward accelerating interest in mission."[238] Consequently, the role of mission education in the training of ministers was also noted for its influence. Ministers who receive specialist training on mission as part of their theological training could pass on this education to their church members. Yet this was not often observed, and interviewees noted that mission education in churches is often lacking.[239] Though the role of the church as mission educator and mobilizer was discussed as an accelerant for mission, the belief that many churches were not living up to their potential in this area was highlighted. Consequently, churches can become something of a retardant to mission involvement. In some cases, the emphasis on local ministry, and particularly the funding of local ministry, was noted as a passive inhibitor of mission involvement.[240] Some interviewees even described overt discouragement from church leaders "who did not see the importance of missions."[241] The authors briefly discuss the impact of wider sociological trends on mission involvement including secularism, individualism, prosperity, and busyness, yet it is through shaping the actions of individuals and church leaders that these have an impact.[242] Though not explicitly studying local church practices, this research highlights a number of factors that may influence local church involvement in mission. The emphasis on significant relationships shows again the influence of organizational practices in local churches on mission involvement. It therefore provides a helpful backdrop to this more focused research on the factors shaping individual churches.

Australian National Church Life Survey

As a contrast to these international empirical studies, the NCLS provides the most comprehensive data on Australian local church practice. Completed by NCLS Research every five years since 1991, the survey draws

237. Matenga and Gold, *Mission in Motion*, 125–27.
238. Matenga and Gold, *Mission in Motion*, 128.
239. Matenga and Gold, *Mission in Motion*, 141.
240. Matenga and Gold, *Mission in Motion*, 178–83.
241. Matenga and Gold, *Mission in Motion*, 222.
242. Matenga and Gold, *Mission in Motion*, 221–31.

participants from twenty denominations, three thousand churches, more than two hundred and fifty thousand church members, and six thousand church leaders.[243] NCLS Research has published a range of reports based on the 2016 NCLS data exploring various aspects of church practice related to mission locally and overseas. Drawing on responses from 2,289 churches in 2016, one report explored the ways in which churches support people in developing countries.[244] Though it is not clear who was being supported or the purposes of the support, it does give an indication of Australian church involvement overseas. The primary way that churches support people is financially (53 percent of churches), through prayer (49 percent), or by providing personal support (35 percent). Only 18 percent of churches provided no support at all. In 2016 there were some notable denominational differences with financial support coming from a higher proportion of Baptist (72 percent), Pentecostal (79 percent), Presbyterian (59 percent), and Salvation Army (67 percent) churches. Similarly, a higher proportion of Anglican (54 percent), Baptist (65 percent), Pentecostal (62 percent), and Presbyterian (65 percent) churches provided prayer support to people in developing countries. Finally, Baptist (58 percent), Pentecostal (61 percent), and Presbyterian (40 percent) churches were the most likely to provide personal support to these people. This high level of involvement among Baptist and Presbyterian churches is relevant to this study given their typically conservative evangelical identity.

The number of churches and church members involved in mission trips has also been explored through the NCLS data. In the 2016 NCLS, 20 percent of churches surveyed had organized an overseas mission trip in the preceding two years, 9 percent had organized a mission trip within Australia, and 6 percent had done both.[245] Pentecostal and Baptist churches reported notably higher levels of trip participation with 33 percent of Baptist and 60 percent of Pentecostal churches organizing trips. It is estimated that these two denominations accounted for 60 percent of all the mission trips organized by Australian churches. Though only 10 percent of Anglican churches reported organizing overseas trips, the high number of Anglican churches means that they account for a further 15 percent of all trips. These denominational emphases were also evident in the numbers of church attenders sent out on short, medium, and long-term mission trips. In 2016, based on the reports of 3,065 churches, it

243. https://www.ncls.org.au/about.
244. Sterland and Hancock, *Support for People*.
245. Sterland and Hancock, *Mission Trips*.

was estimated that in the previous two years, seventeen thousand people had been on short-term mission trips (one to six weeks duration), 1,250 people had been on medium-term trips (seven weeks to two years), and 940 people had headed out long-term (more than two years). While over 35 percent of those who went on short-term trips were from Pentecostal churches, Baptist churches accounted for 37 percent of all long-term missionaries. These numbers not only reflect the size, but also the strong culture of mission participation among these denominations, particularly Pentecostal and Baptist.[246]

The final area of church mission involvement explored through the NCLS data is the number of overseas workers supported by each church.[247] From the responses of 2,916 Protestant churches in the 2016 NCLS it was reported that, on average, each church supported 1.61 overseas workers. Approximately 25 percent of these workers were supported directly, while the rest were sent in partnership with a mission agency. As for the other measures, there was wide variation in the level of participation across the different denominations. Anglican, Baptist, Pentecostal, and Presbyterian churches all supported more than the average number of overseas workers. Anglican churches supported 1.62 workers per church, Presbyterian churches supported 2.71 workers per church, and Baptist churches supported 3.71 workers per church. In each of these denominations there was evidence of close partnerships with mission organizations with more than 80 percent of these workers sent out through an agency. These statistics show the prevalence of mission worker support in various evangelical denominations, yet they give little insight into the cause of difference between individual churches.

In an effort to explore these differences in more depth a report was commissioned from NCLS Research to compare churches that supported high numbers of overseas workers and churches that supported low numbers.[248] The report compared the responses of attenders in evangelical churches that support six or more workers (High Worker Churches—HWCs), attenders in churches that support one or zero workers (Low Worker Churches—LWCs), and all evangelical churches (AEC).[249] De-

---

246. Sterland and Hancock, *Australian Church Attenders*. Anglican churches also contributed 27 percent of all long-term missionaries, yet this is more due to the denomination's size than its culture of mission participation.

247. Sterland and Hancock, *Support for Overseas Workers*.

248. Powell et al., *Research Profile*.

249. Churches included in the report had a weekly attendance of fifty or higher,

mographically there was little difference between the attenders in the three church groups, except that the Low Worker Churches did have a higher proportion of migrants from non-English speaking backgrounds than either of the other two groups.[250] There were more differences among the values of the attenders at these churches with a higher proportion of attenders at LWCs valuing "openness to social or cultural diversity" (LWCs: 15 percent; HWCs: 9 percent), a "traditional style of worship" (LWCs: 20 percent; HWCs: 16 percent), and "sharing in the Lord's Supper" (LWCs: 29 percent; HWCs: 20 percent). By contrast, more attenders in High Worker Churches valued "sermons, preaching, or Bible teaching" (LWCs: 50 percent; HWCs: 58 percent) and "small prayer, discussion, or Bible study groups" (LWCs: 30 percent; HWCs: 34 percent). These differences in values were consistent with the differences in identification with attenders in HWCs more likely to identify as "evangelical" (HWCs: 54 percent; LWCs: 44 percent) and "reformed" (HWCs: 12 percent; LWCs: 8 percent).[251] These differences suggest that churches supporting higher numbers of workers have a greater emphasis on Bible focused ministries and a preference for less liturgy and formality in worship.

Other points of difference between the two groups of churches suggested differences in church culture and vitality. Drawing on multiple years of surveys, NCLS Research has identified "nine core qualities of church life" which reflect the vitality of a church.[252] They define vitality as the extent to which a church is strengthening the faith of its members, deepening relationships within the church, providing inspirational leadership, and stimulating engagement between the church and the wider community.[253] By these measures there are some differences between the HWCs and the LWCs. Attenders at HWCs were more likely to describe God as "the most important reality in [their] life" (HWCs: 66 percent; LWCs: 60 percent) and more likely to state that they always experienced "preaching very helpful to their life" (HWCs: 40 percent;

---

were within the Anglican, Baptist, Churches of Christ, or Presbyterian denominations, and were considered evangelical based on the faith identity of the senior leader. HWC data came from 33,306 attenders from 189 churches; LWC data from 7,561 attenders from 70 churches; AEC data from 63,891 attenders from 486 churches.

250. Powell et al., *Research Profile*, 3.
251. Powell et al., *Research Profile*, 7–9.
252. Bellamy et al., *Enriching Church Life*, 2–29.
253. Bellamy et al., *Enriching Church Life*, 2–5.

LWCs: 36 percent).[254] They were also slightly more likely to be "involved regularly in outreach or evangelistic activity" (HWCs: 29 percent; LWCs: 24 percent) and to see "encouraging people here to share their faith or invite others" as a priority for their church (HWCs: 25 percent; LWCs: 20 percent).[255] These differences suggest a relationship between church vitality and the support of overseas workers, though the nature of this relationship is not clear.

This profile highlights several factors that may be important in shaping local church participation in mission, but the research methodology limits the clarity with which these factors can be assessed. Firstly, though the sample was large, a total of 63,891 attenders from 486 churches, there is no guarantee that it is representative of the wider evangelical church population. Furthermore, the number of missionaries supported by the church is a crude measure of a church's involvement in mission. The church's wealth, size, and cultural context can profoundly impact this number and supporting more missionaries is not necessarily indicative of higher involvement of church members. The statistical significance of the differences between HWC and LWC churches was also not assessed and therefore may not be relevant. Furthermore, the data provided no way to consider the organizational factors previously identified in international research as being influential for mission engagement. Finally, on many of the measures reported, HWCs were more like all evangelical churches than the LWCs were. In other words, it was something of an anomaly for the evangelical churches in this research to support so few overseas workers. This low level of engagement may therefore be an indication of poor church health in general, rather than a reflection of different theology or organizational approaches.

Empirical Research: Interim Conclusions

This survey of existing research of church involvement in mission provides valuable insights into the patterns of participation but limited understanding of the factors that cause it. Empirical studies in North America have demonstrated higher than average participation in international mission among evangelical churches with involvement in short-term mission trips. Analysis of megachurches and Chinese churches in

---

254. Powell et al., *Research Profile*, 10.
255. Powell et al., *Research Profile*, 12, 16.

the United States and a wide range of pastors and church members in Canada has revealed notable engagement with global mission yet wide variation between churches. In Australia, the NCLS data measured the number of overseas workers supported by a church and member participation in STMs noting that evangelical churches similarly showed the highest levels of involvement. These studies provide various benchmarks against which local church practices may be compared, yet the causes for the diversity among churches have received only limited consideration.

There are a few studies that considered the factors stimulating local church participation in mission in other parts of the world. Descriptions of highly engaged model churches in the United States suggest a range of practices related to leadership strategies, organizational structures, relational connections, and patterns for congregation participation that are believed to stimulate church engagement. However, the lack of comparison with less engaged churches limits the credibility of these findings. Wuthnow's examination of US churches identifies the theological convictions and organizational factors correlated with higher levels of mission participation among evangelical churches.[256] Jeanne Wu notes the significance of missiological convictions in shaping church patterns of engagement while Singaporean research suggests that mission organization connections are also important.[257] Matenga and Gold's international study highlights the importance of key relationships for helping individuals become involved in global mission, though they did not compare the involvement of churches as a whole.[258] These studies identify a number of theological, missiological, organizational, and relational factors that have been influential in shaping evangelical church mission involvement in other parts of the world. The only Australian research comparing local church involvement in mission was the report commissioned from NCLS. This indicated that evangelical churches supporting high numbers of overseas workers have attenders that are more likely to identify as evangelical and reformed, they place more value on preaching and small groups than they do on traditional worship and the sacraments, and they are more likely to prioritize their personal faith and the importance of sharing that with others. These findings suggest a relationship between many measures of church vitality and the support of high numbers of overseas workers, though data was unable to consider the theological,

---

256. Wuthnow, *Boundless Faith*.
257. Wu, *Mission through Diaspora*; Syn, *On Being*; Liew, "Partnerships."
258. Matenga and Gold, *Mission in Motion*.

missiological, organizational, or relational factors noted overseas. An exploration of Australian evangelical churches that considers these factors across churches with differing patterns of mission involvement is therefore needed.

CONCLUSIONS

This review of the literature has highlighted a variety of factors that may be influencing the involvement of Sydney evangelical churches in mission. Significant shifts in the theology of church and mission over the last fifty years have transformed the way Christians think about the role of local churches in mission, and the place of mission in the local church. These conversations have impacted Sydney evangelical churches in various ways and contextual responses have arisen. In addition to these theological discussions, missiological conversations have produced a range of practical approaches to church engagement in mission. Some have championed the role of denominational and para-church mission structures, while others have focused more on the missional responsibilities of local churches alone. This latter approach has encouraged churches to embrace their missional responsibility. In some cases, the application of missiological principles to local mission has been the primary focus, while for others it has been the task of supporting overseas mission by sending and partnering with missionaries. The influence of these approaches on evangelical churches in Sydney must be considered as collected data is analyzed, however theological and missiological convictions may not be the only influential factors. International empirical research has highlighted the need to also consider organizational and relational dimensions of church practice, but existing research has not adequately examined these factors in the Australian context. This study addresses that lacuna by employing a grounded theory methodology that allows the factors for consideration to be shaped by quantitative and qualitative data collected in Sydney evangelical churches. In the next chapter, the diversity of church patterns of mission involvement is explored through a survey of Australian evangelical churches to reveal what local evangelical churches are doing in local and distant mission, and how involvement in each arena relates to the other.

3

Patterns of Church Mission Involvement

INTRODUCTION

This study employs an explanatory sequential grounded theory approach to both describe and explain the diverse patterns of involvement in mission among Sydney evangelical churches. The first phase of this research is purely descriptive. The goal is to understand the landscape of local church mission activity before deeper analysis can generate theory. This chapter outlines the findings of this first phase observed through the survey of local church leaders and interviews of church members and leaders from a subset of these churches. These patterns reveal differences in mission involvement between local churches which are influenced by size and wealth but cannot be explained by those factors alone. There is also some evidence of a relationship between the different means of mission involvement that requires deeper analysis.

QUESTIONNAIRE FINDINGS

Distribution and Returns

Questionnaires were distributed and completed between July 2018 and January 2019.[1] Using publicly available details, church leaders were contacted by the author via telephone. The purpose of the research was explained, and they were asked if they were willing to participate. Most church leaders completed the survey themselves, though some forwarded it to other church staff with responsibility for mission activities or church members involved in the church's mission activities. If responses were not received after four to six weeks, a follow up email was sent inviting completion of the questionnaire.

Efforts were made to contact 254 churches and questionnaires were distributed to 242 willing church leaders. There were 215 complete and five partially complete questionnaires returned, providing 220 responses. This was a 91 percent response rate to the 242 questionnaires distributed, affording a high level of confidence in the data received. The denominational mix of the returned questionnaires was equivalent to the mix of the original sample (see table 1). Churches were located throughout NSW and ACT with 65 percent (133) from within the "Significant Urban Area" of Sydney.[2]

Denomination	Full sample	Questionnaire recipients	Returned questionnaires	Evangelical churches
Anglican	105 (41%)	103 (43%)	97 (44%)	96 (47%)
Baptist	85 (34%)	78 (32%)	72 (33%)	67 (33%)
Presbyterian	29 (11%)	27 (11%)	22 (10%)	20 (10%)
Independent	24 (10%)	23 (9%)	20 (9%)	17 (8%)
Other	11 (4%)	11 (5%)	9 (4%)	5 (2%)
TOTAL	254	242	220	205

Table 1. Number of Churches Studied and Percentage of Each Sample, by Denomination

---

1. See Appendix 1 for questionnaire details.

2. A Significant Urban Area is a combination of one or more urban areas that are less than 5km apart. See https://www.abs.gov.au.

Church Identification

Respondents were asked to indicate the adjectives they would use to describe their church by selecting one or more identifier. The options were evangelical, missional, charismatic, reformed, pentecostal, and emerging/emergent. Ninety-three percent (205) of the churches identified as evangelical and thus provided the body of data for this analysis. Of these respondents, 135 (66 percent) selected descriptors in addition to evangelical as indicated in figure 1. Fifty percent (102) of the evangelical churches were also identified as reformed and 37 percent (seventy-five churches) were identified as missional.

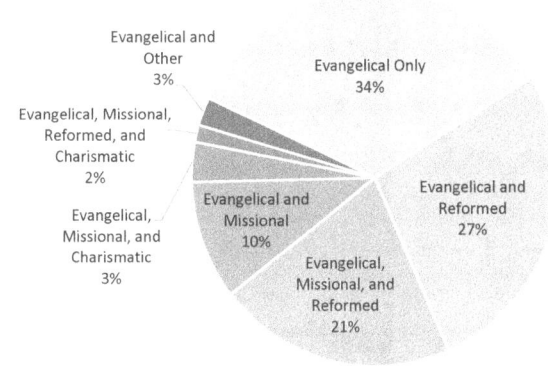

Figure 1. Self-Identification of Evangelical Churches

Of the fifteen churches that did not identify as evangelical, five were reformed, two missional, and six were a unique combination of missional, charismatic, pentecostal, and emerging. Denominationally, six were Baptist, three Presbyterian, two Anglican, two independent, one Reformed, and one Uniting. Though many of these churches may be considered evangelical based on denomination, theology, practice, or attendee identification, they were excluded from the data for the purposes of this research on the grounds of the respondent's selection.

Church Size

Respondents were asked to indicate the number of adults that would attend the church's services on a typical weekend. Five options were provided: less than 50, 50–99, 100–249, 250–499, and more than 500. As evident in figure 2, most churches included in this research had more than one hundred adults in attendance on an average week. Powell and Pepper report that the average weekly attendance at Australian churches was 121 people in 2011, with Catholic and Australian Christian Churches (Pentecostal) churches the largest.[3] This higher representation of larger churches in this sample may be because most of the churches surveyed were in suburban Sydney. Church income was not perfectly correlated with attendance, yet churches with higher attendance generally report higher incomes.

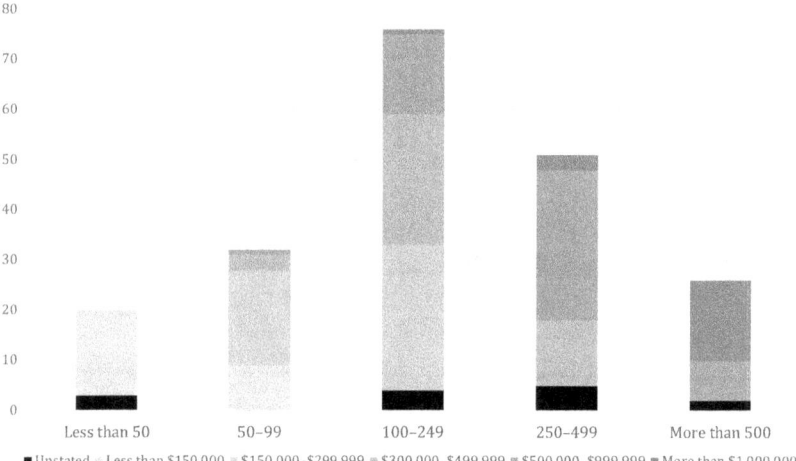

Figure 2. Number of Evangelical Churches by Attendance with Income Evident

Support for Australian Mission Workers

Respondents were asked to indicate the number of people and organizations that the church supports to do mission work in the local community or elsewhere in Australia, as well as the number of missionary units[4] and mission organizations supported that are working outside Australia. The size of the church influenced the number of people and mission organizations that a church supported both locally and overseas, with larger churches displaying higher levels of support than smaller churches. On

3. Powell and Pepper, "Local Churches in Australia."
4. Missionary units were defined as "an individual, a couple or a family serving overseas."

average, churches tend to support more organizations and people doing mission work in Australia than organizations and people working overseas (see table 2). In churches with more than five hundred attendees, there is a stark difference between average and median number of people supported in mission work in Australia. Most churches support fewer than ten people, though there are several churches that support twenty, twenty-five, thirty, or one hundred people! This may be due to differences in the interpretation of the question, or a notable local focus among these larger churches. The number of overseas missionary units supported by each church is higher than those reported in the 2016 National Church Life Survey (NCLS).[5] Sterland and Hancock state that the average number of overseas workers supported by Protestant churches across Australia was 1.61 yet this survey found an average of 4.66 workers per church. This difference may be a consequence of the size of the churches in the sample or may reflect a higher level of support for overseas workers in evangelical churches in Sydney.

Church Attendance	Organizations serving in Australia average (median)	Organizations serving overseas average (median)	People serving in Australia average (median)	Missionary units serving overseas average (median)
<50	2.0 (1)	1.8 (1.5)	2.9 (1.5)	2.8 (2)
50–99	2.6 (2)	2.2 (2.0)	3.3 (3.0)	3.8 (3)
100–249	3.6 (3)	2.6 (2.0)	6.3 (5.0)	4.0 (3)
250–499	5.0 (5)	2.6 (2.0)	10.6 (7.0)	5.4 (4)
500 or more	3.4 (3)	3.4 (3.0)	12.8 (6.0)	7.7 (8)

Table 2. Number of Supported Organizations, People, and Missionary Units Stratified by Church Attendance

In contrast to the number of people supported, the level of financial support tends to be greater for mission overseas than it is locally (see table 3).[6] Churches appear to support mission in Australia practically and

---

5. Sterland and Hancock, *Support for Overseas Workers*.

6. Level of financial support was calculated by taking the mid-point of the item selected under income and money given and is therefore an estimate of the actual percentage. For the extremes the following assumptions were made. Less than $150,000 = $100,000; more than $1,000,000 = $1,200,000; less than $10,000 = $5,000; more than $100,000 = $150,000.

through prayer more than they do financially. One notable trend from this data is that large churches (over five hundred attendees) tend to give a smaller percentage of their total income towards mission in Australia (approximately 4 percent, compared to 6–7 percent for smaller churches). However, the percentage of income given to mission overseas is largely consistent (approximately 8 percent) regardless of the size of the church.

Church Attendance	Support for mission in Australia	Support for mission overseas	Total support for mission
<50[7]	8	9	17
50–99	6	8	14
100–249	6	8	15
250–499	7	7	14
500 or more	4	9	13

Table 3. Financial Support for Mission Overseas and within Australia Stratified by Church Attendance (% of Church Income)

Involvement in Local Mission

Respondents were asked to indicate how often their church had conducted various local mission activities in the previous twelve months. Activities included evangelistic services or events, evangelistic Bible studies or courses, street or shopping center evangelism, door knocking or drop-in centers, or other evangelistic or outreach activities.[8] Respondents could indicate: monthly or more often, every two or three months, at least twice a year, once a year, or none. To facilitate analysis each response was given a score reflecting the number of events the church would therefore hold each year. "Monthly or more often" was considered to be twelve events in a year, "every two or three months" was considered to be six times per year, "at least twice a year" was considered to be two times per year, "once a year" was considered to be one time per year, and "none" was zero. The

---

7. The high number of churches in this group that earned less than $150,000 and gave less than $10,000 may have skewed the results more than in the other categories.

8. An additional question about "other visiting" revealed such a different pattern to the evangelistic activities that it was deemed to be measuring another element of church practice, such as pastoral care.

scores for the four categories were then added to give the approximate number of evangelistic activities that the church conducted in the last year.

The size of the church influenced the number of evangelistic activities that a church conducted with larger churches displaying higher levels of activity than smaller churches. Yet size is not wholly determinative, for example, the lowest number of events for a church with 100–249 regular attenders was one, while the highest was thirty-seven. Table 4 shows the impact of size on activity by displaying the average number of each type of activity for each church size category.

Church attendance	Services and events	Studies and courses	Street outreach/ door-knocking	Other activities	Total
<50	2.7	1.7	3.7	4.4	12.4
50–99	4.0	1.7	1.7	5.7	13.0
100–249	4.5	3.0	1.9	5.8	15.1
250–499	5.5	4.7	2.2	6.6	19.0
500 or more	5.8	5.4	2.9	7.2	21.3

Table 4. Average Number of Local Mission Activities per Church Stratified by Church Attendance

Aggregating these numbers for each church makes it possible to rank churches according to their involvement in local mission and identify the 25 percent most active and the 25 percent least active in each size category. By comparing these most and least active churches some conclusions may be drawn about churches that show above and below average levels of local mission activity while controlling for size. Forty-seven percent of the high local mission (HLM) churches and 27 percent of the low local mission (LLM) churches identified themselves as missional. Given that 37 percent of the whole sample selected this identifier, it suggests that missional churches are more likely to be highly active in local mission than other churches. Half (102) of all the 205 evangelical churches identified as reformed; this appeared to have little relationship to a church's level of local mission activity, with 49 percent of the HLM churches and 45 percent of the LLM churches identified this way.

In addition to high levels of local evangelistic activity, HLM churches displayed higher levels of support for mission in Australia (see table 5). On average, HLM churches were supporting more people and organizations doing mission within Australia than other churches,[9] even though this is not evident in financial terms. This reflects a stronger commitment to Australian based mission in these churches in terms of practical and prayer support which is arguably more reflective of church member participation than financial support is.

Churches level of local mission (LM) activity	Average number of mission workers in Australia	Average number of mission organizations in Australia	Average percent of income for Australian mission
High LM churches	8.6	4.3	6
Mid LM churches	8.0	3.6	6
Low LM churches	4.9	2.9	5

Table 5. Local Church Involvement in Australian Based Mission Stratified by Level of Involvement in Local Mission

The picture is different when overseas mission support is considered. A local church's level of involvement in local mission appeared to show no relationship to its level of support for overseas mission. As can be seen in table 6, there was no significant difference between high, medium, and low local mission churches with regard to the number of overseas mission workers and mission organizations they support, the percent of their income given to overseas mission, or the number of overseas mission trips taken. In other words, churches that are highly engaged in mission to their own community appear to be no more likely than other churches to be supportive of distant mission.[10] Though this data does not show a neglect of distant mission, it does indicate a disconnection between participation in mission in these two arenas.

---

9. The difference in participation is more evident when considering the median number of people supported across the categories. The HLM churches support a median of six people, while the mid LM and LLM churches both have a median of four. The averages are skewed in these latter group by a small number of outliers.

10. This is consistent with the suggestions of Stetzer and others who have observed a lack of engagement in global mission among missional churches. Stetzer, "Five Reasons."

Churches level of local mission (LM) activity	Average number of mission workers overseas	Average number of mission organizations overseas	Average percent of income for overseas mission	Average number of overseas mission trips
High LM churches	5.1	2.8	7	0.9
Mid LM churches	4.9	2.7	8	1
Low LM churches	3.8	2.0	6	0.7

Table 6. Local Church Involvement in Overseas Mission Stratified by Level of Involvement in Local Mission

Overseas Mission Involvement

Church involvement in overseas mission is a multidimensional practice. Consequently, to assess the level of a church's involvement several questionnaire responses needed to be considered. Churches were stratified according to size and then ranked according to the following measures: number of overseas missionary units supported; number of missionary units sent out in the last five years; percentage of income given to overseas mission; regularity of prayer for mission workers; regularity of personal contact with mission workers; and the number of ways in which the church showed a specific commitment to the mission workers over the past twelve months (including personal relationship, visiting, financial commitment, prayer, or another kind of link). The churches were allocated points for each measure in each size category and the points were tallied to identify the 25 percent of churches most highly involved in overseas mission and the 25 percent of churches least engaged in overseas mission. This stratification of churches in each size category identified the 25 percent of churches that displayed the highest levels of involvement in overseas mission across the many dimensions of practice (see table 7). Compared to mid overseas mission churches, on average these high overseas mission (HOM) churches supported 75 percent more mission workers, arranged twice as many overseas mission trips, sent out three times as many mission workers, and gave nearly 60 percent more of their income to overseas mission.

Churches level of overseas mission (OM) activity	Average number of mission workers overseas	Average number of mission organizations overseas	Average percent of income for overseas mission	Average number of overseas mission trips	Average number of mission workers sent out
High OM churches	7.2	3.0	11	1.5	2.9
Mid OM churches	4.1	2.3	7	0.7	0.9
Low OM churches	3	2.5	6	0.7	0.6

Table 7. Local Church Involvement in Overseas Mission Stratified by Level of Involvement in Overseas Mission

These patterns of involvement in overseas mission also correlated to the ways in which churches were involved in supporting mission in Australia. As table 8 shows, churches with high involvement in overseas mission showed higher levels of support for people and organizations working in mission in Australia than did churches with high levels of involvement in local mission (cf. tables 5 and 6). This suggests that there was some relationship between support for overseas mission and support for Australian mission.

Churches level of overseas mission (OM) activity	Average number of mission workers in Australia	Average number of mission organizations in Australia	Average percent of income for Australian mission
High OM churches	10	4.6	7
Mid OM churches	7.1	3.5	5
Low OM churches	5.3	2.9	5

Table 8. Local Church Involvement in Australian Based Mission Stratified by Level of Involvement in Local Mission

There did not appear to be any relationship between the involvement of churches in overseas mission and their identification as missional or reformed. In each category the proportion of churches that were identified as missional or reformed was approximately the same as for the whole sample. This contrasts with the findings of the NCLS profile discussed in chapter 2 which suggested a relationship between being reformed and support of overseas missionaries.

Relationship between Local and Overseas Mission Activity

Having ranked each church on both their level of local mission activity and their level of involvement in overseas mission it was then possible to consider the relationship between the two. Churches that displayed higher levels of involvement in overseas mission reported hosting more local mission events than churches with low levels of involvement in overseas mission. On average high overseas mission churches reported 18.4 events per year, while low overseas mission churches reported only 14.5. This further strengthened the earlier observation, that high levels of involvement in overseas mission correlates more closely with high levels of involvement with local mission though the reverse is less well correlated (see figure 3). Seventeen churches (8.3 percent) were ranked in the top 25 percent for both overseas and local mission. That is, 33 percent of the high overseas mission churches were also ranked as high local mission churches, and vice versa. The fact that this is higher than 25 percent suggests that there is some relationship between overseas and local mission involvement. The direction of this relationship is suggested by the number churches that were ranked high on one scale but low on the other. Specifically, only seven (14 percent) of the high overseas mission churches were ranked low for local mission involvement, whereas twelve (24 percent) of the high local mission churches were ranked low for overseas mission involvement. This suggests that churches with high overseas mission involvement were less likely to show low involvement in local mission, but churches with high local mission involvement were the same as all other churches in terms of overseas mission involvement.

These results provide some insight into the relationship between local and overseas mission involvement. While all mission involvement is driven by the same theological convictions, local and overseas mission cannot be equated and are clearly influenced by other factors. High levels of engagement with mission in one sphere will not automatically result in high level of engagement with mission in the other. The beliefs and practices that stimulate local mission activity will not automatically stimulate overseas mission involvement. Yet, while the two are not perfectly correlated, high levels of involvement in overseas mission were more likely to be associated with high levels of involvement in local mission than vice versa. Overseas mission involvement may therefore stimulate local mission involvement in some way. Though different approaches are required for each sphere of mission involvement, there appears to be some relationship. More in-depth qualitative analysis is required to assess the nature of this relationship.

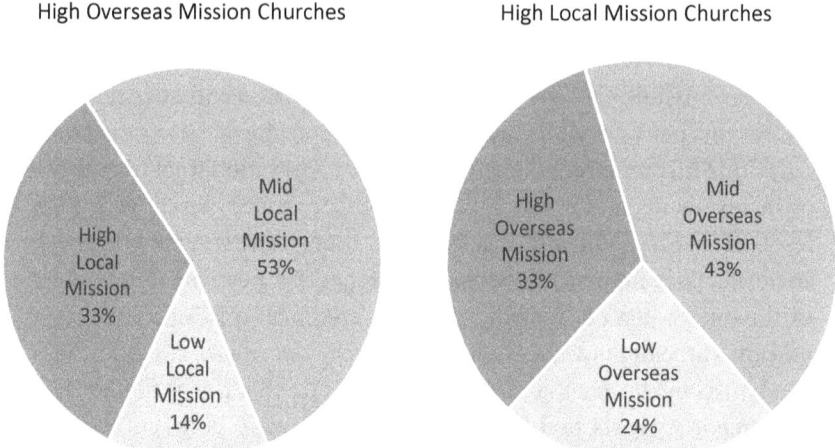

Figure 3. High Overseas Mission Church Involvement in Local Mission and High Local Mission Church Involvement in Overseas Mission

Denominational Differences

The sample of churches included in this research is not representative of all churches. It was a relatively small purposive sample which sought to identify a range of churches in terms of size, location, and level of involvement in mission. Consequently, any differences between denominations may be due to sampling error. With that in mind, there were some differences noted. Anglican and independent churches appeared to be more likely to be highly involved in local mission, while Baptist churches appeared to be less likely to be highly involved (see table 9). However, when considering overseas mission involvement, Anglican churches appeared to be slightly less likely to be highly involved and independent churches were slightly more likely to be highly involved.

	High local mission (%)	Mid local mission (%)	Low local mission (%)	High overseas mission (%)	Mid overseas mission (%)	Low overseas mission (%)	Whole sample (%)
Anglican	55	44	45	43	49	47	47
Baptist	22	37	35	35	30	35	33
Presbyterian	8	12	8	8	12	8	10
Independent	14	5	10	12	8	6	8
Other	2	3	2	2	1	4	1

Table 9. Denominational Representation in Each Category of Involvement in Local and Overseas Mission

Though the sample sizes became smaller and therefore the conclusions more tentative, there were some other notable trends as the overseas mission and local mission categories were combined. As table 10 demonstrates, the churches in the high local mission and high overseas mission category closely reflected the denominational diversity of the whole sample. However, the high local mission and low overseas mission category shows a higher proportion of Anglican churches and a lower proportion of Baptist churches than the whole sample. This was the most apparent difference, though the generalizability of these results cannot be assured.

	High local and overseas mission (%)	High local and low overseas mission (%)	High overseas and low local mission (%)	Low overseas and low local mission (%)	Whole sample (%)
Anglican	47	67	43	37	47
Baptist	29	17	29	42	33
Presbyterian	12	0	14	11	10
Independent	12	8	14	5	8
Other	0	8	0	5	2

Table 10. Denominational Representation in Each of the Extreme Combined Categories of Mission Involvement

Questionnaire Conclusions

This questionnaire has provided a valuable insight into the patterns of mission involvement in 205 evangelical churches across NSW and the ACT predominantly from the Anglican, Baptist, and Presbyterian denominations. All the churches represented by the data identify as evangelical, 50 percent also identified as reformed, and 37 percent as missional. The high response rate (91 percent) gave a high level of confidence in the data, though the purposive sampling limits the generalizability of the findings. Despite this limitation there were several key insights that have been noted.

Firstly, churches tended to support more people doing mission in Australia than they did people overseas, but they gave a greater financial contribution to overseas workers. This may reflect an appreciation of the difference in cost or a tendency to support Australian based mission workers in practical and relational ways rather than financial. Secondly, the size of a church's attendance appeared to impact the level of both local and overseas mission activity. Larger churches did more and gave more both locally and overseas; however, the relationship did not appear to be linear. On average churches gave approximately 8 percent of their income to overseas mission and 6–7 percent to mission in Australia. Yet larger churches—those with more than five hundred regular attendants—tended to give a smaller proportion (around 4 percent) to mission in Australia while maintaining the 8 percent overseas.

There was notable diversity across all sized churches regarding their level of both local and overseas mission activity. The churches with the highest levels of overseas mission involvement were more likely to support people and organizations involved in mission in Australia and to have high levels of involvement in local mission activities. By contrast, though churches with the highest levels of local mission activity were similarly more likely to support a higher number of people and organizations involved in mission within Australia, they did not show higher levels of support for mission overseas. These results suggest that high levels of involvement in overseas mission is related to all means of mission involvement, while high levels of involvement in local mission may happen in isolation. The reasons for these differences are further explored in the following chapters.

QUALITATIVE CATEGORIZATION OF CHURCHES

Guided by the survey findings, ten churches were approached for involvement in the second phase of the research. This entailed semi-structured interviews with three members of each church: a minister or pastor employed by the church, a member of the church who the leader considered to be enthusiastic about distant mission,[11] and another generally active member of the church. These churches were selected because they displayed either high levels of involvement in distant mission, or local mission, or both. Based on the interview findings, the ten churches were categorized in terms of their level of involvement in distant mission and their level of involvement in local mission. Seven of the churches were determined to have the same pattern of mission involvement as determined by the survey, while the interview results of three churches were seen to differ from their survey findings. On interview, these churches were found to have higher levels of involvement than was indicated in the survey.

Church	Survey		Interview	
	Local mission involvement	Overseas mission involvement	Local mission involvement	Distant mission involvement
CH1	High	Low	High	Low
CH2	High	Low	High	Low
CH3	Low	High	High	High
CH4	High	High	High	High
CH5	High	Low	High	Low
CH6	High	Low	High	High
CH7	High	High	High	High
CH8	High	High	High	High
CH9	High	High	High	High
CH10	Low	High	High	High

Table 11. Profiles of Local Church Mission Involvement
Based on Survey and Interviews

Two of the churches (CH3 and CH10) that were determined to have low levels of involvement in local mission based on the survey, were found

11. Distant mission refers to all mission activities that take place away from the church. Most distant mission is overseas, but it may include the support of mission workers in other parts of Australia.

to have comparatively high levels of involvement in local mission through the interviews because of under-reporting of church run evangelistic activities in the survey. This may have been due to a narrower understanding of "evangelistic" events than intended in the survey with both churches reporting "none" when asked about "other evangelistic or outreach activities," although it was evident in the interview that they did many. One church (CH6) that had been determined on the survey to have low levels of involvement in distant mission was found to have high levels of involvement. This was due to apparent under reporting of the various means of support and personal engagement with the mission workers reported in the survey. Though the number of mission workers supported was above the median for churches of that size, and the financial support for mission well above the average, the level of church commitment to direct engagement with mission workers was not fully reported in the questionnaire which led to the church being considered as having low involvement. The high level of involvement evident through the interviews was confirmed by the leader of a mission agency that partners with this church to send numerous mission workers, and who considered the church to be an excellent example of a mission engaged church.[12] These differences between the interview and questionnaire findings show the limitations of questionnaires for describing complex patterns of local church activity. The qualitative data gained through interviews is richer and provides a more nuanced understanding of local church behavior; it is therefore the primary source of data for analyzing different patterns of church mission engagement. For the purposes of this analysis, churches were compared according to their relative level of engagement in mission globally and were designated as less globally engaged (LGE) or more globally engaged (MGE) churches.[13] The core qualities of these LGE and MGE churches will now be reviewed.

Profile of Less Globally Engaged Churches

Three churches (CH1, CH2 and CH5) were determined to be LGE churches on the basis on the survey and interviews. These churches differ from each other greatly in size and location, yet they all showed above

---

12. Personal communication with agency NSW Ministry Leader, May 9, 2018.

13. Though "global mission" often refers to overseas mission, the true sense of the word refers to both local and distant mission. Globally engaged churches are actively involved in their local community and in distant places.

average involvement in local mission and below average involvement in distant mission compared to other churches of equivalent size.[14] All three churches self-identified as evangelical, one of the three also identified as reformed, and another as both missional and reformed. All three churches had experienced some changes in leadership in the previous few years. Two of the churches were led by senior ministers who had been in the church for five years or less and the third had only recently employed an assistant pastor to focus on mission activities. All three leaders referenced the relative recency of their appointments as they spoke of changes to the church's involvement in mission that they were seeking to cultivate.

The three churches all displayed high levels of involvement in local mission, though they had different emphases and employed different methods. The Sunday gatherings were consistently considered core to their local mission activities, together with evangelistic courses for those interested in learning more about the Christian faith. The interviewees from CH5 reported a wide range of programs run by members of the church to engage people from the local community.[15] Many of these sought to address social or economic needs in the context of relationship while seeking opportunities to proclaim the gospel. Members of CH2 also hosted a range of programs to engage local people and address social and relational needs, and similarly prioritized proclamation of the gospel as core to mission.[16] CH1 had limited involvement in programs to address social needs, yet it regularly hosted invitational events to engage non-Christians from the local community.[17] Interviewees from these churches all spoke of efforts to encourage the church members to be active in personal evangelism. All three churches had seen people become Christians and join their church in the previous year and they saw this as a core purpose of the church.

By contrast, these churches displayed lower levels of involvement in distant mission when compared to churches of similar size. There was some participation in distant mission activities in each church but the level of engagement among the members was low. CH2 had a significant history of partnership with distant mission workers, yet this had declined markedly in the previous decade. Many mission workers had been sent

---

14. CH1 had 100–249 regular attenders, CH2 had 250–500 regular attenders, and CH5 had 50–99 regular attenders.

15. Interviews with CH5_SP, June 13, 2019; CH5_CM, July 8, 2019; CH5_MC, July 8, 2019.

16. Interview with CH2_SP, June 24, 2019.

17. Interview with CH1_SP, August 26, 2019.

out from the church previously, yet most of these had returned to Australia and very few new workers had gone out. At the time of the interview, there was only one missionary family supported overseas and three individuals in mission work elsewhere in Australia. Though some of the older members of the church were committed to supporting distant mission, most of the members were disengaged. The church had recently decided to support a new overseas mission worker, but that relationship was in its infancy. CH1 had two missionary families that they had a connection with for many years, though with a relatively low level of engagement among the church members. The senior minister of the church was personally committed to the mission workers and encouraged church members to also be active in their support but, as one church member stated, "[He] has a friendship with [the mission workers]—historic—but we're not there."[18] This church had a strong emphasis on local evangelism, though little emphasis on distant mission involvement.[19] As the mission pastor stated, "I think because we have been heavily focused on local mission, and that's, I think, quite a strength of our church ... but I do wonder if part of it has been, we've been so focused on trying to build things up here, can we spare anything?"[20]

The third LGE church supported two distant mission workers and a global Christian radio ministry, though the significant challenges the church had faced in the last decade had led to a primary emphasis on mission to the local community.[21] The distant mission workers were regularly prayed for in the Sunday services and the minister had visited one worker on location overseas, yet the other interviewees focused primarily on local outreach.[22] All three churches provided some financial support to distant mission workers, though in CH1 and CH5 it was not part of the church's budgeted expenditure. The non-staff interviewees in both these churches either expressed little concern for distant mission,[23] or the belief that distant mission involvement at the church was too low.[24]

---

18. Interview with CH1_CM, September 27, 2019.
19. Interview with CH1_MC, September 27, 2019.
20. Interview with CH1_SP, August 26, 2019.
21. Interview with CH5_SP, June 13, 2019.
22. Interviews with CH5_CM, July 8, 2019; CH5_MC, July 8, 2019.
23. Interviews with CH1_CM, September 26, 2019; CH5_CM, July 8, 2019; CH5_MC, July 8, 2019.
24. Interviews with CH2_MC, August 29, 2019; CH2_CM, September 2, 2019; CH1_MC, September 27, 2019.

Profile of More Globally Engaged Churches

Seven of the ten churches approached for interviews were determined to be highly involved in both local and distant mission and are thus designated more globally engaged (MGE). All of these churches identified themselves as evangelical. Three of the seven also identified as reformed, one as missional, and the final three identified as both missional and reformed. Two of the seven were Anglican, two Baptist, two Presbyterian, and one independent. Two were Chinese churches and had English, Cantonese, and Mandarin speaking congregations. The seven churches varied markedly in size. One had less than fifty regular attendees, two had 100–249, two had 250–499, and the remaining two had over five hundred. The churches were in many different parts of Sydney.

All of these churches displayed high levels of involvement in local mission activities compared to churches of a similar size, though the patterns of involvement were varied. The larger churches hosted a wide range of evangelistic activities including invitational events, evangelistic courses, and Sunday services specifically tailored to ensure accessibility to non-Christians.[25] A number of churches partnered with other churches and para-church ministries to run programs and host outreach events.[26] Interviewees from all churches spoke of intentional efforts of the church leaders to train and equip church members to be active in personal evangelism among their friends and families. Some churches had developed resources specifically for this purpose and used time in church services to encourage and train people further.[27] All but the smallest church hosted mid-week programs open to non-Christians and encouraged their guests to explore the Christian faith. Small group meetings or courses were also run to enable non-Christians to learn about the Christian faith.[28] The majority of the local mission activities that these churches were involved in prioritized the communication of the gospel, yet some did this in the context of addressing social needs.[29] While interviewees from most of these churches saw the regular church meeting as a missional activity that

---

25. Interviews with CH3_SP, August 8, 2019; CH8_SP, April 11, 2019; CH6_MC, June 16, 2019.

26. Interviews with CH6_CM, June 16, 2019; CH8_SP, April 11, 2019.

27. Interviews with CH3_SP, August 8, 2018; CH4_MC, April 4, 2019.

28. Interviews with CH3_SP, August 8, 2019; CH4_SP, March 28, 2019; CH6_SP, May 2, 2019; CH7_SP, August 12, 2019; CH8_SP, April 11, 2019; CH9_SP, October 9, 2019; CH10_SP, June 3, 2019.

29. Interviews with CH8_MC, May 30, 2019; CH10_MC, July 19, 2019.

seeks to communicate the gospel to non-Christians, interviewees from three of the churches indicated that the primary purpose of the Sunday gathering was to build up the faith of the Christians present. Despite a range of local mission activities, interviewees from CH6 and CH7 did not believe that their churches were sufficiently active in local mission because many people found personal evangelism very difficult.[30] This is, however, more a reflection of their personal expectations than an objective measure of church participation.

All of these churches also showed high levels of participation in distant mission activities. As was noted above, one of the churches (CH6) was considered to have low levels of involvement in mission based on the survey, yet this was due to under reporting. The high level of participation was evident in the number of mission workers that the church supported, the regularity and nature of the engagement with these mission workers, the prayer, emotional, and practical support given to the workers, the sending of church members into mission work, and the financial support provided. All the MGE churches supported an above average number of mission workers compared to other churches of the same size. In every case, at least some of these workers had previously attended the church on a regular basis, reflecting the commitment evident in these churches to prepare and send people out for these roles. A notable portion of each church's expenditure went towards the financial support of mission workers and organizations involved in mission away from the church's local community. The primary point of differentiation between LGE and MGE churches was the proportion of the church members that were meaningfully engaged in partnership with mission workers and the depth of that engagement. This included financial support, prayer, personal engagement and, in some cases, visiting the workers in their context.

There was some diversity among these MGE churches in the emphasis and structure of their distant mission involvement. There were different systems employed to provide financial support for the mission workers, and each church had devised structures to share information and facilitate prayer for the workers. The diversity of church size correlated to differences in the capacity to provide financial and practical support of mission workers yet, compared to other churches of equivalent size, these churches showed high support. The churches also displayed different priorities in their mission involvement. The minister of one church spoke of

---

30. Interviews with CH6_CM, June 16, 2019; CH7_CM, September 18, 2019.

their commitment to supporting mission work among Jewish people before anything else.[31] Several churches supported national mission workers where possible,[32] while others only supported Australians who had moved to a specific location for mission work.[33] All but the smallest church supported some distant mission workers who were serving in Australia,[34] but the majority of workers being supported were in other countries. The nature of the work people engaged in was also varied, though there was a consistent emphasis on seeking to communicate the gospel message. Despite this diversity, these churches were similar in their widespread commitment to supporting distant mission work with an emphasis on partnering with individuals and families serving in other countries.

CHURCH MISSION INVOLVEMENT CONCLUSIONS

Through this questionnaire and interviews it has been clearly demonstrated that there are important differences in the way that evangelical local churches in Sydney and NSW are involved in mission activities. These differences are influenced by, but cannot be fully explained by, the size and wealth of the church; other factors are clearly at work. The questionnaire indicated some relationship between different modes of involvement in mission. Churches that displayed high levels of involvement in distant mission were generally active in local mission activities, yet churches that were highly engaged with local mission were not more likely than other churches to be highly involved in distant mission. Through interviews with church leaders and members of ten local churches across Sydney, these patterns of mission involvement were further explored. These churches all displayed high levels of involvement in local mission yet diverse patterns of involvement in distant mission. These differences manifested in a variety of ways, but essentially in MGE churches most church members were engaged in distant mission activities, while very few members of LGE churches were engaged in distant mission. These churches all showed a general commitment to mission,

---

31. Interview with CH9_SP, October 9, 2019.

32. National workers are local to the country in which they serve. Interviews with CH3_MC, September 2, 2019; CH4_MC, April 4, 2019; CH9_SP, October 9, 2019; CH10_MC, July 19, 2019.

33. Interviews with CH6_SP, May 2, 2019; CH7_SP, August 12, 2019; CH8_MC, May 30, 2019.

34. Interview with CH7_SP, August 12, 2019.

yet the differences in distant mission involvement allowed consideration of the factors shaping these approaches to mission involvement. In the following four chapters, the core categories arising from the analysis of this qualitative data are explored. Chapter 4 discusses interviewees' ecclesiological convictions regarding the nature and purpose of the church. In chapter 5, interviewees' beliefs about mission are examined and contrasted. Chapter 6 considers the mission practices of these churches using the dual lenses of organizational culture and organizational climate. Finally, chapter 7 analyzes the differences in relational networks in these churches and how their significance might be understood with social exchange and social capital theories.

4

Ecclesiology of Local Churches

INTRODUCTION

When discussing the involvement of their church in mission, interviewees expressed beliefs about the nature and purpose of the local church. As the significance of this theme became evident, they were asked what they believed the purpose of their church to be. Their responses, together with how they described their churches, reflect fundamental ecclesiological convictions. Considering the significant discussions regarding the relationship between mission and ecclesiology that took place through the twentieth century, one would expect that differences in people's understanding of either the nature or purpose of church would align with the differences in local church activities. However, though interviewees provided a variety of perspectives and emphasized different elements, there were no clear patterns consistent with the church's level of involvement in mission. The only notable difference was in the emphasis that each church placed on the various ministry and mission tasks that they considered important.

ECCLESIOLOGY: NATURE

The specific activities and purposes of a local church are profoundly shaped by the ways in which the church is defined by its members. Through the history of Christianity what constitutes a church has been conceived in a variety of ways. The church may be understood as primarily universal or local, visible or invisible, autonomous or episcopal. These convictions will influence the relationships that a local church develops with other churches, denominational structures, and parachurch entities. Interviewees described their churches in terms of their structure and the connections to other Christian entities. They also employed several metaphors to illustrate the defining characteristics of their church and the priorities that they perceived.

The use of the term "church" among interviewees provides a valuable insight into the relationship between the local church, their denomination, and other Christian structures. All but one of the churches hold more than one service on a Sunday. In most cases interviewees referred to each group that meets as a "congregation" and the group of congregations under a single leadership team as a "church." One of the Chinese churches had seven congregations that met on a Sunday across two locations—three in English, two in Cantonese, and two in Mandarin—yet they were together considered one church. Though each congregation has its own pastoral staff, there was a central leadership team that governed the ministry of the whole church. Similarly, one of the Anglican churches with three different services on a Sunday was led by a unified team of ministers and used the term "church" to describe the entity as a whole. One notable exception to this pattern was a Presbyterian minister who emphasized that in his parish each service is referred to as a church.

> We dropped the word congregations. We use the word churches. With the view that they need to chart their own course. They've all got their own leadership teams. They all have permission to minister and meet on their own basis.[1]

This highlights the fact that the term "church" carries an implication of autonomy. A church has the authority to determine its own identity, purpose, and emphasis whether it is one congregation or many.

Despite the variety of denominations represented, there was no indication from the interviewees that their church was under the direction of denominational structures. Two ministers referred to the "Presbyterian Church" when talking about denominationally administered social ministries or overseas activities.[2] Yet in both cases, they highlighted the autonomy of the local church by noting the ways that their churches

---

1. Interview with CH10_SP, June 3, 2019.
2. Interviews with CH9_SP, October 9, 2019; CH10_SP, June 3, 2019.

differed from the practices of the wider denomination. The only notable way in which denominational connections were referenced by interviewees was regarding the parachurch mission agencies and aid organizations that they supported. All the Anglican churches supported CMS and Anglicare while only Presbyterian churches supported mission workers through APWM. The Baptist and independent churches predominantly supported non-denominational mission organizations with the two Chinese churches having a strong connection to OMF.[3] Despite these trends, all churches supported some organizations outside their denominational affiliation. Overall, the denomination of the church appeared to have little influence on the ecclesiological convictions regarding the nature of the local church. Each church was seen to be an autonomous local community that determined its own approach to mission.[4]

While few of the interviewees explicitly articulated their beliefs about the nature of the church, their use of images to describe their churches provided a valuable insight into their understanding and functional ecclesiology. Images engage the imagination and invite participation in a way that prosaic descriptions do not. Numerous authors have explored the importance of metaphors in describing a biblical ecclesiology. Paul Minear's comprehensive survey identified ninety-six images through the New Testament.[5] Many of these were minor images, though major images included the people of God, the new creation, the fellowship in faith, and the body of Christ. These reviews of biblical metaphors for the church often reflect the theological convictions of their author. Writing from a Roman Catholic perspective, Avery Dulles explored a number of major images highlighting the institutional and sacramental dimensions of the church.[6] These he used to emphasize the relationship between the "churches" and the "Church." Robert Kysar discussed select biblical metaphors to justify his description of the church as "a community of faith on the way home stumbling in the light."[7] John Driver highlighted the images that reveal the missional purposes of the church and arranged

---

3. OMF is a non-denominational evangelical mission organization that works throughout East Asia.

4. This is consistent with Veli-Matti Kärkkäinen's assertion that there is a global trend towards congregationalism across denominations. See Kärkkäinen, *Introduction to Ecclesiology*, 59.

5. Minear, *Images of the Church*.

6. Dulles, *Models of the Church*.

7. Kysar, *Stumbling in the Light*, 87.

them under the four headings "of pilgrimage, of the new order, of peoplehood, and of transformation."[8] Stanley Skreslet also focused on the New Testament images related to mission, though with a greater emphasis on the interpersonal mission of the disciple rather than the communal mission of the church.[9] These examinations provide valuable background on different images while showing the ways that metaphors can be used to depict one's beliefs about the church.

Interviewees used relatively few images to describe their churches and generally employed the term "church" to describe the community of people who met together in one or more congregations. The members of these communities were referred to synonymously as "Christians," "believers," or "the people of God." There was some distinction between the actions of the individuals and the church as a corporate entity, though any activity performed by church members with the support of the leadership was generally considered a church activity.[10] Even when staff were not directly involved in an activity, if they were seen to sanction it then it was considered a church activity. In this way the church was represented by subsets of its members in a variety of endeavors. In addition to this use of the term "church," interviewees employed four other images to describe church: family, body, light, and lifeboat. The family image emphasized the relational connections within the church community, while the body, light, and lifeboat images described the missional nature of the church.

Family

The family metaphor was used by interviewees from three different churches, two of which were more globally engaged (MGE) churches (CH6 and CH7) and one was a less globally engaged (LGE) church (CH1).[11] In each case, the emphasis of the family language was on the relationships between the members of the local church. One interviewee from CH1 spoke of the value of events that brought "the church family together as a community" so that people could encourage one another in

---

8. Driver, *Images of the Church*, 22.

9. Skreslet, *Picturing Christian Witness*.

10. Interviews with CH2_MC, August 29, 2019; CH5_CM, July 8, 2019; CH8_CM, May 22, 2019; CH8_SP, April 11, 2019.

11. The family or brethren metaphor is usually used in the New Testament to describe Christians in all places, not only the local church (Gal 6:10; 1 Thess 4:10; 1 Pet 2:17; 5:9).

their faith.¹² The pastor of this church used the same language to describe the benefit of church membership for those who live away from their own family or who do not have any Christian relatives.¹³ The pastor of CH7, an MGE church, stated that "of all the metaphors, family gets used by far the most" because of the strong relational connectedness in the church due to its small size and stable congregation.¹⁴ CH6 used the family image in its mission statement describing the church as "authentic believers in Jesus, in one family, on mission."¹⁵ All of the interviewees from this church recalled the family language in discussing the purpose of the church.¹⁶ The minister stated that the "one family" phrase reflects a desire to encourage "cross-generational, cross-congregational activities" in a church with multiple language groups and congregations.¹⁷ The members of this church both qualified the term "family" with the adjective "welcoming" and discussed the efforts to encourage the church to be open to outsiders rather than just focusing on their own comfort.¹⁸ This highlights the fact that the primary significance of the family language is on the internal connectedness of the church.

The biblical imagery that shapes this understanding of the church as a family draws on the importance of familial connections in Hebrew thought. In ancient Israel, as in many collective societies today, people were defined by their family identity.¹⁹ Members of a particular family were not simply descended from a particular patriarch, but their character and integrity reflected their familial connections. When Jesus declared that "whoever does God's will is my brother and sister and mother," (Mark 3:35) he was not only making a statement about their relationship to him, but the ways in which they were to behave. This highlights the significance of Christians being part of the "family" (ἀδελφότης—1 Pet 2:17; 5:9; cf. 1 Thess 4:10; Heb 2:11) and the "household of God" (οἰκεῖος/οἶκος τοῦ θεοῦ—Eph 2:19; 1 Tim 3:15; 1 Pet 4:17; cf. Gal 6:10). Membership in the family is a consequence of the redeeming work of Jesus, through whom Christians receive "adoption to sonship" (υἱοθεσία—Rom 8:23; 9:4;

---

12. Interview with CH1_CM, September 26, 2019.
13. Interview with CH1_SP, August 26, 2019.
14. Interview with CH7_SP, August 12, 2019.
15. Interview with CH6_SP, May 2, 2019.
16. Interviews with CH6_MC, June 16, 2019; CH6_CM, June 16, 2019.
17. Interview with CH6_SP, May 2, 2019.
18. Interviews with CH6_MC, June 16, 2019; CH6_CM, June 16, 2019.
19. Minear, *Images of the Church*, 166–69.

Gal 4:5; Eph 1:5). The "unifying presence of the Holy Spirit" then binds believers together in an ongoing way.[20] The practical expression of this unification is mutual love (John 13:34–35; Rom 12:9–10; 15:1–2; 1 Cor 13:4–8; Phil 2:1–4).[21] It is this connection and mutual commitment to each other that the interviewees primarily had in mind in their references to the family language. This was expressed by interviewees from all churches regardless of their approach to mission.

Missional Images

Body

Four interviewees from four different churches used the term "body" to describe the church. Each of these churches showed high levels of involvement in both local and distant mission yet the body image was used to highlight a variety of implications. A church member of CH3 used the phrase "building up the body" four times through his interview to refer to a core activity of his church.[22] He described how this practice of edification "will then enable [the members] to do mission better."[23] This is clearly a reference to Eph 4:11–12, "Christ himself gave the apostles, the prophets, the evangelists, the pastors and teachers, to equip his people for works of service, so that the body of Christ may be built up." This interviewee was using the body language to refer to the local community of Christians that met together so that they might be equipped for ministry. In particular, he saw participation in mission as the primary focus of this equipping.

A second interviewee referred to being "part of one body of Christ" as motivation for participation in mission activities.[24] This echoes the argument of 1 Corinthians 12 in which the apostle Paul uses the image of the body of Christ to emphasize that each member of the church is equally valuable and has a role to play: "you are the body of Christ, and each one of you is a part of it" (1 Cor 12:27). The interviewee's use of the word "one" to define the body suggests that he saw membership in the universal church as cause for involvement in mission. In a similar way another interviewee used the body language to describe the corporate

---

20. Dulles, *Models of the Church*, 49.
21. Banks, *Paul's Idea of Community*, 52–54.
22. Interview with CH3_CM, August 23, 2019.
23. Interview with CH3_CM, August 23, 2019.
24. Interview with CH9_CM, September 10, 2019.

actions of her church in the local community. "We get to do our little local body bit of [our suburb], but of course, we're part of the worldwide body that God is using to bring about his purposes."[25] In each of these cases the interviewees were seeing membership in the "body," either the local or the universal church, as the foundation from which mission involvement happens. The pastor of a fourth church used the term with a slightly different emphasis. At the time the members of his church gave money directly to mission workers, but he would like to see them combining their giving and supporting the mission workers "as a body."[26] In this sense the local church is seen as a corporate entity that can participate in distant mission together. This multidimensional usage of the body imagery reflects the variety of uses in the New Testament.[27]

The image of the church as the body of Christ occurs numerous times in the New Testament and has had a significant influence on ecclesiology. Dulles reviewed the influence of the body image on ecclesiology and noted the emphasis in these passages on connection with Christ. He concluded that, together with the people of God metaphor, the body image portrayed the church as a "mystical communion" that has no missiological significance.[28] Driver, Kysar, and Skreslet similarly gave little consideration to the body metaphor in their discussions on the church's participation in mission.[29] However, Minear went into great depth exploring the many different ways that the body image is employed by Paul in the New Testament.[30] Minear agrees that the dominant themes of the image relate to the unity of the church and its intimate connection to Christ, yet notes that the universal rule of Christ means that his body, the church, "exists for the purpose of the ultimate erasure of the line between the church and the world."[31] This echoes the ecclesiology of Karl Barth who drew heavily upon the body of Christ imagery.[32] For Barth,

---

25. Interview with CH10_MC, July 19, 2019.

26. Interview with CH7_SP, August 12, 2019.

27. Minear notes that this metaphor is predominantly found in the Pauline Epistles where Paul "appeals to the body image in a flexible fashion." Minear, *Images of the Church*, 189.

28. Dulles, *Models of the Church*, 39–54.

29. Driver, *Images of the Church*; Kysar, *Stumbling in the Light*; Skreslet, *Picturing Christian Witness*.

30. Minear, *Images of the Church*, 173–220.

31. Minear, *Images of the Church*, 243.

32. Kärkkäinen, *Introduction to Ecclesiology*, 57.

the church was "the living community of the living Lord Jesus" which was a witness to Christ in the world as it lives in relationship with him.[33]

The interviewees in this study used the body image to highlight similar missiological qualities. They spoke of their church as a body because they believed it to be connected to Christ and because the individual members were spiritually bound to one another. As such, they felt a responsibility to be involved in mission. This reflects a belief that the church as a body exists worldwide as a witness to Jesus (Acts 1:8), and if a local church is going to be faithful to this aspect of its identity, then it will participate in mission. These uses of the body image reflect a close link between Christology and ecclesiology in these churches. These church members believed that the salvific purposes of Christ should be expressed through the local church, particularly in their local community. As the body of Christ, they were to be actively engaged in mission. It is therefore notable that this language was not used by interviewees in less globally engaged (LGE) churches.

Light

The third biblical metaphor employed by interviewees was "light." Five interviewees from five different churches used this image but each person mentioned the term only once.[34] This suggests that it was not a dominant image employed at any of the churches, but a shared concept among evangelicals. Four of the interviewees were from MGE churches and one from an LGE church. In each case the image was used to highlight the missional task of the church. One interviewee from an MGE church spoke of it as a general exhortation to be involved in mission, but all other interviewees connected it to local mission specifically. The church was to be a "light in the community,"[35] a "light . . . open doors welcoming anyone and everyone in,"[36] and "a light to the nations, the nations have come to us."[37] All of these churches were active in local mission and this image was employed to support that activity.

---

33. Barth, *God Here and Now*, 75–104.

34. Interviews with CH5_MC, July 8, 2019; CH6_MC, June 16, 2019; CH7_SP, August 12, 2019; CH9_CM, September 10, 2019; CH10_MC, July 19, 2019.

35. Interview with CH7_SP, August 12, 2019.

36. Interview with CH10_MC, July 19, 2019.

37. Interview with CH5_MC, July 8, 2019.

The light image appears numerous times in the New Testament often drawing on Old Testament references. Throughout Scripture, God is clearly portrayed as the source of both light and life, which are often held together (Gen 1:1; John 8:12; 9:5; 2 Cor 4:6; 1 John 1:5). The prophecy of Isaiah that the Messiah would be "a light for the Gentiles" (Isa 49:6) is referenced in the New Testament and applied to the followers of Jesus (Matt 5:14; Luke 2:32; Acts 13:47). The disciples, and later the church, become the light because of their connection to Jesus and are simply commanded to be that which they are (Phil 2:14; Eph 5:8). The image is employed in the New Testament to emphasize Jesus' transformation of his people so that they might shine his light in the world.[38] This is a predominantly attractional mode of mission whereby the nations are drawn to Jesus by the holiness of his people.[39] Though not elaborating on its significance, these interviewees employed the light image in a similar way. They see their churches as having a responsibility to shine the light of Jesus through their words and deeds, and thereby lead people in their local community him. This is a clearly missional image that was employed in both MGE and LGE churches, though, like the body image, it had a predominantly local application.

Lifeboat

The final image explicitly employed by interviewees to describe their church was that of a lifeboat. This image was referenced by two interviewees from CH1, one of whom described it as "a commonly used analogy of the senior minister."[40] The interviewee explained, "[the] church is like a lifeboat that is placed in [our suburb] and all around us are people drowning. And our job, as people on the lifeboat, is to grab people and bring them into life—into eternal life through Jesus. So that is why we exist."

Though the lifeboat is not a biblical image applied to the church, there is a long tradition of associating the church with a boat that brings salvation. Minear notes that "some exegetes have discovered allusions to the church in the boat scenes of the Gospels." He notes the occasions of Jesus calming the storm (Matt 8:23–27; Mark 4:35–41), walking on the waves (Matt 14:22–27), and teaching from the boat (Mark 4:1), yet

---

38. Minear, *Images of the Church*, 128–29.
39. Driver, *Images of the Church*, 170–82.
40. Interviews with CH1_SP, August 26, 2019; CH1_MC, September 27, 2019.

he concludes that "it is improbable that modern readers will ever agree" on the implications of these biblical references for the church.[41] Another biblical source of the image is the reference to Noah's Ark and baptism as means of salvation in 1 Peter 3:18–22.[42] Yet the clearest parallel to this minister's usage comes from the peaching of D. L. Moody who said, "I look on this world as a wrecked vessel. God has given me a life-boat, and said to me, 'Moody, save all you can.'"[43] This image reflects the belief that people in the local community are spiritually perishing unless they are brought into relationship with Jesus. This implies a moral imperative to prioritize mission activities in the local church. However, just as a lifeboat can only assist people that are near to it, so this image suggests that the church has primary responsibility for the people that live nearby. As one of these interviewees observed regarding her church, "our responsibility as God's people for salvation beyond our patch is not felt."[44]

It is notable that of these four images, family, body, light, and lifeboat, three of them highlight the missional responsibility and actions of the local church. The body, light, and lifeboat images were used by interviewees to discuss the ways in which the church was to be involved in mission activities. Yet, none of these images imply that the local church has a missional responsibility beyond the local community. A number of those who employed the body image indicated an awareness that the universal church had a responsibility to make Christ known, yet the implication of this for their church was that they were to be actively engaged in mission in their own community. Imagery was not used by the interviewees to highlight the role of their church in mission activities further afield.

Church Identity

Though no other key images were employed to describe the churches, there were a number of references to core qualities that explained the

---

41. Minear, *Images of the Church*, 33.

42. This imagery for the church has long historical pedigree. In Tertullian's treatise *On Idolatry* he parallels the church to Noah's Ark as the only place of salvation. Similarly, the church was depicted as a boat on the walls of the catacombs, and the fourth century *Apostolic Constitutions* spoke of the Bishop as "one that is the commander of a great ship," who was to arrange the church gathering like people on a ship. This may also be why the central part of the church building has long been referred to as the nave, from the Latin *navis* (ship).

43. Pell, *Dwight L. Moody*, 516–17,

44. Interview with CH1_MC, September 27, 2019.

"identity" of the churches. The pastor of CH8 described involvement in mission as "part of [the church's] DNA . . . essential to the church's identity."[45] This involvement included local activities as well as sending people out. In a document outlining the missions strategy for his church, another church leader described the churches he leads as "missional churches . . . committed to participating, both individually and as communities, in God's mission."[46] This reflected his belief that all Christians are expected to live "as witnesses and agents of the kingdom" in every aspect of their lives.[47] The minister of CH4 noted several key qualities which he saw as biblical values that should shape the identity of the church. Involvement in mission was one of the values, as well as a commitment to gratitude, the Bible, prayer, care for one another, holiness, and generosity.[48] This reflects an emphasis on the nature rather than the activities of the church. The goal of ministry was to faithfully reflect these values in the life of the church. In each case the interviewees that spoke about mission involvement as an integral dimension of the church's identity were in MGE churches. This missional identity was seen to have implications both locally and further afield.

Overall, statements about the nature of the local church varied between interviewees, yet there was no clear pattern that differentiated MGE from LGE churches. Interviewees from both employed images that highlighted the missional qualities of the churches, yet in each case these images emphasized the responsibility for local missional engagement. Through this variety of descriptions there was a broad consistency to the understanding of the nature of the local church. Interviewees all viewed their churches as autonomous communities of Christians who were spiritually bound to one another and had a shared responsibility for mission. Some interviewees from MGE churches also expressed the view that mission involvement was integral to the church's identity and that the horizon for this involvement extended beyond the local community. As this discussion shows, there is clear overlap between the way interviewees understand the nature and the purpose of a local church, though they also articulated core convictions about the purpose of the church.

---

45. Interview with CH8_SP, April 11, 2019.
46. CH10, Missions Strategy and Directions, August 31, 2017.
47. Interview with CH10_SP, June 3, 2019.
48. Interview with CH4_SP, March 28, 2019.

ECCLESIOLOGY: PURPOSE

Before interviewees were asked about the specific activities of their churches, their beliefs about the purpose of their church were explored. While some interviewees responded to this question by sharing the church's formal mission statement, most expressed what they saw to be the core functions of their church in their own words. These purposes were predominantly focused on serving people and can therefore be categorized according to the recipients of the ministry.[49] Some purposes served the needs of the church's own members, other purposes sought to engage non-members, typically non-Christians, in the local community, and some purposes considered the needs of people beyond the local context—both believers and non-believers. Every interviewee saw serving the local community as one purpose of their church. Most people included serving the church members in their response (twenty-six of thirty, 87 percent), while two-thirds of respondents saw serving people beyond their local context as part of their purpose (twenty of thirty, 67 percent). The majority of interviewees (nineteen of thirty, 63 percent) included all three categories in the purpose of their church. When further questioned about the place of mission in the church's work, all interviewees spoke of involvement in distant mission, that is serving the needs of those beyond the local context, as part of the purpose of the church even if it was not initially mentioned. The primary difference was seen in the relative emphasis that was placed on each sphere of concern.

Serving Members

While most interviewees (87 percent) initially described serving the needs of church members as part of the purpose of their church, every interviewee, from both MGE and LGE churches, spoke about it in further discussions about the church activities. These member-directed activities had three primary goals. Firstly, they sought to edify members and strengthen them in their faith. Secondly, they sought to equip members

---

49. It is interesting to note that none of the interviewees described worship as one of the purposes of the church. Some church members did mention it as one of the elements of their services, but it was not a core purpose. (Interviews with CH6_MC, June 16, 2019; CH9_MC, August 29, 2019; CH10_MC, July 19, 2019.) This reflects a teaching common among evangelicals in Sydney, that Christian worship is primarily a life of service to God and his people, rather than a task of the gathered congregation. See Peterson, *Engaging with God*.

for direct involvement in ministry and mission activities. And finally, they provided care and support for members of the church.

Some interviewees recalled formal mission statements which referred to the goal of strengthening the faith of members. For example, CH6's mission to be "authentic believers in Jesus" reflected a desire for people to be firmly grounded in the "bare bones" of the Christian faith.[50] Similarly, the CH8 mission statement was "to be a people of God, growing in Christ, reaching out with the gospel until he returns."[51] This indicated the goal of encouraging spiritual growth among the members as core to the purpose of the church. While one member of this church could approximately recall the mission statement, another summarized his understanding of the church's purpose as "to love God, follow Christ, and to love others, so that they will know Christ."[52] Interviewees used a range of terms to capture this concept of stimulating spiritual faithfulness among members. A member of CH9 described the church as a place where "we encourage each other to keep living and to keep persevering in the race to the end."[53] The minister of that same church expressed it as helping to "build people in their faith in Christ."[54] The minister of CH4 saw this emphasis as simply a function of encouraging the church to faithfully live out its Christian identity which he did by articulating seven values that he believed were core to the identity of a biblical church.[55] Finally, a member of CH2 expressed the purpose of her church as "to build up the people of God who are there."[56] This focus on the spiritual development of church members was a commonly stated purpose.

In addition to establishing Christians in their faith, many churches also sought to equip members to be involved in ministry themselves, particularly by participating in local mission activities. A church member of CH3 recalled the senior minister saying that the Sunday service was "for building up the body. Which will then enable them do mission better."[57] For the minister of CH4, involvement in mission was one of the core values that the church sought to embody and was something

50. Interview with CH6_SP, May 2, 2019.
51. Interview with CH8_SP, April 11, 2019.
52. Interview with CH8_MC, May 30, 2019.
53. Interview with CH9_CM, September 10, 2019.
54. Interview with CH9_SP, October 9, 2019.
55. Interview with CH4_SP, March 28, 2019.
56. Interview with CH2_MC, August 29, 2019.
57. Interview with CH3_CM, August 23, 2019.

that he wanted to equip the church members to do. He stated, "If I want to lead my church in being faithful disciples of Jesus, then helping them think about how they engage in God's work in the world, locally and globally, seems pretty central to me."[58] The pastor of CH5 explained that the church has a threefold vision captured by the words, "bring, build, [and] send."[59] Build refers to "building disciples of Jesus"[60] which was further explained by one of the church members as "to equip the people of God to be able to reach out to the community."[61] This highlights the close relationship between the activities of the church focused on the needs of the church members and the wider purpose of engaging those outside the church.

Several interviewees referred to *The Vine Project* by Marshall and Payne when describing the building up of believers as a purpose of their church.[62] These two goals of establishing Christians in their faith and equipping them for ministry are key points in Marshall and Payne's framework. This book draws on Matthew 28:19 to argue that the purpose of a local church is to make disciples by engaging and evangelizing non-Christians, establishing Christians in their faith, and then equipping them for the work of ministry.[63] In this framework, "establishing Christians" seeks to deepen the person's commitment to the Christian faith, while "equipping" is focused on preparing people to participate in ministry and mission so that they might engage and evangelize non-Christians too.[64] The language of "making disciples" was also used by a number of church leaders without specific reference to Marshall and Payne.[65] This suggests that the member focused activities may also have an eye to the non-members.

The final dimension of a church's ministry to its own members is mutual care. Some interviewees mentioned this as a key quality of their

---

58. Interview with CH4_SP, March 28, 2019.

59. Interview with CH5_SP, June 13, 2019.

60. Interview with CH5_SP, June 13, 2019.

61. Interview with CH5_CM, July 8, 2019.

62. Marshall and Payne, *Vine Project*. Interviews with CH1_CM, September 26, 2019; CH3_SP, August 8, 2019; CH3_CM, August 23, 2019.

63. Marshall and Payne, *Vine Project*, 146–47.

64. Marshall and Payne, *Vine Project*, 264–95.

65. Interviews with CH2_SP, June 24, 2019; CH5_SP, June 13, 2019. This is consistent with the emphasis on the language of Matthew 28:18–20 in shaping missiological thinking and practice since William Carey's *Enquiry*.

church. One church previously included the phrase "loving each other" in its mission statement.[66] The church which sought to embody seven core values, included "care for one another" as one of these values.[67] Another minister expressed the goal of the church as to "love the people who are here, but not forgetting to love the outsider."[68] To that end he stated that the leaders within the church were equipped and supported to "teach and pastorally care" for the church members.[69] Other interviewees simply expressed mutual care of the members as a key quality of their churches.[70] In some cases this was recognized for its positive impact on the missional engagement with the local community when visitors witnessed the "genuine love of the community,"[71] though for most it was simply considered a worthy goal in itself. Many of these interviewees see this internal work focused on serving the church's members as core to the church's purpose. Of the thirty interviewees, nineteen (63 percent) considered it a primary purpose of the church and another seven (23 percent) considered it to be a secondary purpose. This emphasis on the edification of believers is core to the Knox-Robinson ecclesiology which has been highly influential in evangelical churches across Sydney.[72] In these churches it served the three ultimate goals of strengthening church members in their faith, equipping members for participation in ministry and mission activities, and caring for each other. Though expressed in these diverse ways this priority was evident in all churches regardless of their pattern of mission involvement.

Local Mission: Serving the Local Community

Without exception, every interviewee spoke of serving or reaching the people in the local community when first asked about the purpose of their church. Twenty-six of the thirty (87 percent) interviewees described local engagement as a primary purpose of their church. Despite this consistency, the nature of this engagement varied between churches regarding the

66. Interview with CH1_SP, August 26, 2019.
67. Interview with CH4_SP, March 28, 2019.
68. Interview with CH9_SP, October 9, 2019.
69. Interview with CH9_SP, October 9, 2019.
70. Interview with CH6_CM, June 16, 2019; CH6_MC, June 16, 2019; CH7_SP, August 12, 2019.
71. Interview with CH1_SP, August 26, 2019.
72. Silberman, "Un-Missional Church?"

contexts in which this engagement took place and the *needs* that it sought to address. Regarding the context, some interviewees focused on the attractional dimension of the church's mission whereby it drew people into the church community through events and activities at the church. Others emphasized the responsibility that the church had to engage people out in the local community in groups and as individuals. Responses also differed regarding the needs being addressed; some interviewees highlighted the need to address practical or social needs, while others were purely concerned with addressing spiritual needs. Most churches were engaged in a mix of activities suggesting several needs were being addressed in the local community, though with different emphases.

Contexts for Local Mission

For most interviewees, the primary way that they believed their church should engage members of the local community was by attracting them to church events. Various images were used to highlight this attractional approach. A member of CH7 described their church as seeking to "lift up the name of Jesus"[73] while two members from CH6 spoke of their church's efforts to be a "welcoming family."[74] This latter image reflected the efforts to prioritize the comfort of non-members at their services so that visitors could "come and see what Christians are like and actually explore Jesus."[75] Other interviewees also spoke of their church's intentional efforts to ensure that their regular meetings were accessible for non-members. An interviewee from CH10 spoke of the church's desire to be a "light . . . [and] open doors welcoming anyone and everyone in."[76] This is consistent with the vision of this church to "bring, build, [and] send" in which "bring" refers to "bringing people to come to know and love Jesus."[77] These responses all reflect a belief that a core purpose of the local church is to draw in non-Christians so that they might hear the Christian message and experience Christian community.

By contrast, however, some interviewees explicitly stated that they did not believe their regular Sunday meetings should be intentionally

---

73. Interview with CH7_MC, September 2, 2019.
74. Interviews with CH6_MC, June 16, 2019; CH6_CM, June 16, 2019.
75. Interview with CH6_MC, June 16, 2019.
76. Interview with CH10_MC, July 19, 2019.
77. Interview with CH5_SP, June 13, 2019.

missional activities. A member of CH3 recalls the minister stating that "primarily, [the Sunday service] is for building up the body, which will then enable [church members] to do mission better."[78] Similarly, a member of CH4 stated that the church service was "more geared to members."[79] She understood the minister's view to be that non-Christians may "come in and see the community and [be] attracted to what [they] see, [but] he's not changing it for the outsider."[80] This reflects a belief that, even though non-Christians are welcome, the church meeting is primarily for the benefit of Christians. Nevertheless, even in these churches, attracting people into the church community through other activities was considered a purpose of the church. By hosting special invitational events or evangelistic courses, they engaged in local mission. Therefore, though expressed differently, interviewees from all churches believed that one purpose of the church was to host events and activities through which they could serve non-Christians in their local community.

In addition to these attractional events, many interviewees spoke of the need for church members to engage non-Christians in their own contexts. The minister of CH4 placed a particular emphasis on this as he reflected on past experience:

> I've been in plenty of churches, which run a lot of the evangelistic events through the year. And which leave people feeling like, "We're part of a church that's doing lots of evangelism." When, in actual fact, a lot of people aren't very engaged in thinking about evangelism.[81]

For this reason, the church used training events, small group meetings and segments in their Sunday services to encourage and equip its members to be "engaging with individuals at the school gate, through their friendships, and neighborhoods."[82] Other interviewees similarly spoke of the need to equip church members to engage in mission in the local community. The minister of CH10 shared about his efforts to encourage church members to "view themselves as missionaries" in their daily lives.[83] In a number of churches this was further encouraged by running activities in

---

78. Interview with CH3_CM, August 23, 2019.
79. Interview with CH4_MC, April 4, 2019.
80. Interview with CH4_MC, April 4, 2019.
81. Interview with CH4_SP, March 28, 2019.
82. Interview with CH4_SP, March 28, 2019.
83. Interview with CH10_SP, June 3, 2019.

the local community for the purposes of mission, such as free barbecues, community events, and serving local schools.[84] In all these ways, these interviewees reflect the conviction that the local church must be engaged in mission to members of their local community. Though the ways in which this conviction was expressed differed, it was consistently evident in all the churches regardless of their level of involvement in distant mission.

Local Mission Needs

In addition to the various contexts in which churches sought to connect with people, the kinds of needs that mission activities were focused on were discussed. Without exception, interviewees believed that addressing people's spiritual needs by sharing the Christian faith was the primary purpose driving local church engagement with their community. Church services, evangelistic events, and evangelistic courses were widely recognized to have social and relational benefits, but the emphasis was on meeting spiritual needs. Just as interviewees had discussed the primacy of addressing the spiritual needs of church members, the main concern for non-members was also spiritual. The minister of CH9 summarized this emphasis well when describing the purpose of the church, "we're trying to build people in their faith in Christ, whether that means evangelizing or edifying them."[85] From his perspective, whether people are already Christians or not they need the same thing: spiritual growth. This focus on spiritual needs was expressed by another minister when he said, "the equipping that we want to be doing is for speaking the words of God into each other's lives and the lives of unbelievers."[86] In his view, people's spiritual needs are of paramount importance and are addressed by hearing "the words of God."

The value of addressing the practical and social needs of members of the local community was a secondary priority, even though it was mentioned by several interviewees. One church member at CH5 saw this mode of missional engagement as a priority for her church, stating that "the big focus here is on showing love to the community in service,"[87]

---

84. Interviews with CH5_SP, June 3, 2019; CH6_SP, May 2, 2019; CH8_MC, May 30, 2019.

85. Interview with CH9_SP, October 9, 2019.

86. Interview with CH3_SP, August 8, 2019.

87. Interview with CH5_MC, July 8, 2019.

although she was disappointed that this had not led to many people becoming members of the church. One example of this commitment was the playgroups for parents with young children that were mentioned by interviewees from seven of the ten churches.[88] All of these programs sought to address social needs in the local community while also providing a context in which church members could introduce people to the Christian faith. As the minister of CH8 stated, "people who are running those [playgroups] definitely are running them with a heart that young mums not only have a space to bring their kids in for social interaction but get a chance to hear the gospel . . . [and] experience the love of Christ."[89] Several interviewees spoke of the English as a second language (ESL) programs that they ran in a similar way. The programs sought to meet a practical need among members of the local community, yet the ultimate goal was to see people become members of the church and have their spiritual needs met.[90]

This dual purpose was articulated by a number of interviewees with regard to other community service activities run in their churches. In discussing the programs run by CH2, the minister stated that they provide an opportunity to "bring Christians into contact with non-Christians."[91] It was hoped that this would lead to people hearing the Christian message. This desire was highlighted by the church's previous experience with a local school program which paired volunteers from the church with disadvantaged children needing mentors. Though there was initial enthusiasm for the program, people lost interest because there was "not much opportunity for the gospel and [they were] not even able to invite them to the kids club."[92] Church members wanted to address both spiritual and social needs and were unwilling to participate in a program where spiritual needs were excluded. In a similar way, one interviewee from CH5 expressed disappointment with the impact of many programs run by her church which she described as a "terrific service for the people in the community" but "the relational side hasn't really

---

88. Interviewees from CH1, CH2, CH4, CH5, CH6, CH8, CH10 reported having church run playgroups. CH3 and CH4 also have preschools connected to the church.

89. Interview with CH8_SP, April 11, 2019.

90. Interviews with CH1_CM, September 26, 2019; CH5_CM, July 8, 2019; CH9_MC, August 29, 2019. These programs are discussed in more depth in chapter 6.

91. Interview with CH2_SP, June 24, 2019.

92. Interview with CH2_SP, June 24, 2019.

attracted [the recipients] to invest in actually being a church member."[93] This reflects a wide-spread view that these local churches have a responsibility to meet social needs of people in their local community, but their ultimate purpose was to lead people to learn about, and hopefully accept, the Christian faith. Though the emphasis varied between individuals, this view was expressed by interviewees from all the churches regardless of their level of involvement in distant and overseas mission.

Distant Mission: Serving Those beyond the Local Community

The third purpose of the local church reported by interviewees was the need to serve people beyond the local community through distant mission. When first asked what they believed were the purposes of their church, interviewees from all but one church included this in their initial response.[94] Church leaders were the most likely to speak of this purpose with all but two mentioning distant mission when first asked. The other two described it as a secondary purpose as the interviews progressed.[95] This uniformity of perspective was consistent across leaders regardless of the level of their church's global engagement. Church leaders from all three churches showing lower levels of involvement with distant mission included it as part of the purpose of their church. For example, the minister of CH2 stated that "the purpose is to make disciples . . . not only in [our suburb] but wherever we can reach."[96] This consistency across church leaders suggests that a leader's stated convictions about the role of distant mission in the local church are not always reflected in church activities.

The more notable differences between churches were in the responses of church members. Interviewees from MGE churches spoke about the responsibility that their church had for involvement in distant mission much more so than people from LGE churches. Among the interviewees from MGE churches ten of the fourteen church members (71 percent), representing five of the seven churches, included serving the needs of those beyond the local community as part of their initial statement of

---

93. Interview with CH5_MC, July 8, 2019.

94. None of the interviewees from CH10 mentioned this in the initial response despite the churches high level of involvement in distant mission activities.

95. Leaders from CH3, CH4, CH6, CH7 and CH8 considered it a primary purpose. Leaders from CH9 and CH10 considered it a secondary purpose of the church.

96. Interview with CH2_SP, June 24, 2019.

purpose of their church.[97] By contrast, church members from only one of the three churches with low involvement in distant mission included serving the needs of those beyond the local community in their response.[98] Those interviewees who did speak of distant mission in this way were long-standing members of CH2 which was previously very active in the support of distant mission, though was no longer. Their statements of purpose may therefore represent the past more than the present. These responses suggest that church members' perspectives on the purposes of the church are more consistent with church practices than are the leader's responses. Church leaders' responses tended to be more idealistic and aspirational than the responses of church members and may be more shaped by their espoused beliefs than their practice. This may have been due to the leaders' knowledge of the researcher's identity.

As the interviews progressed, interviewees further discussed the ways in which they believed their churches should be involved in distant mission. For interviewees across all churches, involvement in distant mission was mediated through connection to individuals and organizations that were working in these contexts. The church is believed to have a responsibility to support the work of ministry in other places. As one church leader stated, "we, as a church, are in a position, because of our numbers and our money, to be able to partner with people who are doing stuff, not just for us and with us. But extending the kingdom of God in other places."[99] This highlights the fact that distant mission involvement is an important endeavor that is believed to align with God's priorities, but it may be impacted by beliefs about the church's size and capacity. This involvement in distant mission not only served distant needs but was recognized to have a positive impact on the members of the church. As the minister of CH4 explained, they partner with a variety of people and organizations to help "engage our congregation members in thinking about God's work in the world . . . that they might develop a particular interest in or affection for different things."[100] This reflects a belief that the different purposes of the local church are not independent from each other.

---

97. This included all church members from CH3, CH4, CH6, CH8 and CH9. The church members from CH7 and CH10 did not include this in their initial response to the question about purpose but did speak of it when questioned.

98. The church members from CH1 and CH5 did not refer to serving people beyond their local community in their initial responses to the question of purpose.

99. Interview with CH10_SP, October 9, 2019.

100. Interview with CH4_SP, March 28, 2019.

One notable feature of the distant mission purpose of MGE churches was their desire to send members out to do mission. The pastor of one MGE church believed that this was key to the purpose of the church, noting that the church "need(s) to be reaching out with the gospel . . . to be sending people out."[101] A similar perspective was expressed by one of the members of this church who stated that "raising up the next generation of missionaries"[102] was something they, as a church, were responsible for. Similarly, the minister of another MGE church intentionally avoided making a distinction between local mission efforts and involvement in mission overseas because he believed that the church had an equal responsibility for both. One key expression of this was the desire to see members of the church personally involved in distant mission, noting that "we continue to pray that God would send people from within our church to other places with the gospel."[103] This conviction that inspiring and equipping church members for personal involvement in distant mission is part of the church's purpose was a distinct feature of MGE churches that was not mentioned by people from LGE churches.

By contrast, the mission policy of one of the LGE churches explicitly states that the church's "greatest responsibility is first and foremost to proclaim the gospel of our Lord Jesus Christ in the [local] Parish and in the wider multicultural [region] of Sydney."[104] A member of another LGE church expressed the belief that the church had too much emphasis on mission to the local community, suggesting that they needed to "widen that scope. And feel the responsibility for the world."[105] This clearly demonstrates a difference in the ways that churches understood their responsibility for mission beyond their local community. In MGE churches, people assumed that their church has a responsibility for involvement in mission beyond the local community, while in LGE churches this is a less important purpose of the church. This is the most notable ecclesiological difference between MGE and LGE churches, yet it is a difference of emphasis rather than a fundamental difference of ecclesiological beliefs.

---

101. Interview with CH8_SP, April 11, 2019.
102. Interview with CH8_MC, May 30, 2019.
103. Interview with CH4_SP, March 28, 2019.
104. CH5, Mission Policy, 2019.
105. Interview with CH1_MC, September 27, 2019.

ECCLESIOLOGY CONCLUSIONS

This review of the ecclesiological convictions of interviewees from ten evangelical churches shows that there is little variation between churches despite differences in denominational affiliation and patterns of involvement in mission. The ways in which interviewees understood the nature of their churches was largely consistent. Churches were viewed as autonomous entities that were able to determine their own priorities and goals. Denominations and other external structures were not perceived to have a clear influence on the church other than shaping the parachurch organizations and mission agencies that each church partnered with. There were four images employed to describe the church. One highlighted the internal relational bonds between church members, while the other three emphasized the responsibility of the church to be active in mission to their local communities. The only difference between churches with higher and lower levels of involvement in distant mission was in the way interviewees spoke of their church identity. Three leaders from more globally engaged churches spoke about mission as integral to the identity of their church. More than an activity of the church, mission was considered a core dimension of what the church is. In all these cases, this missional identity was expressed in both local and distant mission involvement.

Interviewees' comments about the purpose of their church showed a similar pattern of general agreement. The greatest emphasis was given to the importance of local mission closely followed by the need to serve the members of the church. There were a variety of approaches to local mission including attractional and outreach activities with concern for practical, social, and spiritual needs. However, the primary purpose was to draw people into the church community and address their spiritual needs. The efforts to serve the needs of church members were primarily concerned with building the faith of the members, caring for them, and equipping them for involvement in ministry and mission activities. Several church leaders stated that this edification of church members was the primary purpose of church, though this was less so the focus of church members. In these two spheres of concern, there was very little difference between MGE and LGE churches.

The third church purpose discussed by interviewees was the need to serve those beyond the local community through involvement in distant mission. It was here that the primary differences were noted between

MGE and LGE churches. While leaders across all churches described this as a key purpose of the church, church members at LGE churches were less likely to speak about it, preferring to emphasize their responsibility for local mission. How interviewees believed their churches should be involved in distant mission also varied. Support for individuals and organizations working at a distance was seen to be part of a church's purpose, to some extent by all interviewees. However, members of MGE churches emphasized this more and expressed the belief that raising up church members to serve in distant mission was another core responsibility of the church. This was not seen to be part of the purpose of LGE churches. These differences in purpose are not simply a consequence of different ecclesiological convictions but suggest different convictions about the practice of mission. For this reason, the following chapter explores the missiological convictions and emphases that interviewees expressed.

5

Missiology of Local Churches

INTRODUCTION

The second core category that became evident through the analysis of the interview data was the missiological convictions underpinning each church's pattern of mission involvement. Four key dimensions of people's understanding of mission became evident as they spoke. Firstly, the nature of mission reflected the activities that were prioritized in the mission endeavor. Secondly, how interviewees conceived the location of mission influenced whether they believed mission takes place in their own context or only at a distance. Thirdly, the agent of mission reflected interviewees' beliefs about who the actors in mission activities are and by inference what role the local church members play. Finally, the motivation for mission is the stated reasons that interviewees gave for the church's involvement. These explicit missiological convictions are foundational in shaping a local church's approach to mission activity yet, surprisingly, there were minimal differences between less globally engaged (LGE) and more globally engaged (MGE) churches in most of these dimensions. The only apparent area of difference noted was in the emphasis that people placed on distant mission and the responsibility expressed for involvement in this area.

THE NATURE AND GOAL OF MISSION

The consistent view among all interviewees was that the primary goal of mission is to address the spiritual needs of non-Christian people. This was described as leading people into a "relationship with Jesus" so that they might "know" and be "reconciled to God" or "become a Christian" and thereby be "saved" from God's judgment.[1] For most interviewees there was an emphasis on promoting an ongoing commitment to Jesus by "making disciples" or "bringing people under the lordship of Christ" rather than simply making converts.[2] Some interviewees spoke of "planting churches" or "supporting a struggling church" as similar expressions of concern for people's spiritual needs.[3] In some cases, "doing good"[4] and "caring for"[5] people were within the scope of mission, but with a consistent emphasis on addressing spiritual needs. This was well summarized in the mission policy of one MGE church which defined mission as "any endeavor that has as its goal the bringing of men and women to worship God alone, through the risen Lord Jesus Christ."[6]

Across all churches, the communication of the Christian faith with an emphasis on the person and work of Jesus was the primary way to engage in mission. This was most often described as the "proclamation of the gospel" or "to declare/spread the gospel,"[7] though synonymous terms included "evangelize," "tell others about Jesus," "gospel ministry," and "preach the word."[8] Some activities were described in more general

---

1. Interviews with CH1_SP, August 26, 2019; CH1_MC, September 27, 2019; CH3_SP, August 8, 2019; CH6_MC, June 16, 2019; CH7_CM, September 18, 2019; CH10_MC, July 19, 2019.

2. Interviews with CH7_SP, August 12, 2019; CH7_MC, September 2, 2019.

3. Interviews with CH7_MC, September 2, 2019; CH8_SP, April 11, 2019; CH8_CM, May 22, 2019; CH3_MC, September 2, 2019.

4. CH5, Mission Policy, 2019.

5. Interview with CH2_SP, June 24, 2019.

6. CH8, Mission Policy, 2014, 20.

7. Interviews with CH1_SP, August 26, 2019; CH2_SP, June 24, 2019; CH5_SP, June 13, 2019; CH2_CM, September 2, 2019; CH2_MC, August 29, 2019; CH5_CM, July 8, 2019; CH3_SP, August 8, 2019; CH3_CM, August 23, 2019; CH6_CM, June 16, 2019; CH7_SP, August 12, 2019; CH8_SP, April 11, 2019; CH9_MC, August 29, 2019.

8. Interviews with CH1_CM, September 26, 2019; CH1_MC, August 29, 2019; CH5_CM, July 8, 2019.

terms such as "share with others"[9] and "engaging with individuals"[10] yet the wider context indicated that the purpose of this engagement was to communicate the gospel. This ministry was described by some interviewees as "word-based" ministry, referring to God's word in the Bible.[11] This reflects a missiological conviction that people's spiritual needs are addressed as they hear the gospel message and respond by becoming Christians. As one church leader summarized, "Through the preaching of the gospel, or the word, we want to see people brought under the authority of Jesus, give their life to Him, until they become Christians, and grow in their faith."[12] Interviewees from all the churches shared this same understanding of mission.

This emphasis on proclamation did not exclude a concern for social and practical needs, with many interviewees describing activities with this goal. The minister of one LGE church spoke of his church's desire to "care for all people who come into the orbit of the church, holistically, as much as we can."[13] Another church's mission policy described their commitment to "doing good by being a blessing in the community" and "seeking justice by relieving suffering."[14] This was expressed in a variety of ways in different churches, including meals and subsidized groceries for disadvantaged people, chaplaincy services, and social activities for the wider community. Some churches ran mental health support groups, homework assistance sessions, grief support groups, language classes, and friendship groups.[15] One non-denominational church partnered with a nearby Anglican church to provide low-cost groceries and took part in an urban ministry run by a parachurch organization that offered food and friendship to people in need.[16] This concern for non-spiritual needs was also evident in overseas missions. Interviewees from one church spoke about their partnership with mission workers providing earthquake relief in Japan.[17] Similarly, another church supported mission work-

9. Interviews with CH3_SP, August 8, 2019; CH8_CM, May 22, 2019; CH9_MC, August 29, 2019.
10. Interview with CH4_SP, March 28, 2019.
11. Interviews with CH9_MC, August 29, 2019; CH9_SP, October 9, 2019.
12. Interview with CH2_SP, June 24, 2019.
13. Interview with CH2_SP, June 24, 2019.
14. CH5, Mission Policy, 2019.
15. Interviews with CH5_MC, July 8, 2019; CH2_SP, June 24, 2019.
16. Interview with CH8_MC, May 30, 2019.
17. Interviews with CH8_SP, April 11, 2019; CH8_MC, May 30, 2019.

ers in Taiwan, who supported disadvantaged women seeking to leave prostitution.[18] Several churches encouraged their members to support children in developing nations through Compassion International.[19] The pastor of one of these churches stated that the church also funds at least one international aid project each year "just for the sake of caring for someone, without necessarily any gospel motive."[20] This demonstrated that concern for practical needs is an important dimension of mission involvement, even though the proclamation of the gospel was the priority.

For some interviewees, the scope of mission involvement extended beyond specific activities to include the daily lives of Christians. One church member from an MGE church described mission as "a twenty-four/seven thing where our lives should align with what we say we believe."[21] Similarly, another MGE church member suggested that people at her church would have a "broad definition of mission" which would include overseas mission work addressing physical and spiritual needs, as well as living faithfully in Australia as a Christian in a secular workplace.[22] Her summary definition of mission was "taking Jesus to wherever you go."[23] This understanding of mission was dominant at CH10 where the minister believes that, for Christians, "all of life is mission" because mission is defined as "what everyone does as witnesses and agents of the kingdom."[24] One member of this church believes that it has a "social function" in the local community: "Our mission is to obviously spread the word. But in spreading the word to give the example to the people that we're a compassionate church as well."[25] This was expressed in a range of different activities at this church including providing an accessible toilet and shower for the local community, modelling good water conservation on the church property, and offering friendship and prayer to anyone in need.[26] The minister stated that there are some members of

18. Interview with CH2_MC, August 29, 2019.

19. Interview with CH1_SP, August 26, 2019; CH2_SP, June 24, 2019. Compassion International is a Christian aid organization which cares for disadvantaged children by partnering with local churches in developing nations. See https://www.compassion.com.au.

20. Interview with CH1_SP, August 26, 2019.

21. Interview with CH3_CM, August 23, 2019.

22. Interview with CH4_CM, May 7, 2019.

23. Interview with CH4_CM, May 7, 2019.

24. Interview with CH10_SP, June 3, 2019.

25. Interview with CH10_CM, July 19, 2019.

26. Interview with CH10_MC, July 19, 2019.

the church for whom mission is "that narrow, tell people the gospel and lead them to Jesus," but he seeks to encourage them to see their "lives as missional."[27] The desire to share the Christian faith with people is evident in this church, yet with a greater willingness to simply care for people and their local community without need for explicit sharing of the Christian faith. Another member of the church described this as seeking to be "a winsome presence . . . treat people with love and respect and as you do, they're going to ask you about Jesus."[28] This suggests there is still a desire to meet people's spiritual needs while recognizing the breadth of means by which that goal might be achieved. Though this emphasis on mission through daily life was much stronger at this church, the same value was evident in all churches to some extent.

The diversity of ways that different churches balanced the desire to address both spiritual and social needs in their mission activities was evident in the different approaches to English as a second language (ESL) classes that three of the churches ran. ESL classes are a common program that evangelical churches in Sydney use to meet community needs.[29] Interviewees from three of the churches reported some form of ESL program at their church, yet with varying levels of emphasis on gospel proclamation. A church member at CH1 stated that the ESL program they ran primarily sought to provide a point of connection between church members and people in the local community.[30] This resulted in at least one person becoming a member of the church, however the program was stopped because it was attracting people from distant parts of Sydney rather than facilitating relational connections with members of the local community who might join the church.[31] An interviewee from a second church spoke about her efforts to increase the amount of "Bible time" in the ESL program they ran, because it was previously "a token ten minutes."[32] Some people attending these ESL classes had gone on from the classes to join an "easy English Bible study group." This appeared to be the desired outcome of the ESL program, though one interviewee expressed disappointment that it has not yet resulted in anyone becoming a

27. Interview with CH10_SP, June 3, 2019.
28. Interview with CH10_MC, July 19, 2019.
29. Anglicare provides ESL training and resources to churches across the Sydney Anglican Diocese.
30. Interview with CH1_CM, September 26, 2019.
31. Interview with CH1_CM, September 26, 2019.
32. Interview with CH5_MC, July 8, 2019.

member of the church.³³ The third church that ran a program for people with limited English was more explicitly focused on meeting spiritual needs. The program was coordinated by a returned overseas mission worker who described it as an "easy English Bible class" stating, "Instead of kind of doing the English class with the optional Bible lesson, like a lot of churches do, we just do straight Bible lessons but in an English class style."³⁴ This explicit emphasis on Bible teaching had resulted in a number of people joining the church and becoming Christians.³⁵ These various approaches reflect the different motivations that churches have in running these programs. For some the emphasis was on meeting a practical need in the local community, for others it was relationally focused with the ultimate desire that these relationships will provide a context for evangelism, while for a third group the motivation is to provide people with low levels of English access to the Christian message. In each case there was a recognition that the church's mission activities should address both spiritual and practical needs, though the emphasis varied from church to church.

Some interviewees leaned more heavily towards the view that clear proclamation of the gospel was essential because meeting spiritual needs was their primary goal. One interviewee queried whether a food van that comes to the church to provide discounted groceries to disadvantaged people should be described as mission, noting that in her church's mission activities, "the focus is more on the gospel rather than charity stuff."³⁶ This prioritization was particularly evident when members of this church were involved in a mentoring program at the local school discussed in the previous chapter. Though there was initially great enthusiasm, as the school limited the volunteers' opportunities to share about their faith or invite children to church events, people progressively lost interest and stopped being involved.³⁷ Likewise, a member of CH6 spoke about the church's support of relief work at times of natural disaster yet noted, "This may not be quite so much missionary, or a specific missionary focus." A member of CH4 also spoke about the variety of endeavors that the mission workers they support are involved in yet noted that, "It's more

33. Interview with CH5_CM, July 8, 2019.
34. Interview with CH9_MC, August 29, 2019.
35. Interview with CH9_MC, August 29, 2019.
36. Interview with CH2_MC, August 29, 2019.
37. Interview with CH2_SP, June 24, 2019.

evangelistic than caring for the poor."[38] This conviction also influenced overseas mission efforts as the pastor of CH1 stated that the church would only form long-term partnerships with distant mission workers who were "faithfully teaching the Bible."[39] This emphasis on people's spiritual needs was evident to varying degrees in all churches due to the shared belief that attending to people's spiritual needs, through the gospel, is the best way to care for them. As the minister of one church stated, "Mission can include a whole gamut of things that at some point will allow the preaching of the gospel. I think if there's no preaching of the gospel, I wouldn't really call it mission."[40] Similarly, the overseas mission policy of CH8 states that they support "integrated ministry of both word and deed; that is . . . holistic ministries with gospel intentionality," while "the goal of our local mission activities is to share the Christian gospel. As such, most activities will be evangelistic in nature, rather than social action alone."[41] Therefore there was a recognition among all interviewees that mission included efforts to address people's spiritual, practical, and social needs, though there was a consistent emphasis on addressing spiritual needs through the proclamation of the gospel.

THE LOCATION OF MISSION

Local and Distant Mission

The second dimension of missiological thinking that shapes the involvement of local churches in mission is whether people see mission as something that happens locally, at a distance, or both. Since the beginning of the modern mission movement in the eighteenth century, the term "mission" has primarily been used with reference to efforts to spread the Christian faith in distant contexts, while activities to spread the faith locally were described as evangelism.[42] More recently, through the influence of Lesslie Newbigin and the missional church movement, the application of mission language has shifted.[43] This is more than a

38. Interview with CH4_MC, April 4, 2019.
39. Interview with CH1_SP, August 26, 2019.
40. Interview with CH2_SP, June 24, 2019.
41. CH8, Mission Policy, 2014, 33.
42. Michael Stroope's review of the language of mission outlines the broad context for current practice. See Stroope, *Transcending Mission*, 291–316.
43. Newbigin, *Gospel*; Guder, *Missional Church*.

semantic argument as the evangelical commitment to mission means that whatever qualifies as mission will be given more attention.

Most interviewees, particularly church leaders, used the language of mission to describe activities that were taking place both locally and at a distance. The minister of one LGE church spoke about mission as something that the church was "doing here with the people around us, but also partnering with people abroad."[44] Similarly another minister sought to avoid a distinction between local and distant mission, saying, "We see ourselves as having a responsibility to proclaim the gospel locally, and to be supporting the proclamation of the gospel globally."[45] The members of this church reflected this conviction as they noted the church's support for mission workers overseas, but predominantly spoke about mission in the local community, with a particular emphasis on local cross-cultural outreach.[46] One minister appealed to Jesus' command in Acts 1:8 as the reason why his church engaged in mission "close to home as well as far away."[47] The minister at CH4 similarly shared how he explicitly encouraged church members to participate in mission on the "three horizons" of the local suburb, their wider relational networks, and overseas, while recognizing it all as one endeavor.[48]

> In other churches I've been in, evangelism and global mission get thought about separately. And we've really tried hard to not do that . . . not to make a sharp distinction between how we are engaged in God's work in [an African nation] and how we're engaged in God's work in [our suburb].[49]

There is also an intentional effort in this church to diversify the contexts of the mission partners they support and to talk regularly about the church members' personal efforts in evangelism to highlight the variety of places that mission is taking place.[50]

In several churches, the shift toward describing both local and distant activities as mission was an intentional, recent development. All

---

44. Interview with CH1_SP, August 26, 2019.

45. Interview with CH5_SP, June 13, 2019. This was echoed in the church's mission policy which stated that mission was to be "done both locally and globally."

46. Interviews with CH5_MC, July 8, 2019; CH5_CM, July 8, 2019.

47. Interview with CH3_SP, August 8, 2019. "You will be my witnesses in Jerusalem, and in all Judea and Samaria, and to the ends of the earth" (Acts 1:8b).

48. Interview with CH4_SP, March 28, 2019.

49. Interview with CH4_SP, March 28, 2019.

50. Interview with CH4_SP, March 28, 2019.

three interviewees from CH8 articulated a belief that the church must be actively engaged in mission activities both locally and at a distance.[51] The pastor noted that historically there had been a greater focus on distant mission but more recently there was "a renewed awareness that we should be considering local mission."[52] The chair of the church's mission committee confirmed that over the last five years there had been a shift in thinking as they were challenged to consider the local dimension of "global mission."[53] A similar shift was intentionally brought about by the minister of CH10 when he had come to the church three years prior. Responding to what he saw as a narrow view of mission that distinguished overseas mission from the service of every Christian in their daily life, he sought to reshape the church's use of the term.

> I actually say to people, I don't want you using the word "mission" only for what's happening in India. Drop that and let's put something in front of it, "overseas missional initiative," or "cross-cultural missional initiative," "indigenous missional work," or something like that. And let's use the word "mission" for kingdom discipleship.[54]

This broader understanding of mission was echoed by the members of the church who affirmed that Christians need to discern how to participate in mission wherever they are living.[55] One member of an LGE church noted that many people in his church would traditionally have equated mission with "going overseas."[56] However, more recently there had been an effort to "recalibrate" people's perspective so that they recognized mission as "being equipped to evangelize pretty much anywhere."[57] Interestingly, another member of this same church felt that this had been overemphasized to the point where mission referred only to what was happening at the church and in the local community.[58]

---

51. Interviews with CH8_SP, April 11, 2019; CH8_CM, May 22, 2019; CH8_MC, May 30, 2019. This was consistent with the church's policies regarding local and distant mission activities.
52. Interview with CH8_SP, April 11, 2019.
53. Interview with CH8_MC, May 30, 2019.
54. Interview with CH10_SP, June 3, 2019.
55. Interviews with CH10_CM, July 19, 2019; CH10_MC, July 19, 2019.
56. Interview with CH1_CM, September 26, 2019.
57. Interview with CH1_CM, September 26, 2019.
58. Interview with CH1_MC, September 27, 2019.

Though all interviewees were aware of mission language being applied to local and distant activities, there were several interviewees who preferred the more traditional use of the term. All three interviewees from one MGE church noted that they primarily used mission language in relation to international activities.[59] One member of the church noted that "we tend to say evangelism if we're talking about local missionary service."[60] This was similar at another MGE church where the minister affirmed that "mission would usually refer to our mission partners who are serving all over the place," even though "our missionaries have the same purpose that we do."[61] The mission coordinator at this church believed that "we evangelize our neighbors here . . . [but] mission is more crosscultural and less reached."[62] This preference to limit mission language to distant activities was more common among older interviewees. For example, an older member of one MGE church spoke primarily of overseas activities as mission and suggested that an evangelistic ministry based in Sydney is "not really mission" even though the church supports it from the mission budget.[63] By contrast, a younger member of this same church primarily spoke about local activities when asked about mission.[64] Similarly, an older interviewee from an LGE church emphasized her church's support of mission workers overseas, while conceding that they would also consider their support for mission workers locally "as mission within Australia" noting that only recently had the mission prayer meeting included prayer for those working in Sydney and Australia.[65] These examples show that there has been a recent shift in the way that mission language is used in evangelical churches in Sydney. Though the difference in usage is not clearly related to the level of a church's engagement with mission in different contexts, there were some people that preferred to use mission language to describe distant activities.

---

59. Interviews with CH7_SP, August 12, 2019; CH7_MC, September 2, 2019; CH7_CM, September 18, 2019.

60. Interview with CH7_MC, September 2, 2019.

61. Interview with CH9_SP, October 9, 2019.

62. Interview with CH9_MC, August 29, 2019.

63. Interview with CH3_MC, September 2, 2019.

64. Interview with CH3_CM, August 23, 2019.

65. Interview with CH2_CM, September 2, 2019.

Attractional and Outreach Mission

A further point of differentiation in the way that interviewees understood the location of mission pertained to whether it took place within the church services and property or outside it. The attractional mode of mission activity seeks to draw people into church activities which are usually held on the church property.[66] Interviewees from all churches spoke of this as a primary way that their church practiced mission in their local context. A member of one LGE church described her church's services as "very seeker friendly" as it was intentionally accessible to non-members.[67] This was an expression of the church's stated goal to increase the number of invited guests attending church events.[68] Members of another LGE church also described how the Sunday services at their church were based on the assumption that non-Christians would be present.[69] This was particularly the case on "invitation Sunday" when church members were encouraged to invite their non-Christian friends and stay after the service for a shared meal.[70] This emphasis was not limited to LGE churches. The leaders of one MGE saw the attractional dimension of mission as so important that they employed a pastor for "welcoming and integration."[71] The senior minister of this church explained that they had previously tried a range of evangelistic strategies to engage non-Christians in the community, but then realized that people were visiting their services and they were not effectively engaging them; "people keep walking in the door week after week."[72] They therefore shifted their focus to welcoming, evangelizing, and integrating these visitors into the life of the church.[73] This belief that the regular church gatherings were an opportunity for attractional mission was commonly held.

Many churches also hosted attractional public events that explicitly sought to engage non-members. Some events addressed topical issues

---

66. Frost and Hirsch critique this mode of mission seeing it as a consequence of a Christendom understanding of the world. See Frost and Hirsch, *Shaping of Things*, 61–64.
67. Interview with CH1_MC, September 27, 2019.
68. Interview with CH1_SP, August 26, 2019.
69. Interview with CH5_MC, July 8, 2019.
70. Interview with CH5_CM, July 8, 2019.
71. Interview with CH9_SP, October 9, 2019.
72. Interview with CH9_SP, October 9, 2019.
73. Interview with CH9_SP, October 9, 2019.

from a Christian perspective,[74] while others aligned with significant cultural occasions such as Christmas, Easter, or Chinese New Year.[75] Interviewees from several churches spoke of holiday clubs for kids or art displays that provided a neutral event for engagement with members of the local community.[76] There were also church youth groups that were tailored to be accessible to non-members.[77] Evangelistic short courses, that provided another opportunity for non-Christians to learn about the Christian faith in an informal and interactive setting, were another popular approach that many churches employed.[78] One MGE church held a Sunday service in a nearby park a few times a year to increase the accessibility for non-members.[79] CH10 utilized its location in the main street of its community by opening the historic church building to the public for a few hours each day, welcoming anyone who would like to come in.[80] This had been highly successful and the minister reflected how it had shown the willingness of people to visit a church, "as long as the church has the reputation of being welcoming and inclusive."[81] These activities were also manifestations of an attractional approach to mission which complemented the regular church services by increasing the accessibility to non-members. They clearly demonstrated the priority that was placed on attractional mission in all the churches.

In addition to this attractional mission, some churches engaged in local mission through church run activities out in the local community. One LGE church sought to engage their community by having free public barbeques in a number of nearby social housing estates.[82] Several people from this church also sought to engage members of the local community through door-knocking and sharing their faith with people on the street.[83]

---

74. Interviews with CH3_SP, August 8, 2019; CH2_CM, September 2, 2019; CH6_CM, June 16, 2019.

75. Interviews with CH1_SP, August 26, 2019; CH4_MC, April 4, 2019; CH6_CM, June 16, 2019; CH8_SP, April 11, 2019.

76. Interviews with CH1_SP, August 26, 2019; CH5_CM, July 8, 2019; CH6_CM, June 16, 2019; CH10_CM, July 19, 2019.

77. Interviews with CH2_MC, August 29, 2019; CH8_SP, April 11, 2019.

78. Interviews with CH1_SP, August 26, 2019; CH2_MC, August 29, 2019; CH3_SP, August 8, 2019.

79. Interview with CH3_CM, August 23, 2019.

80. Interview with CH10_MC, July 19, 2019.

81. Interview with CH10_SP, June 3, 2019.

82. Interview with CH5_SP, June 3, 2019.

83. Interview with CH5_MC, July 8, 2019.

One of the Chinese churches sought to engage Mandarin speaking people in its local community by handing out Chinese Christian literature in the local shopping center.[84] An interviewee from a MGE church shared about a range of missional activities that their church did in partnership with other local churches.[85] This included community events at Christmas and Easter, large evangelistic rallies, and the provision of chaplains for local high schools.[86] This engagement with local school communities through Special Religious Education was another common feature of many churches' local mission activities.[87] Several churches also sought to equip their members for personal evangelism through training events and resources.[88] Interviewees from two other MGE churches spoke about regular interviews of church members in the Sunday services to explore ways in which people can participate in mission in their workplace or local community.[89] These mission activities in the local community were seen to be a more effective way of engaging people who would otherwise not attend a church event. They reflect a firm belief that mission should take place locally through both attractional and outward means and this was evident in both LGE and MGE churches.

AGENTS OF MISSION

In addition to the location and goals of mission, a third point of distinction in how mission is understood relates to who is identified as the agent of mission. There were three primary agents that interviewees referred to as the main actors in mission. For some it was those gifted and identified individuals who have taken ministry or mission as their primary vocation. This would include mission workers serving elsewhere in Australia or overseas, and paid ministry staff in a local church. Some people spoke about this as the church being the agent of mission, yet in these instances they were referring to the church leaders as the primary agent with the support of the church members. Secondly, some interviewees spoke about all Christians as the agents of mission indicating

---

84. Interview with CH6_SP, May 2, 2019.
85. Interview with CH8_MC, May 30, 2019.
86. Interview with CH8_SP, April 11, 2019.
87. Interviews with CH5_MC, July 8, 2019; CH8_SP, April 11, 2019.
88. Interview with CH3_SP, August 8, 2019.
89. Interviews with CH10_SP, June 3, 2019; CH4_SP, March 28, 2019.

that every follower of Jesus was expected to be active in mission to those around them. Finally, some interviewees spoke of God as the primary agent of mission. This reflected *missio Dei* theology, though the language was rarely employed. These three perspectives were not mutually exclusive with many people identifying all three as agents in the mission task. Though there was variety across all the churches, this was one dimension of missiology that showed apparent difference between LGE and MGE churches with interviewees from the latter placing more emphasis on the agency of God.

Agents of Mission in Less Globally Engaged Churches

Interviewees from LGE churches varied in their references to the primary agent of mission, though there was widespread acknowledgement of the central role that gifted individuals play. Interviewees from CH2 spoke at length about the long history that the church had of sending out and supporting mission workers to other countries and other contexts in Australia.[90] These workers were seen as key agents for mission. Church services and invitational events were described as contexts in which church leaders were the agents of mission.[91] The primary role of most church members was to support mission workers and invite people to church events. Interviewees from other LGE churches also noted the primary agency of mission workers and church leaders. Attractional modes of mission, such as "invitation Sundays" made the minister the primary agent of mission as he shared the gospel message, while the rest of the church community invited and welcomed people.[92] Similarly, the emphasis that the leaders at CH1 placed on inviting people to church events highlights the belief that church members are primarily involved in the missional activity in this supporting role.[93] The primary agent of mission in these events is the professional mission worker or church leader.

Even with this emphasis on invitation, there was also a concerted effort at these LGE churches to encourage church members to be personally involved in local mission. A church member from CH1 reported that

---

90. Interviews with CH2_MC, August 29, 2019; CH2_CM, September 2, 2019.

91. Interviews with CH2_SP, June 24, 2019; CH2_MC, August 29, 2019; CH2_CM, September 2, 2019.

92. Interview with CH5_SP, June 13, 2019.

93. Interview with CH1_SP, August 26, 2019.

previously the perception at the church was that distant mission workers were the primary agents of mission, but increasingly people were being "equipped to evangelize" and participate directly in mission themselves.[94] Likewise, the minister from CH5 stated that part of the mission of the church is "seeing ourselves as missionaries in our local area" and there were key lay people recognized as models of this mindset.[95] The church had hosted events to teach its members how to effectively relate to and share the Christian message with people from a Muslim background and to train people in door-knocking.[96] Though this was not a key feature of the approach to mission expressed by the interviewees at CH2, there was an acknowledgement that every believer is called to be active in mission and a small number of individuals within the church were recognized as doing this.[97] Across all these LGE churches, interviewees generally recognized the fact that every Christian is ideally an agent of mission, though the extent to which this happens varies markedly.

Though these two agents of mission were mentioned by all the interviewees from LGE churches, there were only two instances in which God was referred to as an agent of mission. Both comments were made in passing by church leaders. When speaking about the slowness with which new Christians in the church become engaged in the support of distant mission, one leader noted that they were eager to share the message of Jesus themselves, but it "takes time" for them to appreciate "that there is a mission going on around the world that God's making happen."[98] The minister of CH1 made a similar comment referring to "all the great things that God's doing" in the local community.[99] These passing comments suggest that they did believe that God is an agent of mission, however it is not emphasized in these LGE churches.

Agents of Mission in More Globally Engaged Churches

Interviewees across MGE churches also displayed some variety regarding the primary agents for mission. They referred to mission workers, average

---

94. Interview with CH1_CM September 26, 2019.
95. Interview with CH5_SP, June 13, 2019.
96. Interview with CH5_SP, June 13, 2019.
97. Interviews with CH2_SP, June 24, 2019; CH2_MC, August 29, 2019.
98. Interview with CH5_SP, June 13, 2019.
99. Interview with CH1_SP, August 26, 2019.

Christians, and God as agents, though with a greater emphasis on God's agency than in LGE churches. People from all MGE churches recognized distant mission workers as key agents of mission. The minister from CH3 spoke of the esteem that is given to the distant mission workers the church supports, identifying the church's partnership with these people as one way they facilitate "the gospel going forth around the world."[100] The interviewees from churches that primarily use "mission" language to describe distant activities also tended to emphasize mission workers as the primary agents of mission.[101] For example, the minister of CH9, who stated that "mission" language was "slightly more reserved for outside the church,"[102] did not refer to church members as active agents in mission, despite the fact that he considered experience of church community to be a key factor in outsiders becoming Christians. This emphasis on the mission and ministry professionals was often noted by interviewees in MGE churches, though it was not the dominant view.

There were a number of interviewees from MGE churches who explicitly emphasized the agency of every believer in the mission endeavor. Several church leaders spoke of their intentional efforts to encourage this mindset. The ministers of CH3 and CH4 both spoke about including segments in their Sunday services to equip church members to be active in mission in their daily lives.[103] The CH3 staff also developed a website and podcast with training materials to encourage church members in these ways.[104] This perspective was clearly effective as members of both of these churches spoke about the personal involvement in daily mission activities of every Christian.[105] As one of these church members stated, "Mission's a twenty-four/seven thing where our lives should align with what we say we believe and it should be visible to the public, in workplaces, [and] in uni[versity]."[106] Interviewees from CH8 shared this perspective and the minister spoke of many members of the church who personally got involved in local mission activities and then led other

---

100. Interview with CH3_SP, August 8, 2019.

101. Interviews with CH6_MC, June 16, 2019; CH9_CM, September 10, 2019; CH9_SP, October 9, 2019.

102. Interview with CH9_SP, October 9, 2019.

103. Interviews with CH3_SP, August 8, 2019; CH4_SP, March 28, 2019.

104. Interview with CH3_SP, August 8, 2019.

105. Interviews with CH3_CM, August 23, 2019; CH4_CM, May 7, 2019.

106. Interview with CH3_CM, August 23, 2019.

members of the church to join them.[107] This belief that all Christians are agents of mission did not overcome the fact that many people found it difficult.[108] A member of one MGE church stated that "the congregation, myself included, find it more difficult to be the "missionary." Whereas support through prayer, [and] through financial means, it's an easy way out."[109] The minister of CH3 felt that the church members were generally convinced of the need to be personally engaged in mission activities, yet they often felt unsure about how to "practically get out there and do it."[110] This awareness of the barriers to participation highlights the belief that all Christians are agents of mission.

The MGE church with the greatest emphasis on the agency of all Christians in mission also had a strong emphasis on the agency of God. The minister of CH10 spoke of his efforts to encourage this view of mission ever since he joined the church.[111] In a letter he wrote to the church he said, "We become participants in God's mission as we are joined with Jesus in his death and resurrection, and as we walk in the Spirit of new life. We need to understand our lives as missional, in every area of life and work."[112] In the interview he spoke about "what God's doing in [the suburb]" and that mission is "what everyone does as witnesses and agents of the kingdom."[113] This alignment between the agency of God and the believer in the mission task was echoed by the other interviewees from this church. One of the members spoke of "God's mission" five times through their interview and stated that "we're part of God's big mission for the world." This involved a wide variety of activities as another member of the church stated, "I think what I do is mission . . . I'm like a support worker I suppose, I'm not a preacher."[114] Mission is defined broadly and every church member is able to be involved in mission in what God is doing.

Interviewees from many other MGE churches also spoke about God's agency in mission. A congregation member from CH6 spoke of "God's work" in the world on three different occasions.[115] A member of

107. Interviews with CH8_SP, April 11, 2019; CH8_MC, May 30, 2019.
108. Interview with CH6_SP, May 2, 2019.
109. Interview with CH6_CM, June 16, 2019.
110. Interview with CH3_SP, August 8, 2019.
111. Interview with CH10_SP, June 3, 2019.
112. CH10, Mission Letter, 2017.
113. Interview with CH10_SP, June 3, 2019.
114. Interview with CH10_CM, July 19, 2019.
115. Interview with CH6_CM, June 16, 2019.

CH8 similarly spoke about "God's mission" and "God's work" to describe what the church's mission partners are involved in around the world.[116] All three interviewees from CH9 made reference to "God's mission" or "God's plan for the world" highlighting the consistent perspective at this church that they are joining in with God's work.[117] However, the interviewee that most consistently spoke of God's agency in mission was the minister of CH4. On twenty occasions he spoke of "God's mission" or "God's work/working" as well as a number of other references to the direct actions of God in the mission task.[118] As in CH10, this minister saw this as a key motivator for the participation in mission of church members who were expected to "play their part in God's work in the world."[119] This emphasis on God's agency stands in contrast to the interviewees from LGE churches. While members of LGE churches may affirm the belief that God is active in mission, it was not emphasized when they spoke about their church's participation in mission and was not considered a motivator for participation. This is an important theological difference between MGE and LGE churches as it impinges upon the motivation that people feel for mission involvement.

MOTIVATION FOR MISSION INVOLVEMENT

The final missiological dimension to be considered is the motivation for participation in mission reported by interviewees. People were asked why they were involved in mission and what reasons for participation were referenced in their church. The responses in both LGE and MGE churches incorporated biblical teaching, Christian identity, the needs of others, and personal affective drives. These factors can be understood as either intrinsic or extrinsic. Intrinsic motivation exists when people find satisfaction simply from involvement in the activity, while extrinsic motivations involve secondary consequences such as tangible rewards or verbal affirmation. Self-determination theory argues that intrinsic drives are a more powerful motivation for action than extrinsic drives; yet extrinsic factors can effectively drive motivation if they are internalized

---

116. Interview with CH8_MC, May 30, 2019.
117. Interviews with CH9_MC, August 19, 2019; CH9_CM, September 10, 2019; CH9_SP, October 9, 2019.
118. Interview with CH4_SP, March 28, 2019.
119. Interview with CH4_SP, March 28, 2019.

by the actor.[120] Therefore, an extrinsic demand which motivates action purely through secondary benefits, such as payment or affirmation, will have less influence than an extrinsic demand which aligns closely with a person's values or self-identity. People are most likely to engage in activities that are intrinsically motivating, but after that, activities that are seen to align with how they view themselves or the values that they esteem are the next most important. Activities that are motivated purely by secondary benefits are the least likely to be pursued. Interviewees in all churches described a range of extrinsic motivations for involvement in mission locally and at a distance, yet only interviewees from MGE churches reported an intrinsic drive for involvement in distant mission activities.

Motivation in Less Globally Engaged Churches

The reason for participation in mission most often reported among interviewees from LGE churches was the belief that it is commanded in Scripture. Five of the nine interviewees provided this response with reference to the great commission in Matt 28:18–20.[121] Some referred to additional passages of Scripture, including Isa 49:6 and Acts 1:8 as further justification.[122] Other interviewees suggested that the nature of the gospel message itself places an obligation on Christians to share it with others.[123] Three interviewees from LGE churches felt further obligated by their access to other Christian resources. One member of CH2 stated that they had "been given lots, therefore we are expected to give lots."[124] Similarly, the pastor of CH1 spoke about their desire to share widely the access they had to "theological training and wisdom."[125] However, another member of this church felt that people at her church were not involved very much in distant mission because they did not "recognize how richly resourced we are."[126] These commands, obligations, and duties were all extrinsic

---

120. Gagné and Deci, "Self-Determination Theory," 331–62.

121. Interviews with CH1_CM, September 26, 2019; CH2_CM, September 2, 2019; CH2_MC, August 29, 2019; CH5_CM, July 8, 2019; CH5_MC, July 8, 2019.

122. Interviews with CH2_CM, September 2, 2019; CH5_CM, July 8, 2019.

123. Interviews with CH2_CM, September 2, 2019; CH2_MC, August 29, 2019; CH5_CM, July 8, 2019.

124. Interview with CH2_MC, August 29, 2019.

125. Interview with CH1_SP, August 26, 2019.

126. Interview with CH1_MC, September 27, 2019. The issue of perceived capacity for mission involvement is discussed further in chapters 7 and 8.

motivations. Mission involvement was seen by these interviewees to be expected due to the commands of Scripture, the nature of the gospel, and the resources available. This does not mean that mission was engaged begrudgingly, simply that the drive for participation from these motivations is likely to be lower.

There were several interviewees from LGE churches who reported other extrinsic motivations that were more integrated with their values and identity. Some interviewees stated that their care for others led them to participate in mission so that they could share the benefits of their faith.[127] This was felt very strongly by one interviewee due to the large number of non-Christians in her local community.[128] Similarly, others were motivated by their concern for people who were facing God's judgment and their desire to share the gospel message with them so that they might be saved.[129] These dual motivations often went together; interviewees wanted others to experience the benefits of the Christian faith while also avoiding the consequences of rejecting it. In a similar way, interviewees believed that God is concerned for people's wellbeing and are thereby motivated to do what they can to care for them.[130] For some interviewees, mission activities were simply inherent in being a Christian, because mission is a consistent theme through the whole Bible.[131] One minister of an LGE church stated that participation in mission ultimately arises from the desire to glorify God which should be common to all Christians.[132] These motivations are all extrinsic, yet they are integrated with the values and identity of those who shared them. The use of emotional language indicated that they were stronger motivations even though they were connected to secondary consequences. Most interviewees from LGE churches appealed to extrinsic drives with both low and high levels of integration, though there were three interviewees who only appealed to commands and obligations suggesting lower levels of motivational drive.

---

127. Interviews with CH1_MC, September 27, 2019; CH2_MC, August 29, 2019.

128. Interview with CH5_MC, July 8, 2019.

129. Interviews with CH1_MC, September 27, 2019; CH1_SP, August 26, 2019; CH5_CM, July 8, 2019.

130. Interviews with CH1_SP, August 26, 2019; CH5_MC, July 8, 2019,

131. Interviews with CH2_MC, August 29, 2019; CH2_SP, June 24, 2019; CH5_SP, June 13, 2019; CH5_CM, July 8, 2019.

132. Interview with CH5_SP, June 13, 2019.

Motivation in More Globally Engaged Churches

The motivations for mission involvement expressed by members of MGE churches echoed many sentiments of those in LGE churches, yet with the greater emphasis on integrated extrinsic motivators and intrinsic motivators. Many people spoke of the biblical command to be involved in the task of mission.[133] There were specific references to Isaiah, Matt 28, Acts 1:8, and the command to "love your neighbor," while other interviewees recalled the missional storyline of the Bible as evidence that the whole of Scripture indicates a need for Christians to participate in mission.[134] Regardless of the specific biblical justification, many people viewed involvement in mission as an essential component of the Christian life.[135] As one minister stated, "Talking to neighbors and friends and young people about Jesus is just what you do."[136] Like those from LGE churches, interviewees stated that mission involvement was necessary because the gospel needs to reach those who have never heard it.[137] Similarly, the belief that Christians who have received much are expected to share it with others was mentioned by a number of interviewees with joy at the abundance of resources that they were able to share.[138] These motivations are similar to those expressed by interviewees from LGE churches, yet with greater emphasis on the alignment between people's involvement and their personal values indicating more integration.

Several interviewees from MGE churches spoke directly about the need to see mission involvement as more than a Christian duty. One person from CH6 acknowledged that involvement in mission is commanded for followers of Jesus, but this is rarely the primary motivation for people in his church: "I don't think it shows a good understanding of the gospel, and not good maturity, if you're only doing it just because God told you

---

133. Interviews with CH4_CM, May 7, 2019; CH6_CM, June 16, 2019; CH6_MC, June 16, 2019; CH6_SP, May 2, 2019; CH8_CM, May 22, 2019; CH9_CM, September 10, 2019; CH9_SP, October 9, 2019.

134. Interviews with CH3_SP, August 8, 2019; CH4_SP, March 28, 2019; CH6_CM, June 16, 2019.

135. Interviews with CH4_SP, March 28, 2019; CH7_SP, August 12, 2019; CH8_SP, April 11, 2019; CH8_MC, May 30, 2019; CH9_CM, September 10, 2019; CH9_MC, August 29, 2019; CH10_MC, July 19, 2019; CH10_CM, July 19, 2019.

136. Interview with CH10_SP, June 3, 2019.

137. Interviews with CH3_CM, August 23, 2019; CH8_CM, May 22, 2019; CH8_MC, May 30, 2019.

138. Interviews with CH3_CM, August 23, 2019; CH4_SP, March 28, 2019; CH9_MC, August 29, 2019.

to."[139] Rather, he suggested that aligning oneself with God's love for people was a more powerful motivation. Similarly, the minister from CH7 stated that some people's conviction that Christians have a responsibility to participate in mission can have a "pessimistic edge to it."[140] He elaborates, "It can be a little bit discouraging when people see their responsibility to evangelize, but they don't actually expect anything to come from it."[141] These interviewees believed that there is an obligation upon Christians to participate in mission, but they noted that people need to be personally engaged rather than simply acting on the command. As in LGE churches, many interviewees expressed concern for others and referred to people's needs as a motivation for mission involvement, particularly the need for them to hear the gospel.[142] Similarly, many people referenced the belief that non-Christians are facing God's judgment with seven interviewees from six different MGE churches describing this as a significant stimulus for people in their church.[143] One interviewee believed this was a primary motivation and that people in her church needed to grasp it more fully.[144] According to self-determination theory, this greater emphasis on emotionally engaged and integrated motivations in MGE churches accords with a stronger desire for involvement.[145]

The minister of another MGE church noted that, while there were some people in his church who were motivated by the need to "win the lost soul," he believed that those who wanted to share their faith because they "have a great hope [and] a great story" were more highly engaged.[146] These more positive affective drivers were raised by several interviewees from MGE churches. For many of these people, mission involvement arises from a desire to share the benefits of faith that they have experienced.[147] Interviewees spoke of the "goodness" of the gospel and the transformation

---

139. Interview with CH6_CM, June 16, 2019.

140. Interview with CH7_SP, August 12, 2019.

141. Interview with CH7_SP, August 12, 2019.

142. Interviews with CH6_SP, May 2, 2019; CH6_CM, June 16, 2019; CH6_MC, June 16, 2019; CH7_CM, September 18, 2019.

143. Interviews with CH3_SP, August 8, 2019; CH4_SP, March 28, 2019; CH6_MC, June 16, 2019; CH7_MC, September 2, 2019; CH7_SP, August 12, 2019; CH9_SP, October 9, 2019; CH10_SP, June 3, 2019.

144. Interview with CH6_MC, June 16, 2019.

145. Gagné and Deci, "Self-Determination Theory," 338–39.

146. Interview with CH10_SP, June 3, 2019.

147. Interviews with CH6_CM, June 16, 2019; CH3_SP, August 8, 2019; CH6_MC, June 16, 2019; CH8_CM, May 22, 2019; CH10_MC, July 19, 2019.

that it brings.[148] They stated that they are motivated to share these benefits with others because they love them and because they believe that God also loves them.[149] Others expressed this as a purely intrinsic motivation as they spoke of mission as a "privilege" which God "invites" them to participate in.[150] This is a motivational consequence of the emphasis in many MGE churches on God as an agent of mission. These intrinsic motivations were particularly evident when relationships with mission workers were mentioned.[151] Due to the relational connection with the distant worker, interviewees wanted to not only care for the worker but they recognized the opportunity to be personally involved in distant activities as something to be embraced.[152] This distant involvement brought temporal joy, with one interviewee speaking of the "eternal reward of [seeing] someone in heaven" as a consequence of one's actions now.[153] These enduring benefits were often included in the broader motivation of "glorifying God" which was mentioned by four of the interviewees.[154]

This review of the motivations for mission involvement across LGE and MGE churches reveals both similarities and differences. People from both churches spoke about the duty of Christians to be involved in mission which flowed from their understanding of the commands and storyline of Scripture. They believed that it was expected that disciples of Jesus would participate in mission, and numerous people spoke of the need for those who have accepted the gospel to be involved in seeing it spread. Some people spoke of the obligation that comes from having received both spiritual and material benefits from God, though this was more prevalent among members of MGE churches who described it as an opportunity rather than a burden. People from all churches spoke about the alignment between their personal values and involvement in mission. Interviewees from both LGE and MGE churches expressed a desire to share the benefits of faith with others, as well as a concern for those who do not have access

---

148. Interviews with CH6_CM, June 16, 2019; CH10_SP, June 3, 2019.

149. Interviews with CH4_CM, May 7, 2019; CH6_CM, June 16, 2019; CH7_SP, August 12, 2019.

150. Interviews with CH4_SP, March 28, 2019; CH9_MC, August 29, 2019; CH10_MC, July 19, 2019.

151. Interviews with CH3_SP, August 8, 2019; CH8_CM, May 22, 2019.

152. Interviews with CH8_MC, May 30, 2019; CH9_SP, October 9, 2019.

153. Interview with CH9_SP, October 9, 2019.

154. Interviews with CH7_SP, August 12, 2019; CH8_MC, May 30, 2019; CH9_SP, October 9, 2019; CH10_SP, June 3, 2019.

to the message. Despite these similarities, only interviewees from MGE churches spoke of being intrinsically motivated for involvement in distant mission activities. This was often associated with the relational connections to mission workers and the opportunity to be personally involved in their work. They also spoke of the desire to join God in mission activities in a way that people from LGE churches did not. In general, people from MGE churches noted intrinsic and integrated extrinsic motivators more often than those from LGE churches. This was particularly evident with regard to distant mission which they were motivated to participate in because of their relationships with the distant mission workers and their belief that God was inviting them to join him in this work.

DISTANT MISSION NEEDS AND RESPONSIBILITY

While these differences are important, the motivational difference most evident between LGE and MGE churches was in the perceived needs for mission activity in distant contexts and the level of responsibility people felt to address those needs. Interviewees from MGE churches reported higher levels of motivation for involvement in distant mission activities than interviewees from LGE churches. Various motivational factors for this distant involvement were noted by interviewees in MGE churches. The belief that "God is at work throughout the world, and in every part of the world" was one key motivation for Christians to be involved in mission everywhere.[155] This divine universal concern motivated Christians to show interest in both distant and local mission, even though the local needs were more immediately evident.[156] One minister considered involvement in distant mission an essential practice for all followers of Jesus, and therefore sought to encourage all the members of his church to be personally involved.[157] For many interviewees, the relational connection to the distant mission workers further enhanced this motivation to be involved in distant contexts, particularly where the workers were former members of the church. People naturally cared for those that they knew well and were more engaged with the work that they were doing. Yet beyond these relational motivations for involvement, the perceived need for mission activities in different contexts differed between interviewees in LGE and MGE churches.

155. Interview with CH10_MC, July 19, 2019.
156. Interviews with CH9_MC, August 29, 2019; CH6_CM, June 16, 2019.
157. Interview with CH4_SP, March 28, 2019.

Several people from MGE churches referred to the unequal distribution of Christian resources around the world. Some spoke about "unreached people groups" or "under resourced" contexts beyond Australia where there are very few Christians.[158] This perceived inequality of access to the gospel and gospel resources was a stated motivation for participation in those areas.[159] One young interviewee observed that "if no one goes to unreached countries, then there's no way that they can hear the gospel."[160] Interviewees in other MGE churches noted that the gospel needed to be shared in "unreached countries" so that the biblical vision of a multiethnic gathering in heaven might be realized (Rev 7:9).[161] One church leader spoke explicitly about the influence of this global inequality on his church's decisions about missions involvement expressing a desire that his church would be intentionally involved in places with fewer resources.[162] Another interviewee similarly spoke of a desire among the leaders in his church to encourage people to ask, "Where are the needs in the world?"[163] This sensitivity to the differences in access to Christians and Christian resources in distant contexts was a key dimension of the greater sense of responsibility for distant mission observed in MGE churches.

By contrast, most interviewees from LGE churches did not express a strong sense of responsibility for distant mission involvement and they made minimal reference to the needs for mission activity beyond the local community. The pastor of CH2 spoke of previous efforts to encourage prayer for unreached people groups, but this had not had a notable impact and did not shape the church's pattern of missions involvement.[164] By contrast, the leader of CH1 spoke about the "big world of Christians out there," commenting, "Isn't it wonderful what God's doing in people's lives around the world?"[165] Rather than noting the paucity of access to Christianity in other places, they spoke of the encouragement that it can be to Christians in Sydney "to witness places in the world where people are just

---

158. Interviews with CH3_CM, August 23, 2019; CH4_CM, May 7, 2019; CH7_CM, September 18, 2019; CH8_SP, April 11, 2019; CH9_MC, August 29, 2019; CH9_SP, October 9, 2019; CH10_MC, July 19, 2019.

159. Interviews with CH8_SP, April 11, 2019; CH9_SP, October 9, 2019.

160. Interview with CH3_CM, August 23, 2019.

161. Interviews with CH3_CM, August 23, 2019; CH8_MC, May 30, 2019.

162. Interview with CH9_SP, October 9, 2019.

163. Interview with CH8_MC, May 30, 2019.

164. Interview with CH2_SP, June 24, 2019.

165. Interview with CH1_SP, August 26, 2019.

flocking to Jesus."[166] Unlike the concerns expressed by interviewees from MGE churches, this reflects a belief that the needs for mission are essentially equal in all contexts or potentially that there are fewer needs in distant contexts. Instead, interviewees from LGE churches were more likely to speak of their responsibility for local mission and to highlight the needs of the spiritually "lost" in the local community who have never heard the gospel message.[167] Some interviewees spoke of the multiethnic nature of their communities which provided many opportunities for cross-cultural mission. They believed that they could fulfill Jesus' commands to "preach the word to all nations" in their local context because "the nations have come to us."[168] Consequently, there was a greater motivation to focus on mission activities in the local community than there was overseas. The minister of one LGE church expressed the conviction that his church has "responsibilities to proclaim the gospel locally and to be supporting the proclamation of the gospel globally."[169] However, he noted that they had been focusing particularly on local mission activities because "unless you are an effective, fruitful local church, you're probably not going to be particularly effective or fruitful globally."[170] This reflects a greater sense of responsibility for local mission activities than distant on the basis of a different understanding of the spiritual needs around the world.

Therefore, in addition to the difference in motivational integration between interviewees from MGE and LGE churches, there are perceived differences in need which influence the patterns of mission involvement. Interviewees from MGE churches more often expressed the view that they had a responsibility for distant mission, often because of the limited access to Christians and Christian resources in other countries. By contrast, interviewees from LGE churches primarily emphasized their responsibility for mission in their local community, noting the cultural diversity and apparent spiritual needs. This is not a difference in the way mission is defined, but it reflects a difference in belief regarding what is needed. Interviewees in MGE churches were not only driven to mission involvement by more potent motivational forces, but they also perceived

---

166. Interview with CH1_SP, August 26, 2019.

167. Interviews with CH1_SP, August 26, 2019; CH5_CM, July 8, 2019.

168. Interviews with CH1_CM, September 26, 2019; CH5_MC, July 8, 2019; CH5_CM, July 8, 2019. This echoes Jesus' instruction to take the gospel to "all nations" (Matt 24:24; 28:19; Mark 16:15; Luke 24:47).

169. Interview with CH5_SP, June 13, 2019.

170. Interview with CH5_SP, June 13, 2019.

a greater need for mission involvement in distant contexts. This led to a stronger sense of responsibility for distant mission involvement across the church which was reflected in their distant mission activities. By contrast, interviewees from LGE churches felt motivated to mission involvement in their local context where the needs were immediately evident but had less regard for the distant mission needs. These differences in responsibility for local and distant mission have a notable impact upon the patterns of mission involvement.

MISSIOLOGY CONCLUSIONS

This review of the missiological convictions of interviewees in LGE and MGE churches indicates that there is much consistency in the ways that mission is understood with a few notable differences in emphasis. All interviewees believed that mission is primarily concerned with addressing the spiritual needs of those who are not Christians. There was a consistent emphasis on the proclamation of the gospel with the hope that people might become Christians and live as disciples of Jesus. There was a general acknowledgement that the daily actions of Christians are an essential complement to proclamation of the gospel and Christians are to care for people wherever they can, but communicating the gospel is the central task of mission. This consistency across LGE and MGE churches was also evident regarding the location and context of mission. Most interviewees spoke of mission as taking place both locally and at a distance. There were some churches and, particularly older, interviewees that preferred to reserve the language of mission for overseas activities while using the language of evangelism for their local endeavors, but mission was generally accepted as happening in all contexts.

There was some divergence between interviewees from LGE and MGE churches regarding the agent of mission. People from both churches acknowledged that while mission workers and church staff have unique roles to play in mission, every Christian is to be actively involved in mission in their own context. A key dimension of this involvement was inviting people to church events, though being an active member of the church community and living in ways that are consistent with the Christian faith were also noted. The greatest difference was in reference to the agency of God. While a wide range of interviewees from MGE churches spoke of God's sovereignty over and participation in mission, there were only two passing comments from interviewees in LGE churches suggesting that God was an agent of mission. Though this did not clearly influence the nature or location of mission, there were interviewees in MGE churches who saw God's direct involvement in mission as a source of motivation. Differences in motivation for mission involvement across the LGE and MGE churches showed greater significance for patterns of mission involvement than these definitional issues.

Interviewees from both MGE and LGE churches referred to a range of motivations for mission involvement, yet interviewees from MGE churches placed a greater emphasis on their own intrinsic motivations as well as the alignment between mission involvement and the church identity and core values. Interviewees from MGE churches were more likely to speak about the needs for mission activity in other countries and distant contexts, while interviewees from LGE churches were more likely to emphasize the needs in the local community. These differences in perceived need shaped the responsibility that people felt for mission in different contexts. Interviewees from LGE churches emphasized their responsibility for local mission activities, while interviewees from MGE churches spoke of the responsibility for mission involvement both locally and overseas. Together with the belief that God is actively engaged in mission in all contexts, interviewees from MGE churches were more likely to consider involvement in distant mission as a privilege and opportunity to be embraced. These differences in missiological motivation and perceived responsibility partially explain the greater emphasis on distant mission involvement in these churches noted in the previous chapter. Interviewees from MGE churches were more likely to see involvement in distant mission as one of the core purposes of their church because they were intrinsically motivated for mission involvement and saw it as a core dimension of their identity. Furthermore, they perceived a greater need for mission involvement in distant contexts which they and their church had a responsibility to address. This was strengthened by an emphasis on the agency of God in mission and the belief among interviewees that it is a privilege to be personally involved. Though these differences in ecclesiological and missiological convictions are limited, they appear to have some influence on a local church's practices and processes regarding mission. To understand these implications a careful analysis of these practices and processes follows.

6

Church Mission Practices and Organizational Analysis

INTRODUCTION

Analysis of the interview data thus far has explored the ecclesiological and missiological convictions of both the leaders and members of these churches. This attention to interviewees' stated beliefs has highlighted many similarities between churches despite the differences in their patterns of mission involvement. Beliefs about the nature and purpose of the church as well as the nature and location of mission were essentially the same with differences of emphasis rather than differences of great theological substance. The more important differences between LGE and MGE churches became evident as the practices and processes related to mission involvement were explored. Careful consideration of these differences provides valuable insight into the possible causes of these differences. The core areas of difference were in the mission-related practices of prayer and information distribution, the use of finances, the mobilization and equipping of people for mission involvement, the mission activities in the local community, and the internal leadership structures related to mission involvement.

As these differences in practice were categorized, it became evident that the internal social dynamics of the local churches being examined were shaping these patterns of mission involvement. To understand the full implications of these differences, the perspectives of organizational theory were employed. These perspectives draw insights from several disciplines to explain the behavior of social groups. The use of organizational perspectives in the analysis of congregations is not new, even though the organizational models employed in the private sector do not transfer directly to the local church context.[1] Organizational insights provide a helpful complement to theological analysis by viewing the local church as a social unit shaped by human actions and relationships.[2] The perspectives found to be of greatest relevance to this study were the related concepts of organizational culture and organizational climate. These will first be described and then employed in the examination of the practices and processes of mission involvement evident in the interviews.

ORGANIZATIONAL CULTURE

Studies in organizational culture seek to apply the cultural lenses of anthropology to the actions of groups of people. This approach is often traced back to Andrew Pettigrew's 1979 longitudinal study of a British boarding school which recognized the development and maintenance of cultural norms over many decades.[3] Through the nineteen eighties and nineteen nineties, examinations of organizational culture grew in popularity and the practice was developed and regularly applied to the corporate sector. One commonly referenced framework for organizational cultural analysis is described by Edgar Schein.[4] Schein applies an anthropological perspective to organizations describing culture in three layers: artefacts, espoused beliefs and values, and basic underlying assumptions.[5] Artefacts are the easily observable features of the organization including buildings, decorations, products, practices, and policies. The espoused beliefs and values express what is important and how things should be done within the organization. These beliefs and values are shaped by the convictions of leaders and can usually be articulated by group members when questioned.[6] The underlying assumptions are more difficult to elicit, yet they

---

1. Cameron, "Are Congregations Associations?," 139–51; Harris, *Organising God's Work.*

2. Cameron et al., *Studying Local Churches*, 65–75.

3. Pettigrew, "On Studying Organizational Cultures," 570–81.

4. Schein, *Organizational Culture*; also Ehrhart et al., *Organizational Climate and Culture.*

5. Schein, *Organizational Culture*, 22–23.

6. Schein, *Organizational Culture*, 38–40.

determine the values, beliefs, and practices of the organization. Bringing these three levels together, Schein defined organizational culture as:

> A pattern of shared basic assumptions learned by a group as it solved its problems of external adaption and internal integration, which has worked well enough to be considered valid and, therefore, to be taught to new members as the correct way to perceive, think, and feel in relation to those problems.[7]

The culture of an organization shapes everything that it does, it is "pervasive and influences all aspects of how an organization deals with its primary task, its various environments, and its internal operations."[8]

Schein's cultural framework provides a valuable tool in the analysis of churches as organizations, yet benefits from the refinement brought by other perspectives. It is widely agreed that both deep and superficial layers of organizational culture must be considered.[9] However, the use of the term "assumptions" to describe the deepest layer of organizational culture is potentially misleading as it implies subconscious elements of worldview.[10] It is preferable to describe this deepest level as core beliefs rather than assumptions. Schein's middle layer of culture, described as "espoused values," is the most problematic when applied to a local church setting. While Schein identifies these values as having been endorsed by the leadership and utilized in the formation of vision statements and policies, the cultural values of volunteer associations like churches do not follow bureaucratic managerial principles.[11] The true cultural values of a church are not necessarily those that are espoused, but those that are evident in group member behavior. At this point they may be described as "enacted values" as they reflect the actual shared culture of the group.[12]

The core cultural beliefs of a particular church will be shaped by a wide range of factors including shared theological convictions, societal norms, the members' individual backgrounds, and the shared experiences of the church as a community. Leadership plays an important role in the formation and development of organizational culture, yet these

7. Schein, *Organizational Culture*, 17.
8. Schein, *Organizational Culture*, 17.
9. Ostroff et al., "Organizational Culture," 647–48.
10. See Hiebert's anthropological framework for the relationship between assumptions and worldview. Hiebert, *Transforming Worldviews*.
11. Cameron, "Are Congregations Associations?," 141.
12. Ostroff et al., "Organizational Culture," 648; Zohar and Hofmann, "Organizational Culture," 646–47.

other influences combine to shape the culture of the group in more substantial ways than in commercial settings.[13] It is beyond the scope of this research to comprehensively describe the cultures of these churches, yet consideration of the cultural differences between churches is key to understanding what shapes involvement in mission.

ORGANIZATIONAL CLIMATE

A related approach to examining the function of social groups is organizational climate. Climate is a more specific concept than culture as it explores the perceptions of group members regarding the way things are done within the organization. It has been defined as "the shared meaning organizational members attach to the events, policies, practices, and procedures they experience and the behaviors they see being rewarded, supported, and expected."[14] While research into organizational culture draws on anthropological foundations, organizational climate research developed from a psychological perspective.[15] Cultural analysis often utilizes ethnographic approaches to provide a thick description of an organization, including the assumptions and values that shape behavior, while climate studies typically use surveys to identify the shared perceptions of group members. These shared perceptions are determined by the members' experience of the organization's practices and procedures. They thereby explain what the group members see as appropriate and expected behavior within the organization. In this way, organizational climate provides a bottom-up perspective on an organization, and organizational culture a top-down perspective.

Early climate research sought to provide a global understanding of organizations by exploring multiple dimensions influencing every aspect of organizational function.[16] More recently, climate research has typically focused on the strategic "climate for" a particular dimension of interest, such as a climate for safety, or a climate for service.[17] While focusing on a single dimension gives clarity, these dimensions can only be fully understood in relation to other organizational priorities. For example,

---

13. Schein, *Organizational Culture*, 7–21.
14. Ehrhart et al., *Organizational Climate and Culture*, 286.
15. Ostroff et al., "Organizational Culture."
16. Zohar and Hofmann, "Organizational Culture," 644.
17. Ostroff et al., "Organizational Culture," 653.

if maintaining a safe workplace was seen to be an obstacle to productivity, an employee's perceptions of organizational policies, procedures, and practices would determine whether safety or productivity was prioritized. This provides a powerful insight into the core values and beliefs that are shaping behavior within an organization.

INTEGRATING CULTURE AND CLIMATE

Due to the value of both the culture and climate perspectives, attempts have been made to bring them together as complementary ways of understanding a social unit. Both approaches describe factors that influence an organization, yet they highlight different perspectives. Ostroff, Kinicki, and Muhammad suggest that climate describes the group members' perception of "*what* happens" while culture is the underlying reasons "*why* these things happen."[18] Climate is therefore a consequence of the organizational culture whereby the core beliefs, values, and artefacts of the organization are expressed through structures, policies, and procedures. The group members' perception of these practices can be described as the climate of the organization (see figure 4). In this way "organizational practices are the linking mechanism that mediates the relationship between culture and climate."[19]

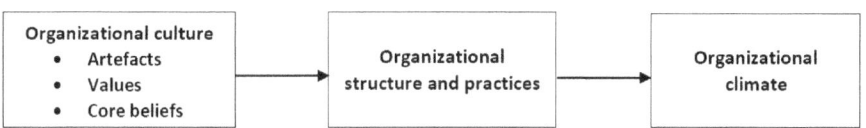

Figure 4. Relationship between Culture and Climate[20]

The advantage of the climate construct is that it draws on more easily accessible data, namely the perceptions of group members, to explain the priorities and values that shape group member behavior. It thereby provides a way to "decipher the deep layer of organizational culture" without the need for expert anthropological observation.[21] Furthermore, it highlights points at which the stated values of the organization are out

---

18. Ostroff et al., "Organizational Culture," 644.
19. Ostroff et al., "Organizational Culture," 656.
20. Ostroff et al., "Organizational Culture," 645.
21. Zohar and Hofmann, "Organizational Culture," 661.

of step with what group members feel is expected behavior. It does this by drawing on group members' ability to negotiate the relative priority given to different organizational goals. These misalignments highlight points at which the espoused values of the organization may not faithfully reflect the fundamental assumptions shaping organizational behavior.

METHODOLOGICAL CONSIDERATIONS

Though the interview data gathered for this research cannot provide a comprehensive description of the culture or climate of the churches examined, these perspectives provide valuable insights into what shapes a church's pattern of involvement in mission. Drawing these perspectives together, it is suggested that a church's missional practices are an expression of its missional assumptions. These practices in turn shape the church members' shared perceptions of how they should be involved in mission, which is the climate for mission (see figure 5). To understand the beliefs and values shaping the involvement of the churches in mission, this model of culture and climate was applied in reverse. The climate for mission in the churches was explored by drawing on the church members' description of church practices in their interviews. Key dimensions of church practice that were highlighted in the interviews were examined and their relationship to the stated values and priorities considered. Analysis revealed a greater difference of practice than would be expected based on the stated ecclesiological and missiological convictions of church leaders discussed in the previous chapters. The possible causes of this misalignment will be discussed.

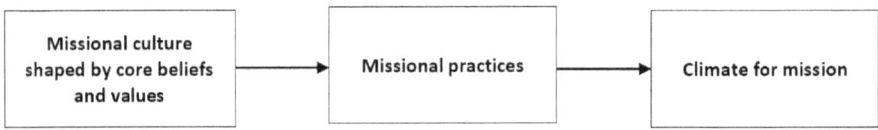

Figure 5. Relationship between Missional Culture, Practices, and Climate for Mission

CHURCH PRACTICES AND CLIMATE FOR MISSION

The practices and structures of a church are the artefacts manifesting the underlying core beliefs and values. Church members' experience of these practices and structures determines the climate for mission as it shapes their perceptions of the appropriate and expected patterns of mission involvement within the church. To understand the climate for mission in these churches, the practices related to prayer and information distribution, use of finance, mobilization of members for mission, local outreach activity, and the leadership structures related to mission were noted to be important. Though a comprehensive assessment of the climate for mission would require an exhaustive survey of church members, this exploration of various church practices provides clear evidence of the differences in the climate for mission involvement, both local and distant, between MGE and LGE churches. The nature of these differences is discussed, and the causal factors examined.

Prayer and Information

The practices of prayer and the sharing of information related to mission are core aspects of missional practice in local churches. In the survey of evangelical churches across NSW and ACT, over 94 percent of respondents indicated that their church was committed to regular prayer for distant mission workers. Interviewees from every church described some level of commitment to prayer for mission in their church. There were times of corporate prayer for mission locally and at a distance, with a particular focus on prayer for distant mission workers. Information from mission workers and organizations was often shared to guide and stimulate prayer. Interviewees described vastly different patterns of practice across the churches. It was a core feature of church life in some churches and an irregular practice in others. Interviewees from MGE churches consistently described practices of prayer and information sharing that reflect a stronger climate for mission involvement than in LGE churches.

Though all interviewees reported prayer for distant mission workers as one of their church's missional practices, the emphasis on this kind of prayer in MGE churches was notable. Interviewees in all MGE churches reported public prayers for at least one distant mission worker being included in each week's Sunday service. These times of prayer were often accompanied by a short update on the workers' situation and any specific prayer requests they may have.[22] Many MGE churches had additional regular prayer meetings outside of the Sunday gathering which included

22. Interview with CH7_SP, August 12, 2019; CH10_MC, July 19, 2019.

prayers for distant mission workers alongside other local church mission and ministry needs.[23] In some churches these happened quarterly, in others bimonthly, and in one case weekly. When mission workers could attend the services at MGE churches, they were given opportunity to speak to the whole church as part of the Sunday gathering and time was given to pray for them and their ministry. Interviewees from several churches described events hosted by the church which gave the workers opportunity to share in more depth about their life and ministry as well as time for the church members to corporately pray for them.[24] Three of the MGE churches had one month each year with a dedicated focus on mission. During this time, they gave comprehensive updates on each of the mission workers they supported and spent significant time in prayer for them.[25] Many of the MGE churches also utilized the mid-week small groups to ensure regular prayer for distant mission workers. In CH4 and CH9, each small group identified one of the church's mission workers they would focus their attention on for the year. They were provided guidelines for support, and they committed to communicate regularly with the workers and to pray for them each time they met.[26] These practices of regular prayer created a strong climate for mission prayer at church gatherings across the MGE churches such that prayer for mission was an expected part of the meeting.

In addition to these opportunities for corporate prayer, all MGE churches sought to facilitate personal prayer for mission workers by circulating regular information about the workers and their requests for prayer. This information was distributed each week via email or physical church bulletins.[27] In some churches, members were encouraged to register to receive specific prayer information about mission workers directly from the worker. In all these ways, church members' perceptions of the importance of being informed about the mission workers and spending time in prayer for them was highlighted. The members of MGE churches were consistently able to speak about the distant mission workers and

23. Interviews with CH3_SP, August 8, 2019; CH4_CM, May 7, 2019; CH6_MC, June 16, 2019; CH7_CM, September 18, 2019; CH10_MC, July 19, 2019.

24. Interviews with CH3_MC, September 2, 2019; CH4_CM, May 7, 2019.

25. Interviews with CH6_CM, June 16, 2019; CH8_MC, May 30, 2019; CH9_MC, August 29, 2019.

26. Interviews with CH4_SP, March 28, 2019, CH6_CM, June 16, 2019; CH8_CM, May 22, 2019; CH9_CM, September 10, 2019.

27. Interviews with CH3_SP, August 8, 2019; CH4_MC, April 4, 2019; CH6_SP, May 2, 2019; CH8_MC, May 30, 2019; CH9_MC, August 29, 2019.

ministries that their church was involved in and were committed to pray for them. This reflected a strong climate for distant mission involvement where church members saw regular prayer for distant mission as a behavioral norm.

The means of prayer and information distribution described by interviewees in LGE churches reflected similar practices as MGE churches, though with less regularity and lower profile. Interviewees from all LGE churches reported having mission workers share with the whole church when they were able to attend the church service, including time for prayer.[28] Some interviewees reported other opportunities workers had to share with the church such as special events or attending small groups.[29] Interviewees from two of the LGE churches reported the occasional use of videos from distant mission workers in the Sunday service to provide updates and guide the church in their corporate prayer.[30] All of the LGE churches had systems for distributing prayer information either by email or in hardcopy, though the church members at two of these churches expressed little confidence that this information was utilized.[31] One of the churches had encouraged each mid-week small group to appoint a mission advocate, yet as one church member stated, "I don't think it's been that successful."[32] The minister of the same church stated that it was their desire to have someone share about distant mission as a part of the church service at least once a month, though they admitted this had not been happening consistently.[33]

Though there were many similarities between these practices and the means employed at MGE churches, there were clear indications from the interviewees that there was little emphasis placed on them. As a church member at one LGE church stated, "there is prayer support, but kind of not organized, if that makes sense. Like, ad hoc or those who are kind of more passionate about it."[34] These practices of prayer and information distribution provide some impetus to prayer, yet they did not develop the same climate for distant mission involvement as in MGE churches. This highlights

---

28. Interviews with CH1_CM, September 26, 2019; CH2_MC, August 29, 2019; CH5_SP, June 13, 2019.
29. Interviews with CH2_MC, August 29, 2019; CH5_SP, June 13, 2019.
30. Interviews with CH1_CM, September 26, 2019; CH5_CM, July 8, 2019.
31. Interviews with CH2_MC, August 29, 2019; CH5_MC, July 8, 2019.
32. Interview with CH1_CM, September 26, 2019.
33. Interview with CH1_SP, August 26, 2019.
34. Interview with CH1_MC, September 27, 2019.

the fact that the presence of systems for information dissemination or public opportunities for prayer do not automatically create a climate for prayer. The LGE churches had these practices to varying degrees, but the emphasis that was placed on them by clergy and other influential leaders was lacking. In MGE churches this emphasis created a climate for mission involvement through prayer that was lacking in LGE churches.

Finances

The systems that churches employ around the financial support of mission and mission workers were another powerful influence on the perceptions of church members regarding the relative importance of mission. Both MGE and LGE churches use a range of different approaches in both the collection and distribution of money for mission suggesting there is no best practice in this area. However, different approaches do have an impact on the climate for mission. The ways in which an organization uses its money reflects its values. In MGE churches the practices of financial support are another key dimension of the climate for mission involvement that is lacking in LGE churches.

In all churches, funding for local mission activities was taken out of the regular offertory and income sources of the church, yet interviewees described various means by which money was collected for the support of distant mission. In some churches, money for distant mission was a portion of the general offertory collected, in others it was from specific donations from church members for the purpose of mission support, while in other churches it was a combination of the two. Three of the seven MGE churches received most of the money they sent to mission from the general offertory. CH4 and CH10 designated approximately 10 percent of their annual expenditure to the support of distant mission and CH3 designated 20 percent. In each case, church members were also invited to give specified donations which the church would pass on.[35] In some cases these additional specified gifts made up a large proportion of the total amount. In the case of CH4, approximately 20 percent of the total received for distant mission came through specified gifts.[36] One church identified specific projects for the church to support

---

35. Interviews with CH3_MC, September 2, 2019; CH4_SP, March 28, 2019; CH10_MC, July 19, 2019.

36. Interview with CH4_MC, April 4, 2019.

and encouraged members to give one-off gifts.[37] A fourth, smaller MGE church used a combination of methods to collect money for distant mission needs. A small portion was set aside from the general offertory and church members were encouraged to either give specified gifts through the church or to support mission partners directly through their mission organizations.[38] Though this meant the amount given to mission from the church members could not be quantified, church members demonstrated a clear commitment to giving generously.[39] Three other MGE churches only used specified gifts to support distant mission. In two of these churches a "faith promise" system was used which invited people to anonymously indicate at the beginning of the year how much they intended to give.[40] This allowed the churches to set the budget for the year ahead and then to give regular feedback to the congregation and encouragement to be generous towards mission needs.[41] One of the churches utilizing this method reported 15–16 percent of its budget went to distant mission, while the other was closer to 18 percent.[42] The third church that only gave specified gifts to the support of distant mission used its mission month each year to encourage congregation members to give to the cause. During the month there was regular encouragement through the sermons and the other mission focused activities including regular updates on the growing total.[43] Over the most recent decade the amount given to distant mission had increased from $20,000 to over $110,000, which was nearly 15 percent of total church expenditure in 2019.[44] Despite this variety of giving methods across these churches, in each case interviewees spoke of an intentional effort to see financial support as part of the broader relational connection to and support of the mission workers. There was a strong climate for the financial support of distant mission in these MGE churches as an expression of a broader commitment to partner with mission workers and organizations in other places.

37. Interview with CH10_MC, July 19, 2019.
38. Interview with CH7_MC, September 2, 2019.
39. Interview with CH7_SP, August 12, 2019.
40. Interviews with CH8_MC, May 30, 2019; CH6_MC, June 16, 2019.
41. This practice is recommended by several Australian authors as the preferred way to support distant mission in a local church. See Dipple, *Becoming Global*, 73–83; Webb, *Your Church*, 89–101.
42. Interviews with CH6_SP, May 2, 2019; CH8_SP, April 11, 2019.
43. Interview with CH9_MC, August 29, 2019.
44. Interview with CH9_SP, October 9, 2019.

The three LGE churches all employed different methods to direct money to distant mission needs. The largest of the three churches designated a portion of its general offertory to distant mission together with any specified donations that come in.[45] These specified gifts primarily came from the older members of the church who continue previous patterns of mission involvement that are no longer widely accepted in the church.[46] The smallest of the three churches only collected specified gifts for distant mission, though there was a portion of general offertory directed to the support of Scripture teachers in the local schools.[47] The total amount of specified gifts had been growing in the five years since the minister had arrived and was approximately 7 percent of the total offertory income in 2019. The third of the three LGE churches did not collect funds for distant mission workers at all but rather encouraged church members to give directly to their mission organizations.[48] One church member noted that this was given little emphasis in the church and was only mentioned publicly once or twice a year.[49] The church also encouraged church members to sponsor children in developing countries through Compassion International. More than 40 percent of the regular attendees did this and the church had developed a strategic partnership with this organization focused on one region overseas.[50] Occasionally the church members were invited to donate to a specific mission project, such as caring for refugees, supporting an overseas theological student, or grants for new churches in Western Sydney, yet these were not ongoing.[51] In this case, the financial systems encouraged members to view the support of mission as an individual task, rather than the role of the church as a corporate body. As one church member noted, "I kind of feel sad about part of our church budget not being allocated towards causes outside of our church."[52] In all three churches there were systems for the collection of funds for distant mission, yet the church members reported that they were not promoted or regularly spoken about. This lack of encouragement reflected a weak

---

45. Interview with CH2_MC, August 29, 2019.
46. Interviews with CH2_MC, August 29, 2019; CH2_SP, June 24, 2019.
47. Interview with CH5_SP, June 13, 2019.
48. Interview with CH1_MC, September 27, 2019.
49. Interview with CH1_MC, September 27, 2019.
50. Interview with CH1_SP, August 26, 2019.
51. Interview with CH1_MC, September 27, 2019.
52. Interview with CH1_MC, September 27, 2019.

climate for the financial support of distant mission. Church members did not see financial support of mission as a high priority behavior.

The ways in which funds were spent further shaped church members' perceptions of the church's emphasis on mission support. Some MGE churches had financial policies that reflected their commitment to overseas mission by limiting the proportion of their expenditure that stayed in Australia or by giving larger amounts of money to mission workers serving overseas.[53] Other MGE churches committed to funding a set portion of a mission worker's total budget, up to one third in one case, but only in the context of a long-term relationship with the worker.[54] Two church leaders noted the impact that financial policies have on church member engagement, as they spoke about the appreciation that people developed for different kinds of mission work as a consequence of their church supporting a variety of ministries.[55] In each case, the church members saw the distribution of funds as a reflection of the importance of mission involvement which created a climate for mission that stimulated involvement.

These various examples indicate that no single approach to the financial support for distant missionaries guaranteed a strong climate for mission. In some MGE churches, the financial support for mission was encouraged by devoting a notable portion of the general offertory to work overseas.[56] This budgetary commitment showed the priority that distant mission had in the church in a way that strengthened the climate for mission. As one church member said, "About 20 percent of our budget goes to mission, so it is an important part of the church's reason for being."[57] By contrast, an LGE church that committed a portion of its budget to distant mission lacked this strong climate for mission because members felt disconnected from the financial processes which were "not talked about regularly."[58] Similarly, in some churches that encouraged direct support for mission workers, this giving stimulated the climate for mission, while in other churches it weakened it. Some MGE churches, that only sent

53. Interview with CH4_MC, April 4, 2019; personal communication with CH9_MC, March 18, 2020.
54. Interview with CH10_SP, June 3, 2019; CH8, Guidelines and Policies Document, 2014.
55. Interviews with CH4_SP, March 28, 2019; CH2_SP, June 24, 2019.
56. Interviews with CH4_SP, March 28, 2019; CH10_MC, July 19, 2019.
57. Interview with CH3_MC, September 2, 2019.
58. Interview with CH2_MC, August 29, 2019.

specified gifts to mission workers, saw generous giving and high levels of engagement in the financial support of distant mission.[59] An LGE church that encouraged individuals to support distant mission workers by giving directly to their mission organizations had a weak climate for mission and distant mission support was not considered a core church activity.[60] Therefore, the impact on climate for mission is not dependent on the financial processes employed, but on the ways in which financial support for mission was integrated with the wider purposes of the church such that the members considered it a key expression of the church's values.

Encouragement and Equipping for Mission Participation

The third area of church practice that provided an insight into the climate of mission involvement is the mobilization and equipping of church members to be agents of mission. Interviewees from MGE churches reported several ways in which people were encouraged to consider serving as distant mission workers. Churches hosted discussion groups,[61] training from visiting mission workers,[62] or short-term mission trips overseas.[63] Some church leaders encouraged attendance at mission conferences,[64] while others sought to develop the relationships between church members and visiting distant mission workers.[65] A number of MGE church leaders spoke of their desire to see members of their church commit to long-term distant mission work and their intentional efforts to encourage it.[66] As one pastor stated, "we continue to pray that God would send people from within our church to other places with the gospel."[67] These practices stimulated the climate for mission as church members considered their own involvement to be a worthwhile activity.

59. Interview with CH9_MC, August 29, 2019.
60. Interview with CH1_MC, September 27, 2019.
61. Interview with CH3_CM, August 23, 2019.
62. Interview with CH6_CM, June 16, 2019.
63. Interviews with CH6_SP, May 2, 2019; CH8_MC, May 30, 2019.
64. Interviews with CH6_MC, June 16, 2019; CH9_CM, September 10, 2019.
65. Interviews with CH8_CM, May 22, 2019; CH3_CM, August 23, 2019. Previous research has found this to be the most potent means of mobilizing people towards cross-cultural mission. See Hibbert et al., "Journey towards Long-Term," 469–82.
66. Interviews with CH3_SP, August 8, 2019; CH4_SP, March 28, 2019; CH6_SP, May 2, 2019; CH8_SP, April 11, 2019; CH9_SP, October 9, 2019.
67. Interview with CH4_SP, March 28, 2019.

Interviewees from several MGE churches reported that, if a church member had expressed a desire to become a distant mission worker, there were systems to help these people make the necessary preparations. The mission committee at CH8 saw it as their responsibility to not only assess the suitability of church members to become mission workers, but also to assist them financially and practically through the preparation process.[68] Similarly, CH4 had been financially supporting a number of their members as they did formal and non-formal ministry training with the goal of heading overseas.[69] A staff member at CH3 described their active ministry trainee program which had been running for many years and through which a number of distant mission workers had been prepared.[70] As another example of this practice, CH9 gave one of their junior staff members extended paid leave while they travelled overseas to visit a mission context where they were considering serving long-term.[71] In all these ways, members of these churches saw people being supported and encouraged as they moved towards distant mission work. This was an important stimulus to the climate for personal involvement in mission.

For many of these churches, this support for people considering distant mission work was accompanied by training and encouragement for church members to be actively involved in local mission. Members from three of the MGE churches reported having regular segments in the Sunday service which sought to equip church members for evangelism and missional engagement.[72] Interviewees from five of the MGE churches reported that evangelism training events for congregation members were run in the previous year, with one church developing a website and podcast to equip church members for local mission.[73] There were programmed opportunities for church members to meet and share their own efforts in local mission, together with encouragement to participate in the local mission activities that the churches were running in the local community, often in partnership with other churches

---

68. Interview with CH8_SP, April 11, 2019.
69. Interview with CH4_MC, April 4, 2019.
70. Interview with CH3_SP, August 8, 2019.
71. Interview with CH9_CM, September 10, 2019,
72. Interviews with CH3_CM, August 23, 2019; CH4_MC, April 4, 2019; CH10_SP, June 3, 2019.
73. Interviews with CH3_SP, August 8, 2019; CH4_MC, April 4, 2019; CH6_CM, June 16, 2019; CH8_CM, May 22, 2019; CH9_MC, August 29, 2019.

and organizations.⁷⁴ These activities brought a climate for local mission engagement that complemented the climate for involvement in distant mission in these MGE churches. The two were fostered though different activities, but typically went together in MGE churches. This is consistent with the pattern of local church mission involvement observed in the survey findings reported in chapter 3.

By contrast, the interviewees from LGE churches described practices that strengthened a climate for local mission involvement, but not for participation in distant mission. The minister at CH5 had sought to equip the church members for mission in the local community.⁷⁵ He provided training in how to use personal evangelism tools including how to share the gospel with people from a Muslim background.⁷⁶ This had encouraged church members to visit people in the local community and to share their faith with people in the town center.⁷⁷ This increased engagement in local mission was not reflected in distant mission involvement. Interviewees from CH1 spoke at length about their church's strong emphasis on engaging people in the local community.⁷⁸ The various ministries of the church, including welcoming and music, were run by teams of church members under the leadership and guidance of staff to ensure they were appealing to outsiders. Training was provided to church members who were running community outreach events and evangelistic courses, and there was frequent encouragement to invite non-Christians to church-run events.⁷⁹ Like some of the MGE churches, this church had a long history of training people for professional ministry and supporting them through the process. One church member noted that the senior minister of the church "has an incredible ability to train ministers . . . and we have a lot of trainees."⁸⁰ Many of these former trainees had continued into paid pastoral ministry in Australia, but interviewees were not aware of any former trainees who had gone into distant mission.⁸¹ A congregation member from CH2 similarly noted that in recent years there had

74. Interviews with CH8_SP, April 11, 2019; CH3_CM, August 23, 2019; CH4_SP, March 28, 2019.
75. Interview with CH5_SP, June 13, 2019.
76. Interview with CH5_SP, June 13, 2019; CH5_CM, July 8, 2019.
77. Interview with CH5_MC, July 8, 2019.
78. Interviews with CH1_CM, September 26, 2019; CH1_SP, August 26, 2019.
79. Interview with CH1_SP, August 26, 2019.
80. Interview with CH1_CM, September 26, 2019.
81. Interviews with CH1_CM, September 26, 2019; CH1_MC, September 27, 2019.

been a number of young people from the church who had transitioned into ministry in Australia, "but maybe not as many have actually become missionaries."[82] When asked why she thought this was the case she observed, "if they're interested in taking up life in ministry, MTS is a pathway, and I think probably that pathway tends to lead into ministry."[83] In these LGE churches, the trainee programs strengthened the climate for involvement in local mission, yet did not encourage involvement in distant mission. Consequently, church members did not feel encouraged toward personal involvement in distant mission, even though mission locally was valued.

Local Mission Activities

The fourth area of church practice that was evident for its impact on climate for mission was local mission activity. Interviewees reported a range of events, programs, and practices that their churches pursued with the goal of engaging non-Christians in their local communities. All the churches approached for interview displayed higher than average levels of local mission activity and had a theological and practical commitment to mission, even though they differed greatly in their involvement in distant mission. The practices employed varied greatly across the churches. Some churches prioritized invitational events hosted at the church, while others focused on the members' personal missional practices. Some churches sought to address a range of social as well as spiritual needs, others only focused on addressing spiritual needs through evangelism. These different patterns of engagement reflect different climates for mission shaped by the church members' understanding of the needs of their local community and the best ways to address them.

Some interviewees indicated that their church's approach to local mission was primarily focused on hosting events to which church members could invite their non-Christian friends. CH3 hosted a week of special events for non-believers which sought to address key questions about life and faith.[84] As Chinese churches, CH6 and CH8 chose to host events that aligned with key Chinese celebrations including Chinese New

---

82. Interview with CH2_CM, September 2, 2019.

83. Interview with CH2_CM, September 2, 2019. For information on MTS see ch. 2, n90.

84. Interviews with CH3_SP, August 8, 2019; CH3_CM, August 23, 2019.

Year and the mid-autumn festival.[85] Several churches hosted events to coincide with key annual celebrations, including Easter and Christmas, as well as hosting additional events through the year to engage the wider community, such as art displays or cooking events.[86] These events created a climate that encouraged church members to invite their friends. As one interviewee said, "[church members] would be strongly encouraged to be inviting people or bring people along to those events."[87] Churches that regularly held these events were similarly noted for their commitment to considering the comfort and needs of outsiders when planning their weekly services. In this way the key events stimulated a climate of invitational mission that was expected to generally encourage church members to invite people to church.[88] These practices reflected an implicit conviction that bringing non-Christians to church events was a primary way of doing local mission. These convictions stimulated the practices which, in turn, strengthened the climate. There was no indication that this conviction influenced a church's level of global engagement, as it was evident in both MGE and LGE churches.

In contrast to this invitational approach, the minister of one MGE church considered the church members' daily interactions with non-Christians as the heart of the church's local mission efforts.[89] The church had a preschool on site and there were some programmed events to facilitate engagement with the families connected to the preschool, but the minister's primary emphasis was on helping church members engage in mission to the non-Christian people in their networks. Through previous experience at other churches, he had concluded that a comprehensive program of church run mission activities could often result in church members being disengaged from mission.[90] He stated,

> We really are trying hard to encourage people to think about their local [suburb] mission, not just in terms of being part of those church programs, but really engaging with individuals at the school gate, through their friendships, and neighborhoods.[91]

85. Interviews with CH6_MC, June 16, 2019; CH8_SP, April 11, 2019.
86. Interviews with CH1_SP, August 26, 2019; CH3_SP, August 8, 2019; CH8_SP, April 11, 2019.
87. Interview with CH1_MC, September 27, 2019.
88. Interview with CH1_MC, September 27, 2019.
89. Interview with CH4_SP, March 28, 2019.
90. Interview with CH4_SP, March 28, 2019.
91. Interview with CH4_SP, March 28, 2019.

CHURCH MISSION PRACTICES AND ORGANIZATIONAL ANALYSIS   157

This was encouraged through training sessions, gathering church members together to talk about their efforts in local mission, and occasionally inviting people to share stories of their evangelistic efforts during the Sunday service.[92] One member of this church reported that this encouraged her greatly in her own involvement in local mission. She stated, "The whole mission is day to day life, day to day living as a Christian in the workplace."[93] By contrast, another member of the church reported that she would like the church to host more invitational events, because she felt that the regular Sunday services were "not necessarily geared for the outsider."[94] In this case the minister's beliefs about the preferred mode of local mission engagement stimulated a climate of personal involvement in mission, but without a strong focus on collective action.

Interviewees from another MGE church noted ways in which their church emphasized partnership with other churches and Christian organizations for the sake of local mission. This church hosted several evangelistic events and activities, but it also partnered with other churches and Christian groups to reach the wider community. This included combined church events around Easter and Christmas, involvement in large inter-church evangelistic events, partnership with other churches in caring for people experiencing poverty and homelessness in the inner city, and active involvement in Scripture classes in nearby high schools.[95] This approach to local mission motivated church members to pursue involvement in a range of activities, many of which were not directly connected to their church.[96] A member of the church staff reflected on this emphasis noting that, "it's never been about make our church big . . . or expand our brand . . . It's an independent church, it's just got a heart for the gospel."[97] These practices led church members to see working with other groups as a good way to engage in local mission. It thereby created a climate of corporate involvement that was not present in all MGE churches. This again demonstrates the effect of implicit convictions about the preferred way to engage in mission practice on the climate for local mission activity. Some churches displayed a strong climate for invitational mission,

---

92. Interview with CH4_CM, May 7, 2019.
93. Interview with CH4_CM, May 7, 2019.
94. Interview with CH4_MC, April 4, 2019.
95. Interviews with CH8_SP, April 11, 2019; CH8_MC, May 30, 2019.
96. Interview with CH8_MC, May 30, 2019.
97. Interview with CH8_SP, April 11, 2019.

others a climate encouraging personal evangelism, and another a climate of corporate mission beyond the local church.

In addition to the diverse modes of local missional practice, interviewees reported a wide variety of perceived needs in their local community. The minister of CH10, an MGE church, had noticed the prevalence of poor mental health and homelessness in his community and chose to open the church building during the week for people to drop in.[98] During these times people from the community were welcome to walk into the church building, talk to a church member, and receive prayer if they wanted to.[99] The church had also begun a mid-week healing service for people with physical sickness or life controlling issues, such as addiction, poor mental health, family dysfunction, or homelessness.[100] In a similar way, interviewees from CH5, an LGE church, spoke of the significant socioeconomic needs in the local community as a key stimulus to the church's local mission approach. There was a lot of social housing in the area with many people on very low incomes, often with poor mental health, and a large number of recent migrants.[101] Consequently, the church ran a range of community oriented programs which were led by enthusiastic lay people with a desire to serve the community.[102] The church partnered with denominational and para-church organizations to provide discounted groceries and free financial counselling.[103] One of the congregation members observed that "service type ministry" and running "programs" was a high priority for many members of the church.[104] Similarly a church member at CH10 spoke about the need for the church to be a "winsome presence" in the community, "we want to be this open door welcoming anyone and everyone in."[105] These local mission practices encouraged church members to see the value in caring for the wider community. There was a strong climate of concern which motivated involvement in these service activities, but not necessarily in personal evangelism or invitation to church events. The perceived needs shaped the climate for mission.

98. Interview with CH10_SP, June 3, 2019.
99. Interview with CH10_MC, July 19, 2019.
100. Interview with CH10_MC, July 19, 2019.
101. Interview with CH5_SP, June 13, 2019.
102. Interview with CH5_CM, July 8, 2019.
103. Interviews with CH5_CM, July 8, 2019; CH5_MC, July 8, 2019.
104. Interview with CH5_CM, July 8, 2019.
105. Interview with CH10_MC, July 19, 2019.

The approach to local mission at CH9, an MGE church, was also shaped by the perceived needs of the local community, yet in a vastly different way. Like CH5, this church had a high proportion of migrants in its local community with 34 percent of residents claiming Chinese heritage and over 6 percent claiming Korean heritage.[106] However, unlike CH5, this was a wealthy area of Sydney where most people earned above average wages and the only community service activity the church ran was an ESL program.[107] This program had introduced many people to the church and the weekly church attendance had increased dramatically over the previous ten years, including many people who became Christians. According to the minister, however, this was not primarily due to the ESL program or any other intentional evangelistic strategy, but a consequence of "the amazing thing that God is doing amongst, particularly, Chinese and Korean people in Sydney . . . [P]eople just keep walking in the door week after week after week."[108] When asked about those who had recently become Christians at the church he noted, "It's kind of happening through regular Sunday services. Connections made through ESL, that sort of thing."[109] These beliefs about what people in the community need results in practices that create a climate for mission through welcoming and integrating people into church.

In all these churches there was a strong climate of local mission activity, even though they varied greatly in their level of global engagement. The approaches to local mission also varied according to people's shared missiological convictions. Though the foundational missiological principles were the same, beliefs about where mission should ideally take place, whether it was a corporate or individual activity, and what needs the church should address shaped the climate for mission. This variety reflects the power of these secondary missiological convictions in shaping church practice.

---

106. Australian Bureau of Statistics, *2016 Census*.

107. The median household income is 26 percent higher than the state median household income. Australian Bureau of Statistics, *2016 Census*.

108. Interview with CH9_SP, October 9, 2019.

109. Interview with CH9_CM, September 10, 2019.

Missional Leadership Structures

In addition to the influence of the church leader's missional beliefs, analysis of the interview data highlighted the mission-related leadership structures and processes that shape a church's mission activities. Among the churches examined there was great diversity in the processes and systems in place. Some of this variety reflected the differences in church governance structures across the different denominations. In churches with episcopal governance structures, the mission activities were more heavily dependent on the actions of the clergy than in churches with congregational governance structures which typically had mission committees in place. The missional leadership structures described in MGE and LGE churches will be considered separately and their impact on climate for mission explored.

Missional Leadership in More Globally Engaged Churches

Of the seven churches that displayed high levels of involvement in distant mission (MGE) there were three discernible patterns of mission leadership. In three of the churches there was a single key individual that was recognized for their influence, in two others there was an identified mission committee that brought together several key leaders, and in the other two there was a shared pattern of mission involvement across the church. These differences were influenced to some extent by the size and governance structures of the church.

Two of the three MGE churches with a key individual shaping the mission activities were Anglican. In both cases it was the church's senior minister that interviewees described as having the greatest influence on mission involvement.[110] Both leaders showed a deep personal commitment to local and distant mission involvement. They led efforts to train and equip church members for personal evangelism including the development of specific evangelistic resources for people to use.[111] Interviewees from one church noted that it was the senior minister who typically chaired the mission events where overseas mission workers would share about their work.[112] He would also interview mission workers when

---

110. Interviews with CH3_SP, August 8, 2019; CH3_MC, September 2, 2019; CH4_CM, May 7, 2019.

111. Interview with CH3_SP, August 8, 2019.

112. Interview with CH3_MC, September 2, 2019.

they visited the services such that their ministry was emphasized for its significance, as the assistant minister in this church noted, "he's lauding them, and praising them, and going, 'How great is this?'"[113] This senior minister's commitment to mission was further reflected in the attitudes and roles of the four assistant ministers he had appointed. One previously served as an overseas mission worker, and another had lived overseas as the child of mission workers. The third was employed by the church as a full-time evangelist, while the fourth was responsible for facilitating church member involvement in personal evangelism and mission support.[114] Consequently, though a single individual was noted for his influence, the commitment to mission was evident at every level of leadership. This church also had a mission committee of non-staff church members who made decisions about mission worker support and served to raise the profile of distant mission throughout the church, but in the words of one church member, "I don't think the committee's that visible."[115] A similar pattern was evident in another Anglican church where there was a committee that made decisions regarding mission finance but the senior minister was the most active supporter of mission.[116] He stated that "our engagement in global mission is so important, that it's not an area of my work that I want to delegate."[117] Nonetheless, there were many other church members that were also deeply committed to mission involvement including a few people employed by mission organizations or preparing to go overseas as mission workers. This pattern in both churches, of a strongly committed single leader together with a plurality of mission enthusiasts, provided a consistent perception among church members that participation in mission activities was expected. This was articulated by one interviewee who stated that "if [the senior minister] were to leave the church tomorrow, most of these [mission] things would continue."[118]

This is less so the case in an MGE Presbyterian church which benefitted from the work of one highly engaged volunteer mission coordinator but didn't have the same plurality of mission involvement among church members. The mission coordinator was fully supported by the

113. Interview with CH3_SP, 8 August 2019.
114. Interview with CH3_CM, August 23, 2019.
115. Interview with CH3_CM, August 23, 2019.
116. Interviews with CH4_SP, March 28, 2019; CH4_MC, April 4, 2019; CH4_CM, May 7, 2019.
117. Interview with CH4_SP, March 28, 2019.
118. Interview with CH4_CM, May 7, 2019.

clergy, who regularly encouraged mission involvement through their preaching and leadership.[119] However, the senior minister described the coordinator as "the engine room" of the church's distant mission involvement noting that it was potentially too dependent on them.[120] The senior minister had been leading the church for many years and in that time had seen it grow from fifty to over five hundred regular attendants.[121] Yet when the mission coordinator joined the church more recently, distant mission involvement was limited.[122] The coordinator developed mission support systems which included the appointment of "mission advocates" in each of the church's mid-week small groups.[123] These systems and processes produced a strong climate for mission involvement, though the minister hoped they would become less dependent on the coordinator's input over time.[124]

Two other MGE churches were less dependent on individuals but had highly engaged mission committees that worked with the pastoral staff to encourage involvement in mission. These two churches had multiple congregations and similar governance structures with multiple pastors, a management committee, and a mission committee consisting of the pastors, a key lay leader, and representatives from each congregation. In both churches the pastors worked closely with these committees to guide and stimulate the churches' involvement in mission; however, both churches had a long history of involvement in distant mission that was lay-led and predated many of the pastoral staff.[125] Pastors at both churches spoke of the enormous positive impact of lay leaders in the mission committees.[126] These lay leaders were personally committed to mission involvement and were encouraged to lead the churches in this way. One pastor confessed that he played a minor role in the mission committee.[127] The influence of these committees was enhanced by the participation of

---

119. Interview with CH9_MC, August 29, 2019.
120. Interview with CH9_SP, October 9, 2019.
121. Interview with CH9_SP, October 9, 2019.
122. Interview with CH9_MC, August 29, 2019.
123. Interviews with CH9_MC, August 29, 2019; CH9_CM, September 10, 2019.
124. Interview with CH9_SP, October 9, 2019.
125. Interviews with CH8_SP, April 11, 2019; CH6_MC, June 16, 2019; CH6_CM, June 16, 2019; CH6_SP, May 2, 2019.
126. Interviews with CH8_SP, April 11, 2019; CH6_SP, May 2, 2019.
127. Interview with CH8_SP, April 11, 2019.

representatives from each congregation who then facilitated the flow of information between the church members and the mission leaders.

This plurality of lay leaders and pastoral staff effectively guided these churches' involvement in distant mission, though there was less structural support for local mission. Efforts to engage the local community were generally coordinated by the clergy with groups of church members coming together to organize evangelistic events targeted for different language groups.[128] For a time, CH8 did establish a local mission committee to strengthen their local mission activities, including school scripture and major outreach events, but the structure was ultimately absorbed into the mission committee.[129] Though the clergy saw this as a worthwhile amalgamation, the well-established practices of the distant mission committee and the difference in the nature of the tasks meant that local mission activities progressively fell off the agenda and became the responsibility of the pastoral staff again. These structures were effective in strengthening the climate of involvement in distant mission, yet the climate for local mission involvement was seen to be weaker.[130]

The final two MGE churches had less explicit mission leadership structures but displayed a high level of mission involvement among all church members with the support and encouragement of the pastoral staff. Both churches had a long history of mission involvement predating their present clergy with strong relational connections between the church members and the mission partners.[131] The minister of one church reported regular contact with the mission partners to keep the church members informed, yet he noted that many other church members were also in touch with them.[132] The minister of the other church described a similarly long history of connection between the church and the distant mission workers, though he had instituted significant changes when he arrived.[133] He disbanded the lay mission committee because he felt that it created an unhelpful distinction between local and distant mission.[134] Instead, he encouraged church members to be actively engaged with their own communities while maintaining strong relationships with

128. Interview with CH6_MC, June 16, 2019.
129. Interview with CH8_SP, April 11, 2019.
130. Interviews with CH6_SP, May 2, 2019; CH8_SP, April 11, 2019.
131. Interviews with CH7_SP, August 12, 2019; CH10_SP, June 3, 2019.
132. Interviews with CH7_SP, August 12, 2019; CH7_MC, September 2, 2019.
133. Interview with CH10_SP, June 3, 2019.
134. Interview with CH10_SP, June 3, 2019.

distant mission partners. The church had a number of present members with direct involvement in mission through previous overseas mission service or current work with mission organizations in Australia.[135] These members had an ongoing impact by connecting the church members to a range of different mission activities locally and overseas, and to foster a culture of participation across the church.[136] Consequently, both these churches displayed a general pattern of mission involvement across the membership with the intentional support of pastoral leaders resulting in a strong and self-perpetuating climate for mission involvement.

In all these churches the missional leadership structures highlighted the priority given to mission involvement which strengthened the climate for distant mission. Though the governance structures of the churches varied, in each case people with a strong commitment to involvement in distant mission had formal recognition among the leadership. In Anglican churches with centralized leadership structures the attitude of the senior minister was key. In churches with a plurality of leadership, the support of the senior leadership was important, yet the mission involvement was often directed by lay leaders. In each case the structures gave legitimacy and influence to the church's mission enthusiasts which strengthened the perception among all church members that mission involvement was a priority. This supported the climate for distant mission and reinforced the expectation that mission involvement was a valuable exercise.

Missional Leadership in Less Globally Engaged Churches

The pastoral staff from each of the less globally engaged churches described structures within their church to encourage distant mission, yet they were not effective in creating a strong climate of mission involvement.[137] These three churches differed markedly in size and location. CH1 was a medium-sized church (approximately two hundred attendees) in a wealthy suburb, CH2 was a large church (approximately four hundred attendees) in an equally wealthy suburb, and CH5 was a small church (less than one hundred attendees) in a more multi-cultural and disadvantaged community. The leaders in each church expressed a commitment to

---

135. Interviews with CH10_SP, June 3, 2019; CH10_CM, 19 July 2019.

136. Interview with CH10_MC, July 19, 2019.

137. Interviews with CH1_SP, August 26, 2019; CH2_SP, June 24, 2019; CH5_SP, June 13, 2019.

mission locally and at a distance, yet they noted that the church members were not consistently committed to distant mission.

In each case there had been a change in the church's leadership in the previous five years. The ministers of CH2 and CH5 both described their churches as being in a rebuilding phase after significant financial and leadership issues prior to their arrival. CH2 had previously had very high levels of involvement in distant mission and some of the older members continued to meet to pray and raise money for mission work.[138] Many former members had left the church and new people had come who the minister said "just aren't interested" in distant mission.[139] The church had a mission committee chaired by the senior minister, but it did not include any newer church members.[140] There was a high level of interest in local mission with enthusiastic church members hosting a range of local outreach activities, but those that were committed to distant mission tended to be elderly with limited influence on the climate for mission across the church.[141] A similar pattern was evident in CH5 though without the previous high level of involvement. The minister had come to the church several years ago when attendance and income had fallen to unsustainable levels. Since coming he had sought to clarify the church's purpose with a particular emphasis on its involvement in mission.[142] Though not wanting to separate local and distant mission, the minister stated that "there's been a big focus on building the kingdom [of God] here locally."[143] There were no key leaders or leadership structures dedicated to distant mission aside from the minister and the parish council and when asked about who, in the church, was most active in mission, the interviewees named those focused on local mission activities only.[144] The minister noted a few individuals in the church who he thought had an interest in distant mission, though he noted that he was "probably the missions committee at the moment."[145] In both these cases the church leaders were supportive of distant mission, yet there were very few church members who reinforced the focus among the rest of the congregation.

138. Interview with CH2_CM, September 2, 2019.
139. Interview with CH2_SP, June 24, 2019.
140. Interview with CH2_MC, August 29, 2019.
141. Interview with CH2_SP, June 24, 2019.
142. Interview with CH5_SP, June 13, 2019.
143. Interview with CH5_SP, June 13, 2019.
144. Interviews with CH5_CM, July 8, 2019; CH5_MC, July 8, 2019.
145. Interview with CH5_SP, June 13, 2019.

The third church showing lower levels of engagement with distant mission had been led by the same senior minister for many years. In this time the church has been heavily involved in local evangelism and had seen many people become Christians.[146] The church was structured according to the "5M" model which was focused on the five key purposes of "magnification, maturity, membership, ministry, and mission."[147] There were paid staff with specific responsibility for each of the "5Ms," though the mission pastor position was only recently established.[148] This person was responsible for the oversight of mission activities in the local community, elsewhere in Australia, and overseas. The leadership encouraged church members to join ministry teams which were responsible for specific aspects of the "5Ms."[149] There were a number of teams focused on local mission activities, including evangelistic courses and community outreach events, and there were plans to establish a ministry team focused on mission beyond the local community, though this had not yet happened.[150] There were some church members enthusiastic about distant mission, but as one of them shared, "there's nothing official, but there's a few people at [the church] who just have a certain passion."[151] This lack of structure weakened the climate for distant mission involvement.

These missional leadership structures did not encourage a climate for distant mission involvement to the same degree that they supported a climate for local mission activity. In each case formal church leadership affirmed the importance of distant mission involvement, yet there were few other prominent church members who reinforced this priority. There were individuals in the churches who were committed to supporting distant mission, yet the leadership structures did not support their influence or legitimacy. Consequently, there was not a shared perception among church members that involvement in distant mission was a priority for the church. Though there is no single leadership structure required to have a strong climate for mission involvement, the church's practices

146. Interview with CH1_SP, August 26, 2019.

147. The "5M" model was originally proposed by American Baptist pastor Rick Warren, but has been reinterpreted by Australian evangelicals, particularly in the Fellowship of Independent Evangelical Churches. See Warren, *Purpose Driven Church*; Lynch, "Dissecting."

148. Interview with CH1_SP, August 26, 2019.

149. Interview with CH1_SP, August 26, 2019.

150. Interviews with CH1_MC, September 27, 2019; CH1_SP, August 26, 2019.

151. Interview with CH1_MC, September 27, 2019.

regarding missional leadership had a profound impact on distant mission involvement among the churches.

SUMMARY OF CLIMATE FOR MISSION

This review of the key missional practices in each of the churches provides a valuable insight into the climate for mission involvement that resulted from the practices, processes, and policies of the church. Although climate is ideally assessed through a survey of group members, this review of interviewee responses across a range of churches helps to explain the causes for the mission climate in these MGE and LGE churches. The diversity in church approaches to prayer, finances for mission, equipping for mission involvement, and mission leadership structures all had a notable impact on the climate for distant mission involvement.

The one factor that did not have a clear impact on the climate for distant mission involvement was local mission involvement. Though all churches displayed a moderate to strong climate for local mission, in several of these churches involvement in distant mission was weak. This revealed the power of missional beliefs to shape missional climate and practice. The patterns of local mission engagement in each church clearly reflected the beliefs of the church members regarding the needs to be addressed and the strategies to be used. Churches in which people believed that attractional mission was the preferred model hosted numerous public events and had a missional climate which encouraged members to invite non-Christian people from the community. Churches in which people believed that mission required addressing the social needs of their community ran multiple programs to meet social needs and displayed a climate of volunteerism among members. Churches in which people believed that their context was best approached through personal evangelism sought to train their members in this area and developed a climate that stimulated this behavior. This demonstrates the fact that climate for mission is task-specific and profoundly shaped by the missiological beliefs of the leaders and members. Regarding local mission, the shape of a group member's involvement was strongly influenced by the convictions and practices of the leadership, yet this was not consistently the case regarding distant mission involvement. All the leaders interviewed expressed a personal commitment to distant mission, yet the climate for involvement in some of the churches was weak.

Members of MGE churches described a range of factors that encouraged them towards involvement in distant mission. From an organizational perspective, these factors included structures and practices that supported a strong climate of involvement. MGE churches had clear systems for the dissemination of information about the church's distant mission partners and they stimulated engagement with this material through public prayers, prayer meetings, and prayer in small groups. Church members were aware of the distant mission workers and felt encouraged to pray for them. The financial systems for collecting and sending money to distant mission workers varied between MGE churches, yet in each case the importance of these finances was emphasized, giving church members a sense of personal ownership and sacrifice toward these gifts. The climate for distant mission involvement was further stimulated in MGE churches through the mobilization and training activities that encouraged church members to consider serving as distant mission workers themselves. For those who decided to pursue these opportunities the churches supported them financially and practically. The missional leadership structures also influenced the climate for mission in MGE churches. Though they differed greatly depending on the size and governance structures of the church, they each had several key people with a commitment to active church involvement in distant mission influencing the membership. In many cases the most active mission enthusiasts were not paid pastoral staff, yet they had recognized roles in the church and were supported and given legitimacy by the leadership. Because of these various structures and practices, the members of MGE churches consistently reported a climate of mission that encouraged active involvement in the support and promotion of distant mission activities.

By contrast, LGE church interviewees revealed that many of the structures and practices evident in MGE churches were not present. Though formal church leadership espoused support for distant mission activities, there were very few church members enthusiastic about distant mission, and those that were lacked the support to reinforce and enact their convictions. Consequently, distant mission involvement was not a perceived priority among the wider church membership. There were generally systems and procedures for the distribution of information and prayer requests from distant mission workers, yet the information was not engaged with in ways that stimulated involvement. Though some members utilized the information and committed to prayer, it was not considered an important church activity. Similarly, the approach to the financial support of distant mission workers did not actively engage church membership as they were not encouraged to see it as a shared responsibility of the church. Finally, there was little support or encouragement for church members to personally consider distant mission work even though they were strongly encouraged to be engaged locally. Though some LGE churches had highly developed processes for training members for Christian ministry, those pathways did not encourage consideration of distant mission work. This pattern of church practices resulted in a weak climate for distant mission involvement even though church leaders, and some church members, expressed a personal commitment to distant mission. These organizational features of the churches had a much greater impact on mission activities than the espoused priorities.

ESPOUSED AND ENACTED PRIORITIES

This apparent disconnection between the leader's stated priorities and the practices of the church can best be understood through the lens of organizational culture and climate. Organizational climate provides a useful lens to consider how church structures and practices shape the behaviors that church members feel encouraged to perform. In many cases, these behaviors were clearly in line with the church leaders' priorities, while at other times there appeared to be a disconnect between the stated purposes of the church and the actual practices of the membership. Zohar and Hofmann describe this disconnect in terms of "espoused" and "enacted" priorities.[152] Espoused priorities reflect the core values that the leadership of an organization is seeking to prioritize. They are often enshrined in vision statements, goals, or policies and can be articulated by those in leadership and, in some cases, group members (see figure 6). Enacted priorities are those that are evident in the activities, procedures, and daily decisions that determine group member behavior. These enacted priorities are therefore the true priorities of the organization as they determine the climate for action in a specific domain.[153] Having reviewed the diversity in these churches' climate for mission, and by implication their true values, it is appropriate to review the espoused values that these churches hold to and to consider points of difference between the two.

---

152. Zohar and Hofmann, "Organizational Culture," 646–47.
153. Zohar and Hofmann, "Organizational Culture," 647.

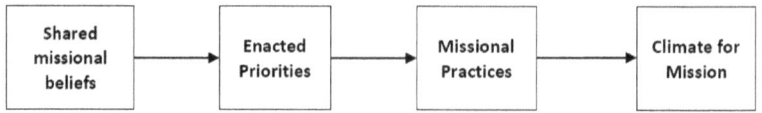

Figure 6. Relationship between Missional Beliefs and Climate for Mission

Chapter 4 explored interviewees' responses when asked about the purpose of their church. Responses highlighted three purposes across all churches: the edification of church members, mission to people in the local community, and support for distant and overseas mission. Interviewees from every church referred to the building up of believers' faith through the ministry of the church, noting the role of both church staff and church members in these activities.[154] Local mission was regularly reported to be another core purpose of the church, in some cases it was described as one of the anticipated outcomes of the edification of church members.[155] Consistently across all churches among both leaders and members the need to engage people locally through mission was a central priority. The third purpose, which was to participate in mission beyond the local community, was also noted by interviewees from all churches. Church leaders all described it as something that their church was committed to in both LGE and MGE churches. Therefore, across all churches the commitment to these three priorities was clearly stated by the leaders. If these espoused priorities were perfectly aligned with the enacted priorities, then all these churches would have a strong climate for local and distant mission involvement. Given that this was not the case, more careful analysis of these patterns of priorities is needed.

Several leaders from MGE churches stated that their church placed an equal emphasis on local and distant mission activities. Some leaders spoke of it as core to their church's identity and a central emphasis of their ministry.[156] A pastor at CH8 expressed this in terms of concern for distant places with fewer Christians. "We need to be reaching out with the gospel, we need to be sending people out to the unreached, or the less reached, the less resourced."[157] Similarly, the minister of CH9 believed

154. Interviews with CH1_SP, August 26, 2019; CH3_SP, August 8, 2019; CH5_CM, July 8, 2019; CH9_MC, August 29, 2019.

155. Interviews with CH3_CM, August 23, 2019; CH6_SP, May 2, 2019; CH8_SP, April 11, 2019.

156. Interviews with CH8_SP, April 11, 2019; CH4_MC, April 4, 2019.

157. Interview with CH8_SP, April 11, 2019.

that the church needed to "start with the people close to you. But in terms of mission, we also want to focus our attention on less reached areas. Places like India and Japan, the Middle East, even Europe."[158] This equal emphasis on local and distant mission also shaped the approach of CH4 where the minister encouraged people to hold together the need for mission on the three "horizons" of the local suburb, the church members' relational networks, and the nations of the world.[159] This equal prioritization of distant mission was expressed by a congregation member from CH6 who stated that, "we've always supported missionaries a lot. And we've, as a church, tried to make that a strong emphasis. Mission work is important."[160] The leaders of these MGE churches espoused an equal emphasis on local and distant mission involvement which was reflected in the views of the church's members. In these churches, the stated purposes were clearly reflected in the climate for mission, yet this was not the case in LGE churches. The minister of CH2, one of the LGE churches, also expressed a commitment to both local and distant mission. He summarized the purpose as to "make disciples not only in [the local suburb] but wherever we can reach."[161] However, the climate for distant mission involvement across this church was weak. Members were actively engaged in local mission activities but not consistently in distant mission activities.[162] Therefore, an equal emphasis on the priority of local and distant mission by church leaders does not ensure a strong climate of distant mission involvement.

Furthermore, there were several LGE church leaders that espoused a greater emphasis on local mission than on distant mission, even though they said both were important. The minister of one LGE stated that he had been helping the church members "to think about mission, and how we do that locally, and globally, but in particular, how do we do that locally."[163] This was reflected in the church's mission policy which stated that "our greatest responsibility is first and foremost to proclaim the gospel of our Lord Jesus Christ in the [local] Parish and in the wider [region] of Sydney."[164] Similarly, the minister of another LGE church stated that

158. Interview with CH9_SP, October 9, 2019.
159. Interview with CH4_SP, March 28, 2019.
160. Interview with CH6_CM, June 16, 2019.
161. Interview with CH2_SP, June 24, 2019.
162. Interviews with CH2_SP, June 24, 2019; CH2_MC, August 29, 2019.
163. Interview with CH5_SP, June 13, 2019.
164. CH5, Mission Policy, 2019.

the purpose of their church was "loving Jesus, loving each other . . . and blessing our community" noting "we have been heavily focused on local mission."[165] A member of this church affirmed this emphasis which they believed was reflected in the senior minister's use of the lifeboat imagery which emphasized saving people in the local community.[166] This focus on local mission activities was consistent with the strong climate for local mission involvement that was evident in both these churches. However, both leaders espoused a commitment to distant mission. For example, the minister of CH1 stated that "our community is not restricted to what is physically around us. And we do have a global responsibility."[167] This was therefore an espoused commitment to distant mission, but it was not reflected in the climate for mission. This was highlighted by the fact that the members of these LGE churches did not speak about the priority of distant mission in the same way as their leaders. They also spoke about it notably less than the members of MGE churches. When asked about the mission purposes of their church they emphasized the spiritual and social needs of the local community and the emphasis that their church placed on addressing these needs through local mission.[168] Though the leaders of these churches did espouse the importance of distant mission, it appears that there was disconnection between this and the climate of mission involvement. The emphasis on one mission priority appears to have led to the neglect of another.

By contrast, there were two MGE churches in which leaders similarly stated that their church had a relative emphasis on local mission, and yet there was a strong climate for both local and distant mission involvement. A minister at CH3 said, "we obviously want to keep supporting the people we sent, prayerfully, financially, and keeping our people informed. But we're more focused on the mission here in the local area."[169] Similarly, the minister at CH10 reported that when he joined the church, he was concerned that the church was placing too much emphasis on the support of distant mission but was neglecting its mission to the local community. He therefore said to the church, "The most important thing you guys are

165. Interview with CH1_SP, August 26, 2019.
166. Interview with CH1_MC, September 27, 2019.
167. Interview with CH1_SP, August 26, 2019.
168. Interviews with CH1_CM, September 26, 2019; CH5_CM, July 8, 2019; CH5_MC, July 8, 2019.
169. Interview with CH3_SP, August 8, 2019.

doing is here."[170] Since this time he has done a lot to invigorate the local mission activities and there is a strong climate for local mission involvement, yet the climate for distant mission involvement remains strong in both churches.[171] Therefore, in some churches where the leaders place a greater emphasis on local mission, the climate for distant mission is strong, yet in others the climate for distant mission is weak. In the former, the importance of both purposes is reflected in the climate for mission, yet in the latter the importance of distant mission is lost in practice. This highlights the disconnection between espoused and enacted priorities.

All the church leaders interviewed identified distant mission involvement as one of the purposes of their church. In the churches that displayed a strong climate for distant mission involvement this espoused priority was also an enacted priority. The stated priorities of the leaders were also the enacted priorities of the church members. However, in churches with a weak climate for distant mission there was clearly a lack of alignment between the espoused priorities of the leaders and the enacted priorities of the rest of the church. Given that enacted priorities are a faithful reflection of underlying missional beliefs, this situation can have two possible causes.

Firstly, the missional beliefs of the leaders may be different to the missional beliefs of the church members (see figure 7). The leader's espoused priorities may clearly reflect their own beliefs, yet the members of the church are acting on their own different set of missional beliefs. There is therefore a disconnect between the missional beliefs and priorities of the leaders and the missional beliefs and priorities of the church.

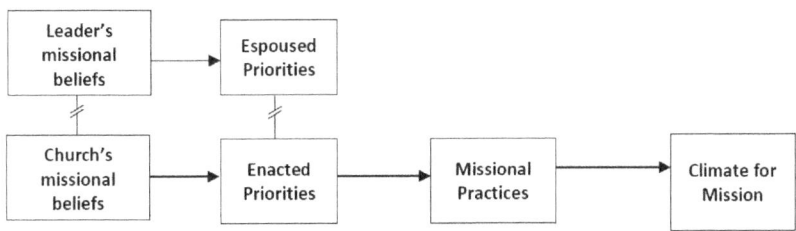

Figure 7. Espoused and Enacted Priorities Differ Due to Differing Beliefs

The second possible situation is that the leader and the church have the same missional beliefs, but the espoused priorities do not faithfully

---

170. Interview with CH10_SP, June 3, 2019.
171. Interview with CH10_MC, July 19, 2019.

reflect these beliefs (see figure 8). In this situation the leaders may state that distant mission involvement is a priority, yet their practices, processes, and policies do not reflect this. The missional climate that results reflects the true missional beliefs of leaders and members but is not consistent with the espoused priorities. In both cases there is a misalignment between the espoused priorities and the climate for mission.

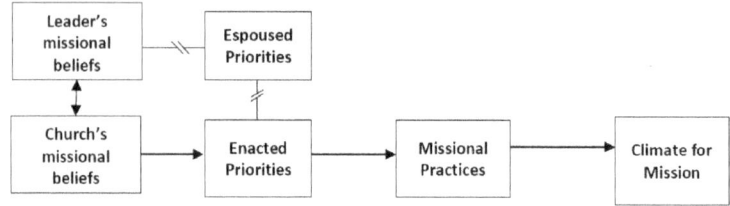

Figure 8. Misalignment between Espoused Priorities and Missional Beliefs

Cultural Integration

This misalignment between the espoused and enacted priorities may be understood as a lack of cultural integration. The concept of cultural integration comes from the work of Joanne Martin who rejects the monolithic view of organizational culture, suggesting instead that it consists of "in-depth, subjective interpretations of a wide range of cultural manifestations, both ideational and material."[172] Martin recommends assessing an organization's culture from three perspectives. An "integration view" emphasizes the dimensions of cultural consistency across the organization in which integration is defined as "those manifestations of a culture that have mutually consistent interpretations."[173] Involvement in distant mission in MGE churches could be described as an integrated dimension of the culture. A "differentiation perspective" pays greater attention to the voices of the different subcultures within an organization, noting the presence of cultural variation. An example of cultural differentiation may be evident in a church where all the elderly church members are committed to consistent prayer for mission workers, while younger members are not. Finally, a "fragmentation view" notes the ambiguity and tension around aspects of a group's culture, whereby different members of the

172. Martin, *Organizational Culture*, 120.
173. Martin, *Organizational Culture*, 93.

group will interpret different artefacts in contradictory ways.[174] Martin argues that all three perspectives may be evident at the same time within an organization, and they are all needed to fully appreciate the cultural dynamics at work.[175]

This perspective can be used to explain the cultural differences observed between MGE and LGE churches. With regards to involvement in distant mission, it could be argued that there is more cultural differentiation and fragmentation in LGE churches than there is in MGE churches. There are members and sub-groups within LGE churches that are committed to distant mission, but it is not a consistent or integrated view across the organization. In cases where these committed members are key leaders, the espoused values of the church may affirm the value of distant mission involvement, even though this value is not consistently enacted. By contrast, in MGE churches where a high degree of cultural integration is evident around mission, the patterns of mission involvement are so embedded in the culture of the church that the practices would continue even in the case of leadership change.

Martin's approach helps to explain how cultural integration may be present around one aspect of the culture, while differentiation or fragmentation may be evident around others. Those who take a monolithic view of organizational culture employ the concept of cultural strength to understand this variance. Though scholars operationalize this concept in various ways, the strength of a culture refers to the degree to which cultural values are shared among members of the group.[176] Research in the corporate sector has suggested cultural strength can be correlated with organizational success.[177] Martin's three perspectives highlight the fact that the culture may be strong (integrated) in some ways but weak (differentiated and fragmented) in others. This can be used to describe well the cultural patterns in LGE churches which show high levels of commitment to local mission activities, yet low levels of involvement in distant mission. In some ways the culture is strong. They have a high level of shared values across many dimensions of church life, yet there is notable variance when it comes to the church's approach to distant mission. It is not that distant mission is absent from the culture of the church, rather it may be more accurate to suggest that there is a weak or fragmented

174. Martin, *Organizational Culture*, 120.
175. Martin, *Organizational Culture*, 121.
176. Ehrhart et al., *Organizational Climate and Culture*, 173–74.
177. Ehrhart et al., *Organizational Climate and Culture*, 175.

culture of involvement in distant mission which manifests as a weak climate for mission.

One potential source of this cultural fragmentation regarding mission may be the changes in leadership reported in the LGE churches examined. Two of the three LGE churches had experienced a change in the church's senior leadership in the previous five years. The third had completed a recent leadership restructure including the appointment of a mission pastor. In all three cases the leaders interviewed espoused a commitment to distant mission involvement while acknowledging that this was not evident throughout the church.[178] By contrast, all but two of the MGE churches have had minimal change in leadership over the last ten years. The two that have had significant change both displayed a long history of active lay involvement in distant mission which has served to maintain the culture of involvement (CH7 and CH10). Organizational culture is slow to change.[179] Leaders can have a profound impact on the culture of a group, especially when the organization is beginning;[180] however, once established, cultural change requires far more than new actions from a senior leader.[181] The group will only change its values and priorities as experiences and insights challenge the underlying cultural assumptions. These new leaders in the LGE churches espouse a commitment to distant mission involvement, yet this aspect of the culture is currently fragmented and weak. For this to become an integrated dimension of the church's culture the missional beliefs of the leaders and members need to align with a high value of involvement in distant mission. Then it will be consistently evident in the enacted priorities and missional climate of the church.

ORGANIZATIONAL ANALYSIS CONCLUSIONS

Organizational culture and climate provide valuable perspectives from which to analyze the involvement of local churches in mission. Like any social unit, the actions of a local church are powerfully shaped by the cultural beliefs of its members. When beliefs are shared among all the

---

178. Interviews with CH1_SP, August 26, 2019; CH2_SP, June 24, 2019; CH5_SP, June 13, 2019.
179. Ehrhart et al., *Organizational Climate and Culture*, 183–84.
180. Schein, *Organizational Culture*, 235–58.
181. Ehrhart et al., *Organizational Climate and Culture*, 187–88.

members, they become evident in the priorities of the group. They inform the practices, processes, and policies which then determine the behaviors that members feel are expected of them. These expectations may be described as the climate for action. This chapter has considered the culture and climate for mission involvement among the members of MGE and LGE churches by considering the practices and processes described. Interviewees' responses across all the churches revealed clear diversity in practice in several aspects of mission involvement. In the cases of prayer, finances, training, and leadership for distant mission involvement, MGE churches displayed consistently strong climates for participation even though they employed a variety of approaches. The common feature was that church members saw participation as a natural part of group membership, and they believed that their contribution was worthwhile. By contrast, LGE church practices produced a weak climate for distant mission involvement. The ways that these churches approached these various activities led members of these churches to see participation in distant mission as an optional activity that was often supplanted by local mission needs.

This weak climate was evident in LGE churches even though the leaders espoused a commitment to distant mission. There was a lack of alignment between the espoused priorities of the leaders and the enacted priorities of the members. The beliefs and values shaping behavior were inconsistent with the espoused values resulting in cultural fragmentation and a weak climate for mission. In some cases, this fragmentation had been exacerbated by leadership changes but the practices around prayer, finances, training for mission, and missional leadership were not strengthening the climate. This organizational analysis of these churches has demonstrated several key factors that influence the involvement of these evangelical churches in mission. Chapters 4 and 5 demonstrated the similarity of both ecclesiological and missiological beliefs among all these churches while noting some differences of emphasis. In this chapter the impact of these differences was evident in the practices and processes shaping the culture and climate for mission; however, the causes of these differences have not been discussed. In the next chapter, the final core category identified through the analysis of interview data is explored and its role in shaping these missiological emphases considered.

7

Relational Networks and Social Capital

INTRODUCTION

The preceding chapters have explored the impact of ecclesiology, missiology, and organizational practices, cultures, and climates on local church mission involvement. Through these analyses, it was noted that there is great theological similarity among all the churches examined, yet differences in missiological emphasis which shape the culture and climate for mission involvement through a variety of church practices. The fourth core category identified through data analysis was relational network differences between LGE and MGE churches. The relationships between the church's leaders and members have already been discussed regarding the culture and climate of mission involvement. Yet, it was the relationships that extended beyond the church's local community that were noted to be most different between LGE and MGE churches. There were differences in the objects of these relationships. Some people highlighted the recipients of the mission activity and others focused on the mission agent. Some interviewees spoke about the individuals serving as mission workers and others only the organizations. Different terms were employed to describe these relationships. While most people spoke of "support" for mission workers or organizations, some interviewees intentionally used the language of "partnership." However, the most important differences between MGE and LGE churches were in the history, depth, and vitality of these relationships. MGE churches not only had connections to more distant mission workers than LGE churches, but these relationships were deeper, had greater historical significance, richer communication patterns, and committed patterns of mutuality. This chapter explores these relational differences and employs the perspectives of social exchange and social capital theory to understand the profound influence that they have in shaping the missiological emphases and patterns of mission involvement of these churches.

MISSION AGENTS AND RECIPIENTS

When discussing the involvement of churches in distant mission, interviewees in both MGE and LGE churches spoke about connections that they had to people and organizations that were engaged in these activities. These contacts were primarily the agents of mission through whom the churches worked in distant contexts. As one member of an LGE church said, "I think our main [mission] involvement is through partners . . . like missionaries or missionary families . . . [W]e also have a partnership with Compassion."[1] The primary focus of these discussions was on processes employed to support and care for mission workers. In MGE churches, interviewees tended to highlight the relational and prayer processes through which they related to the mission agents,[2] while interviewees from LGE churches were more likely to focus on the financial dimension of their mission support and to equate the level of their involvement with the amount of money that was being given.[3] As one minister of an LGE church said, "the way we show . . . our support, one of the big ways, is obviously financially."[4] This financial support lens made the mission involvement task more discrete and easier to measure. Interviewees from all churches spoke about their connections to mission organizations, missionaries, and mission partners when describing their involvement in distant mission. The language of "sending" was used by some interviewees to encompass the various elements of the connection between their church and a distant mission worker, particularly where the worker had

1. Interview with CH1_MC, September 27, 2019.
2. Interviews with CH8_MC, May 30, 2019; CH9_MC, August 29, 2019; CH4_SP, March 28, 2019.
3. Interviews with CH3_MC, September 2, 2019; CH5_SP, June 13, 2019; CH1_CM, September 26, 2019. This was also evident among some members of MGE churches, though it was less common.
4. Interview with CH5_SP, June 13, 2019.

been a member of the church.⁵ As one MGE church leader said, "We're kind of sending people out ... [and we] want to keep supporting the people we sent: prayerfully, financially, and keeping our people informed."⁶ Another MGE church leader spoke of sending people out as a goal for his church, "We want to raise up missionaries from this church to send out."⁷ Therefore, in all these churches, both LGE and MGE, the distant mission involvement happened primarily through relational connection to mission workers with notably less emphasis on the people that these workers were living and serving amongst. In other words, it was the mission agent rather than the recipient that was primarily considered.

There were a limited number of cases in which interviewees spoke about the recipients, rather than the agents, of mission. This was most often when they were speaking about short-term mission trips and prayer. Several interviewees spoke of their church sending teams of church members on short-term mission trips to serve in regional parts of Australia or overseas.⁸ In most cases these trips were described as ways to either support distant mission workers or to inform and inspire members of the church to be more engaged in mission, in these ways they were primarily focused on the mission agent. However, in some MGE churches short-term trips were described as a way that the church was directly involved in distant mission work. For example, the minister at CH6 encouraged participation in short-term mission trips because "the mission committee is keen for our missionary involvement to not simply be in sending other people and financing other people, but the church actually recognizing that this is central to who we are."⁹ This reflects a realization that direct participation in distant mission is a highly valued activity and short-term mission was considered a way to achieve this. Prayer was another way that interviewees spoke about being directly involved in mission to the recipients rather than just the agents, particularly when praying for Christians living in contexts of persecution or places where

---

5. The minister at CH5 (an LGE church) also uses the "sending" language to describe efforts to mobilize the members of the church to engage in mission in their local community. Though this was an uncommon usage amongst interviewees. Interviews with CH5_SP, June 13, 2019; CH6_SP, May 2, 2019; CH3_SP, August 8, 2019; CH8_MC, May 30, 2019.

6. Interview with CH3_SP, August 8, 2019.

7. Interview with CH8_SP, April 11, 2019.

8. Interviews with CH1_SP, August 26, 2019; CH4_MC, April 4, 2019; CH6_CM, June 16, 2019; CH8_SP, April 11, 2019.

9. Interview with CH6_SP, May 2, 2019.

there was very little access to Christian teaching.[10] Therefore, through prayer and short-term mission church members were able to be directly involved in distant mission, but generally they participated through mission agents.

These opportunities for direct involvement, though mentioned less often, were seen to be highly valued. Some interviewees even expressed the view that concern for the recipients, as well as the agents, was evidence of a more meaningful engagement.[11] As one MGE church member stated,

> I think it used to be more, "I'm supporting the missionary" but I think we've grown to understand God's mission better ... I would like to see more people understand what ministry is for our missionaries and pray for the ministry as much as our missionary.[12]

This emphasis on the contexts and recipients of the distant mission worker was only evident in churches that showed high levels of engagement with distant mission. One paradoxical exception was a leader from an LGE church who described how he had highlighted the work that a particular mission worker was doing to motivate church members to support her.[13] He felt that this was needed because the worker did not attend the church and there was no relational motivation for involvement. By helping the church to see the value of the work being done, he believed it would help them to commit and the relationship could develop over time. Therefore, distant mission involvement was invariably mediated through agents of distant mission rather than church members attending to the recipients of mission directly. This was evident in both LGE and MGE churches, though among some interviewees from MGE churches the desire for greater engagement with the recipients was noted as a valuable goal.

INDIVIDUALS AND ORGANIZATIONS IN MISSION

Though interviewees from both LGE and MGE churches spoke about the agents of mission they supported for the purposes of distant mission, there were some differences regarding whether the agents were individuals or

10. Interviews with CH1_SP, August 26, 2019; CH10_MC, July 19, 2019.
11. Interviews with CH6_CM, June 16, 2019; CH8_MC, May 30, 2019.
12. Interview with CH8_MC, May 30, 2019.
13. Interview with CH2_SP, June 24, 2019.

organizations. The preference for supporting individuals rather than organizations was particularly strong in MGE churches. When asked about his church's connection to mission organizations one interviewee from an MGE church said, "We lean towards more of the people, rather than the organizations."[14] Similarly another MGE church interviewee said, "I know [our mission workers] are with [a mission agency], but we partner with the individuals more than the organization."[15] One church leader suggested that this reflected a generational change that his church was adjusting to, "I think we're discovering it is hard for people under forty to actually support missionaries they don't know. People aren't committed to the [one mission organization]. They're not committed to the [another mission organization]."[16] This observation is consistent with what was seen in other churches. There were several churches that gave financial support to organizations but identified key members of those organizations, who were known to the church members, as representatives of that organization.[17] In one MGE church, their support of a denominational social service organization was associated with a chaplain within the organization who was known to many of the church members. As the minister said, "It's an organization that we're supporting but we try to put a personal face to it."[18] This was consistent with this church's policy documents which stated "we aim to focus on particular people rather than organizations."[19] Similarly, a church member from another MGE church spoke about their support of a theological college in India which had been strengthened by having had one of the staff from the college attend the church a number of times. She said, "It's really nice for there to be a warm personal connection. Not just throwing money at a college, but this is [this person's] school."[20] These MGE church members emphasized the individuals because they had a significant relational connection with them; they were more than a means to participating in distant mission.

This emphasis on individuals was much less evident in LGE churches where interviewees more often spoke about their church's connection to organizations. When asked how their church was involved

14. Interview with CH8_CM, May 22, 2019.
15. Interview with CH3_CM, August 23, 2019.
16. Interview with CH2_SP, June 24, 2019.
17. Interviews with CH4_SP, March 28, 2019; CH3_MC, September 2, 2019.
18. Interview with CH4_SP, March 28, 2019.
19. CH4, Mission Partnership Principles, December 2013.
20. Interview with CH9_MC, August 29, 2019.

in mission beyond the local community, one church member from an LGE church replied, "It's focused around probably the work of [a mission organization]."[21] This church supported two overseas mission workers with this organization, neither of whom had a prior association with the church. The minister stated that the connection with these workers began when he approached the organization asking them to recommend people to support.[22] When asked why they approached this organization, both the minister and another church member stated that it was expected because of the denominational connections between their church and the organization.[23] The interviewees from this church also spoke of their support for a Christian radio organization without any reference to individuals associated with it.[24] The minister of another LGE church similarly described the strong historical connections that his church had to organizations, "So, traditionally [this church] has been very strongly supporting [this organization], [that organization], and . . . [another organization] as well."[25] He later commented on the difficulty he sees in engaging younger people in organizational support and is therefore seeking to focus more on individual mission workers in the future. The minister of the third LGE church also emphasized the church's connections to organizations. The first reference made to involvement in distant mission was in discussing the church's support for Compassion.[26] When asked about other ways that the church was involved in distant mission they responded, "We have missionaries that we support both with [one organization] and [another organization]."[27] A member of this church responded to this question in a similar way, emphasizing the mission workers' organizational affiliations.[28] This emphasis on the organization was not evident among interviewees from MGE churches.

This tendency to emphasize the organization rather than the individual suggests a lower level of personal connectedness to distant mission in general. Interviewees from churches with high levels of involvement

21. Interview with CH5_CM, July 8, 2019.
22. Interview with CH5_SP, June 13, 2019.
23. Interviews with CH5_SP, June 13, 2019; CH5_MC, July 8, 2019.
24. Interviews with CH5_SP, June 13, 2019; CH5_MC, July 8, 2019; CH5_CM, July 8, 2019.
25. Interview with CH2_SP, June 24, 2019.
26. Interview with CH1_SP, August 26, 2019.
27. Interview with CH1_SP, August 26, 2019.
28. Interview with CH1_MC, September 27, 2019.

in distant mission were more likely to speak of the individuals that they partnered with. They did mention the organizations that they are connected to, but their emphasis was on the people. The minister of one MGE church suggested this was because of the mutual nature of these connections, "Our mission partners contribute something significant to the life of our church, not just that our church contributes something significant to the life of their work in another place."[29] However, the interviewees from LGE churches did not speak of benefits that came from their organizational connections. It was simply spoken of as the way that the church contributed to distant mission. There was a recognition in these churches that distant mission was an important activity for a church, but due to the differing missiological emphasis it was considered a secondary purpose which is best accomplished by specialist organizations. This emphasis on organizations in LGE churches reflects a tendency to delegate responsibility for distant mission to these independent organizations. The churches could give some money and pray, but the organization would meet the need. In churches that emphasized the personal relationship with individual mission workers, the church members felt a greater level of engagement with the distant mission task.

HISTORY OF CHURCH—WORKER RELATIONSHIPS

The strength of these personal relationships between a church and a distant mission worker was often a consequence of the long time that the mission worker had been connected to the church. Interviewees from MGE churches consistently reported more significant historical associations with mission workers than interviewees from LGE churches. All the MGE churches supported mission workers that were previously members of the church. For many of them the workers had previously been employed by the church in a formal ministry capacity before they began their distant mission role.[30] For one of these churches it was a policy requirement that they only supported mission workers who had been members of their church.[31] Although some MGE churches would support workers that had not previously attended, there was always another

---

29. Interview with CH4_SP, March 28, 2019.

30. Interviews with CH3_MC, September 2, 2019; CH4_SP, March 28, 2019; CH6_MC, June 16, 2019; CH7_SP, August 12, 2019; CH9_SP, October 9, 2019.

31. CH8, Mission Guidelines and Policies, Version 5, 2014.

important relational connection. For example, in addition to supporting several former church members, one MGE church supported the daughter of a couple who had attended the church for many years.[32] These personal relationships were considered necessary to facilitate meaningful engagement. As an MGE minister stated, "You've got much better communication and insight and stories back and forth and encouragement, and I think it works."[33] This was not easy to facilitate where the relationship was missing, as one MGE church members noted, "When someone from our church goes, there's always a lot of support, because we know them ... but as a complete stranger, it's hard."[34] For this reason, the relationships between the MGE churches and the mission workers invariably predated their missionary service.

The one exception to this pattern was in MGE churches that supported national mission workers who were indigenous to their context of service. One church supported a national church leader in an African nation and listed him as one of their mission partners alongside Australians serving in various countries.[35] This person had never attended the church but the relationship began after a key member of the church worked in his country and recommended that the church commit to supporting him.[36] Similarly, another MGE church supported European workers based in their home country who had a long relationship with the wife of the church's senior minister.[37] These indigenous workers were already engaged in ministry before the relationship with the church member began, yet it was the relationship that led to the church's connection and support.

These substantial relational connections between the church and the mission worker provided significant depth to the relational bond. Members of the congregation tended to value these relational bonds and build upon them through ongoing communication while the worker was away. Several interviewees noted that relational connections like these were a prerequisite when considering whether to support a new distant mission worker. One member of the mission committee at CH3 stated that when considering a mission worker for support, the strength of the relational

32. Interview with CH9_MC, August 29, 2019.
33. Interview with CH10_SP, June 3, 2019.
34. Interview with CH6_CM, June 16, 2019.
35. CH4, Mission Partners, 2019.
36. Interview with CH4_MC, April 4, 2019.
37. Interview with CH9_SP, October 9, 2019.

connection was one of the first criteria they considered. The reason given was that "it just makes it easier to get people behind them."[38]

The typical pattern described by the interviewees in LGE churches suggests a much less significant background relationship with mission workers. In one LGE church the workers had no relationship to the church at all before they began their missionary service.[39] In another LGE church that supported two mission workers neither had previously attended the church. One was a relative of a former member of the church and the other was known to the senior minister and serving with a trusted mission organization.[40] The third LGE church did support former members serving as distant mission workers, yet had not maintained those relational connections with the current church members.[41] Previously this church had a very high level of involvement in distant mission and its policy was to only support mission workers that had attended the church.[42] Several mission workers had been sent out from the church in the past and several returned mission workers still attend. However, in the previous five to ten years many of these mission workers had completed their mission service and the relationship with the church has ceased. It had been many years since the church sent out any of its own members to serve in distant mission work. There were only two remaining supported distant mission workers, both of whom were previously members of the church, however, they were sent out many years ago and most of the current church attendees did not know them.[43] In this situation, whatever relational strength may have been present due to the prior connection had been lost though limited ongoing contact.

COMMUNICATION AND CHURCH—WORKER RELATIONSHIPS

The deterioration in these relationships highlights the importance of ongoing communication to maintain these long-term connections. Interviewees from churches with high levels of engagement in distant mission

38. Interview with CH3_MC, September 2, 2019.
39. Interview with CH5_SP, June 13, 2019.
40. Interview with CH1_CM, September 26, 2019.
41. Interview with CH2_MC, August 29, 2019.
42. Interview with CH2_MC, August 29, 2019.
43. Interview with CH2_MC, August 29, 2019.

reported more regular and meaningful communication with distant mission workers than those from churches with lower levels of engagement. This communication took a range of different forms, utilized a variety of media, and differed in how many church members it engaged. LGE church interviewees described channels of communication through which they were kept informed about the progress and needs of the mission worker. This was primarily informational and was given for the express purpose of guiding the church members' prayers.[44] Interviewees from MGE churches also received this kind of communication but spoke of various other opportunities through which they were encouraged to engage with the mission workers personally.[45] This stimulus to relationship was evident across the MGE churches with a particular emphasis on providing opportunities for mission workers to communicate directly with the whole church. One MGE church required that mission workers, "be presented to each congregation to share their ministry and be affirmed by the whole church" before they would agree to support them.[46] Even though this church would only partner with mission workers that were members of the church, they did this to ensure that they were known by all the congregations.[47] While the worker was away, there were opportunities to bring communication from them to the whole church. This included regular updates in the Sunday gatherings through a short presentation or video.[48] This served to maintain the relational connection between the church and the mission worker.

Interviewees from all churches described systems to provide updates and other communication from the mission workers; however, in MGE churches these systems were more fully developed and effective. All churches gave mission workers opportunity to share in a church service when they were able to attend. Many MGE churches also hosted extra events that profiled the mission workers and provided opportunities to engage directly with the church members.[49] One large MGE church would host a mission breakfast three or four times a year at which distant mission workers could give an extended presentation about their work.[50]

44. Interviews with CH2_MC, August 29, 2019; CH5_SP, June 13, 2019.
45. Interviews with CH9_CM, September 10, 2019; CH3_MC, September 2, 2019.
46. CH8, Mission Guidelines and Policies, Version 5, 2014.
47. Interview with CH8_MC, May 30, 2019.
48. Interview with CH8_MC, May 30, 2019.
49. Interviews with CH4_SP, March 28, 2019.
50. Interviews with CH3_MC, September 2, 2019.

Those who attended would not only hear from and engage with the mission workers but would spend time together in prayer for them and their ministry. Several MGE churches incorporated communication from the mission workers into their regular prayer meetings and devoted a significant portion of the time to prayer for these distant needs.[51] The minister of one MGE church would contact their mission partners at least monthly to ensure they were aware of current prayer needs, though he noted that the church members were also regularly in communication with the partners.[52] The mission coordinator at another MGE church encouraged the mission workers to provide personal stories from their ministry that could be shared with the congregation to stimulate connection.[53] Three other MGE churches had one month a year during which there was a focus on distant mission and during the Sunday gatherings, in addition to mission focused teaching, there were detailed updates from the workers they supported.[54] The frequency and depth of communication in MGE churches was notably greater than in similar-sized LGE churches, even where similar modes of communication were being employed.

In addition to this broadcast communication, interviewees from MGE churches spoke of the encouragement towards direct personal communication with mission workers. This was often facilitated through the mid-week small group meetings of church members. Interviewees from five of the MGE churches said their small groups were encouraged to "adopt" a mission worker each year and commit to supporting them directly.[55] This support included regular communication, such as personal emails, sending gift packages, or video calls. The mission coordinator at one MGE church encouraged the small groups to "pray weekly, write quarterly, [and] Skype yearly."[56] The minister of another MGE church spoke of the connections between small groups and mission workers as key to the relationship between the church and the mission worker. He stated that these connections "would really try to develop . . . a more

---

51. Interviews with CH3_SP, August 8, 2019; CH4_CM, May 7, 2019; CH6_MC, June 16, 2019; CH10_MC, July 19, 2019.

52. Interview with CH7_SP, August 12, 2019.

53. Interview with CH10_MC, July 19, 2019.

54. Interviews with CH6_SP, May 2, 2019; CH8_MC, May 30, 2019; CH9_MC, August 29, 2019.

55. Interviews with CH3_MC, September 2, 2019; CH4_SP, March 28, 2019: CH6_SP, May 2, 2019; CH8_SP, April 11, 2019; CH9_CM, September 10, 2019.

56. Interview with CH9_MC, August 29, 2019.

regular, communicative sort of relationship."[57] The mission coordinator at CH8 similarly spoke of "a more grassroots level" of engagement between the church members and the mission workers, "People actually have connections with our missionaries. And personal connections so that they know who they are."[58] A congregation member of CH9 noted his appreciation for the video calls between his small group and a mission worker overseas, "because a prayer letter will only tell you so much . . . it's great to sort of hear from her what's going on."[59]

This emphasis on mutual communication was a core dimension of the strong relational connection between MGE churches and their mission workers. The mission coordinator at CH9 helped the church members to communicate via birthday cards, letters, gifts, and video calls.[60] The pastor at CH8 spoke of an evening that the youth group spent writing letters to the mission workers and their children.[61] Several other MGE churches also sought to keep workers informed about the significant events and activities of the church by sending regular updates to the workers. The importance of this two-way communication was highlighted by the experience of one MGE church that showed a lower score for distant mission involvement in the survey.[62] This was a large church with multiple congregations that supported a significant number of workers, most of whom had previously been members of the church. There was a comparatively high level of financial support and regular reports in the church from the mission workers. Yet, all three interviewees noted that the communication from the church to the mission workers had been lacking. They reported how one of the mission workers had told them that they had felt unsupported by the church because of this lack of mutual communication. This was one of the factors reflected in the survey result. All churches supporting distant mission had some means of communication with their workers, yet the churches with higher levels of distant mission engagement had rich channels of mutual communication. Church members were kept well informed about the needs and situation of the distant workers and were encouraged to engage with these workers directly. This communication engaged people from across the church

57. Interview with CH4_SP, March 28, 2019.
58. Interview with CH8_MC, May 30, 2019.
59. Interview with CH9_CM, September 10, 2019.
60. Interview with CH9_MC, August 29, 2019.
61. Interview with CH8_SP, April 11, 2019.
62. Interview with CH6_SP, May 2, 2019.

membership and they intentionally employed diverse means of two-way communication to help church members feel meaningfully connected to the mission workers.

PARTNERSHIP IN CHURCH—WORKER RELATIONSHIPS

This desire for meaningful engagement reflects the perceived emphasis in MGE churches on the desire for partnership with their mission workers.[63] The language of mission partners was used by several interviewees in both MGE and LGE churches to highlight the belief that distant mission workers were an extension of the mission of the local church.[64] Four of the ten church leaders intentionally used partner and partnership language to describe their connections to distant mission. Three of these were MGE churches and one was an LGE church.[65] This language was clarified by one MGE church leader in an internal church document.

> Partnerships need to be thought about in terms of, for example, commitment over time, deepening relationships, persevering prayer, clear communication. They are not characterized by patronage or distance, rather by covenantal commitment and genuine relationship.[66]

The pastor from one of the LGE churches also referred to the people and organizations that the church worked with as mission partners and had recently renamed the church's mission committee the mission partnership team.[67] Similarly, the minister of another LGE church talked about his efforts to establish a connection with a new mission worker because he believed that they "would do really well in partnering [with her] and [it would] be mutually beneficial."[68] This concept of mutuality was key to

---

63. This language is adopted from Philippians 1:5 where the term καινωνία is translated as "partnership" (NIV11, ESV, CSB), "fellowship" (ASV, NKJV), or "sharing" (NRSV). See O'Brien, "Fellowship Theme," 9–18.

64. This is the language used at CH3, CH4, CH6, CH9, and CH10.

65. Interviews with CH1_SP, August 26, 2019; CH4_SP, March 28, 2019; CH9_SP, October 9, 2019; CH10_SP, June 3, 2019.

66. CH10, Missions Strategy and Direction, August 31, 2017.

67. Interview with CH1_SP, August 26, 2019.

68. Interview with CH2_SP, June 24, 2019.

the partnership language, even though in both cases in LGE churches it was spoken of as a future goal rather than a present reality.[69]

In some MGE churches the partnership language was only used to describe the relationships with churches and organizations working within Australia. A church member from one MGE church spoke about a partnership with a nearby Christian school in which students from the school were encouraged to visit the church as part of their Christian studies classes.[70] A church member from another MGE church spoke about a partnership that they had with a refugee support service which involved donating food and clothing as well as visiting some of the refugees.[71] Interviewees from a third MGE church used the partnership language to describe their collaborations with other churches to host events and run evangelistic activities.[72] This makes it clear that the partnership language refers to relationships in which both parties are meaningfully engaged in the same task.

Though partnership language was used by several interviewees, the more common language employed to describe connections with mission workers beyond the church was "support." Interviewees from both LGE and MGE churches spoke of supporting mission workers and mission organizations. In many cases support was used as a synonym for financial support. However, the terms have apparent semantic overlap as interviewees in churches that preferred the language of partnership often spoke of supporting their partners. Nevertheless, the preference for partnership terms did reflect a greater desire for mutuality and deeper engagement with the mission worker. It indicated that the church members were seeking to participate in the mission work rather than simply enable someone else to do it.

Some of the MGE churches sought to formalize their partnership relationships through written agreements. These documents detailed the responsibilities of both the church and the mission worker through the time of their association. One MGE church had a two-page document which listed their commitment to pray, give financially, and care for the mission worker, together with their expectation that the worker would "serve Christ faithfully," communicate regularly, pray for the church,

---

69. Interview with CH2_SP, June 24, 2019. It is notable that neither of the members of this church used the language of partnership in their interviews.

70. Interview with CH3_CM, August 23, 2019.

71. Interview with CH7_MC, September 2, 2019.

72. Interview with CH8_SP, April 11, 2019; CH8_MC, May 30, 2019.

and visit whenever possible.[73] As a particular expression of the church's desire for mutuality this document contained an explicit request for honest communication.[74] Another MGE church expressed its desire for partnership through a detailed policy outlining the ways in which the church's mission committee would prepare, support, and care for the mission workers.[75] Workers were expected to communicate regularly with the church including efforts to serve the church directly by seeking to "promote mission mindedness in church members" when they could.[76]

Another key expression of partnership articulated by interviewees from MGE churches was the regular encouragement from church leaders for members to personally participate in the ministry of the mission workers. The small groups at one MGE were asked to host breakfast events for their adopted mission workers when they were visiting the church.[77] In this way, the group members helped the whole church to partner with the mission workers. The mission coordinator from another MGE church reported how a small group from her church was involved in an information night that the worker they supported had put on for the benefit of the wider Christian community.[78] The worker had commented to the mission coordinator that no other church had ever been so engaged with his ministry.[79] Some MGE churches sought to strengthen their partnerships with mission workers by visiting them. The minister of CH4 was sent overseas with the support of the church to visit the mission workers in their own contexts.[80] These visits not only encouraged the worker but helped the minister to inform the church about the specific issues that the mission worker faced.[81] He felt this trip was so valuable that he intended to do similar trips in the future. Interviewees at three other MGE churches also reported that church members or staff had visited their mission workers.[82] These visits and practical expressions of

---

73. CH4, Mission Partner Relationships, June 2015.
74. CH4, Mission Partner Relationships, June 2015.
75. CH8, Mission Guidelines and Policies, Version 5, 2014.
76. CH8, Mission Guidelines and Policies, Version 5, 2014.
77. Interview with CH3_MC, September 2, 2019.
78. Interview with CH9_MC, August 29, 2019.
79. Interview with CH9_MC, August 29, 2019.
80. Interview with CH4_SP, March 28, 2019.
81. Interview with CH4_SP, March 28, 2019.
82. Interviews with CH6_SP, May 2, 2019; CH7_MC, September 2, 2019; CH9_SP, October 9, 2019.

partnership further deepened the relational bonds between the churches and the mission workers, even when only a few members were involved.

Several MGE churches demonstrated their desire for partnership by structuring their support of mission workers in ways that encouraged meaningful relationships to develop. The mission coordinator of CH9 noted that the church had eleven distant mission partners, however members were encouraged to prioritize their relationship with the worker that their small group had adopted.[83] "We say, 'You don't have to know all of them, . . . just focus on your one and know them well.'"[84] Another MGE church had a total of nineteen individuals or organizations that were considered mission partners, yet they categorized them as either first or second tier.[85] There was a limit of eight first tier, or "special focus," partners who had a higher profile, were prayed for and spoken of more often, and received a higher level of funding. According to the church policy documents, "this option enables us to be generous out of our wealth in support of good ministry elsewhere, without overwhelming the congregations with too many "special focus" partners and thereby diluting engagement."[86] A third MGE church encouraged each of its four congregations to develop "covenantal commitment and genuine relationship" with five or six mission partners for similar reasons.[87] There were ten to twelve mission partners supported across the whole parish, but the primary focus was on the relationships from each congregation. The minister described this as "relational prioritization" because he wanted to make personal commitment to the mission partners of greater importance than the financial support.[88] In all these ways the goal of partnership with distant mission workers was encouraged in MGE churches. This emphasis on relational connections in MGE churches was a key dimension of their approach to mission involvement that was not evident in LGE churches.

83. Interview with CH9_MC, August 29, 2019.
84. Interview with CH9_MC, August 29, 2019.
85. Interview with CH4_SP, March 28, 2019.
86. CH4, Mission Partnership Principles, December 2013.
87. CH10, Missions Strategy and Directions, August 31, 2017.
88. Interview with CH10_SP, June 3, 2019.

ORGANIZATIONAL CONNECTIONS

In addition to the relational connections to mission workers reported by interviewees, there were several Christian parachurch organizations that played a role in the mission involvement of these local churches. Though relationships with individual mission workers were the primary means by which the churches engaged in distant mission, most of these workers were members of mission organizations. Several churches even required that the mission workers they partner with be associated with an evangelical mission organization which provided the logistical systems to support the workers.[89] Interviewees named ten international mission organizations that they partnered with.[90] Two churches had partners serving overseas with Pioneers, two had partners serving with SIM, and two had partners serving with ECM. Five churches had partners serving overseas with OMF and all ten churches had partners either currently serving overseas with CMS or they had previously. Though Compassion does not send partners overseas, interviewees from four churches reported having regular engagement with this organization. There were an additional three organizations that were mentioned which work only within Australia.[91] Although these many organizations were identified as involved in the mission activities of the church, only four organizations were seen by interviewees as influencing the way their churches behaved. Two of these are mission sending organizations, CMS and OMF, one an international child development organization, Compassion, and the fourth is a network of trainers, consultants and organizations focused on multiplying healthy churches in Australia, Reach Australia.

CMS is one of the largest and oldest missionary organizations in Australia. Descended from the Church Missionary Society founded in England in 1799, it was founded as an Australian mission society in 1916.[92] Though not officially an Anglican organization, CMS has a strong relationship with the Sydney Anglican Diocese and was seen by

---

89. Interview with CH4_MC, April 4, 2019; CH2, Mission Policy; CH8, Mission Policy and Guidelines.

90. These were Global Interaction (now Baptist Mission Australia), CMS, European Christian Mission (ECM), Far East Broadcasting Company, Interserve, OMF, Pioneers, SIM, WEC, and Compassion.

91. These were Australian Indigenous Ministries (AIM), Australian Fellowship of Evangelical Students (AFES), and Reach Australia.

92. CMS Australia, "History."

many interviewees in Anglican churches as their default organization.[93] One Anglican minister described this as "the Sydney Diocese and CMS connection."[94] The influence of CMS on Sydney evangelical churches is evidenced by the fact that every church approached for interviews either presently or previously had supported mission workers through the organization. Several church leaders reported approaching CMS when they were looking for new mission workers to support.[95] These mission workers are typically linked to six or eight churches that give donations to CMS for their financial support. There was a perception among some interviewees that the model of missionary support that CMS previously employed assumed relational distance between the church and the mission worker. One minister spoke of "CMS kind of missionaries" and stated,

> In the old days they'd go, "Right! This church, this church, this church—you'll support this person." And everyone goes, "Yeah, awesome." Now days if you told me, "Here's a ten thousand dollar tax on your church to support this person," you'd go, "Thank you very much, no thanks."

Though he did not suggest this is how the organization works now, it was a model of mission involvement historically associated with the organization.

One of the regular points of contact between church members and CMS mentioned by interviewees from both LGE and MGE churches was the annual CMS conference. Many of the interviewees reported that church members and ministers would attend the conference every year.[96] One church member spoke of how this helped her to understand the contexts of the mission workers and to encourage others at the church to pray for them.[97] However, an interviewee from another church had not observed any significant impact on those who attend. She said, "Even when they come back from [the conference], I haven't heard much

---

93. Interview with CH2_MC, August 29, 2019.

94. Interview with CH5_SP, June 13, 2019.

95. Interviews with CH5_SP, June 13, 2019; CH2_SP, June 24, 2019; CH1_SP, August 26, 2019.

96. Interviews with CH2_MC, August 29, 2019; CH2_CM, September 2, 2019; CH3_SP, August 8, 2019; CH3_MC, September 2, 2019; CH5_SP, June 13, 2019; CH5_CM, July 8, 2019; CH5_MC, July 8, 2019.

97. Interview with CH5_CM, July 8, 2019.

enthusiasm."[98] These organizational connections between the churches and CMS had therefore been important for establishing relationships with mission workers, but there was little indication that they strengthened the climate of mission involvement in the church.

The other organization that was discussed by interviewees as being more than just a structure for sending mission workers was OMF.[99] Formerly known as the China Inland Mission, OMF has mission workers throughout East Asia and among Asian diaspora communities all over the world. Interviewees from five churches reported a connection between their church and OMF. The two Chinese MGE churches had particularly strong connections to the organization. Both churches had several members serving as mission workers with OMF and the pastor from one of these churches described OMF as "our natural ally or contact."[100] In both cases the organization had been involved in coordinating short term mission trips and prayer meetings that church members had been involved in.[101] Involvement in these OMF activities had strengthened these people's understanding of mission and encouraged them to get more involved.[102] Church members from both churches noted that the relational connections with OMF had led to church members becoming mission workers overseas with the organization. As one noted, "We've built good connections with various people in OMF. And I think that lends people to more easily go to OMF."[103] Another member of this church referred to the "OMF ways to be involved" as a resource that the church used to inform their efforts to encourage people to participate more fully in distant mission.[104] In these ways the interactions with OMF in these churches appear to have strengthened the climate for mission in some ways.

One non-sending international mission organization that was noted for its relationship with several churches was Compassion. Compassion is a "Christian international holistic child development organization" that provides child sponsorship opportunities which are administered by

---

98. Interview with CH2_MC, August 29, 2019.

99. https://omf.org.

100. Interview with CH6_SP, May 2, 2019.

101. Interviews with CH6_CM, June 16, 2019; CH8_MC, May 30, 2019.

102. Interviews with CH6_CM, June 16, 2019; CH8_CM, May 22, 2019.

103. Interview with CH6_CM, June 16, 2019.

104. Interview with CH6_MC, June 16, 2019. This is a reference to OMF, "6 Ways to Reach God's World."

local churches in developing countries.¹⁰⁵ Interviewees from four of the churches, one LGE and three MGE, described a connection to Compassion.¹⁰⁶ This included presentations from Compassion representatives annually or less often and a number of church members sponsoring children directly. An interviewee from one of these churches was the "church's representative for Compassion," a role which she said, "doesn't involve much except for a once-a-year slot, just reminding everyone about the work of Compassion and giving them the opportunity to sponsor people if they haven't."¹⁰⁷ These limited relationships were not described as a key part of these churches' mission involvement. However, one LGE church had a much more significant relationship with Compassion which had been growing in intensity over the previous couple of years.¹⁰⁸ Church staff had been meeting with Compassion staff regularly, each congregation had church members who were designated Compassion advocates, and a Compassion staff member had been invited to preach in the church services.¹⁰⁹ This input had resulted in more than 40 percent of the church members becoming child sponsors through the organization.¹¹⁰ The church also formed a regional partnership with Compassion which sought to focus on one overseas region to develop more direct relationships between their church and the churches overseas that worked with Compassion. The church was planning its first short term mission trip to visit these churches, until it was cancelled due to the COVID-19 pandemic. The minister's hope for this partnership was that it would result in church members "getting to know churches in [that country], and praying for the pastors there, and being encouraged by the work of the gospel in that place." Though this was expressed as a future hope, if it were to happen then these experiences may well have strengthened the climate for distant mission involvement in this LGE church.

The final organization, Reach Australia, was only mentioned by interviewees from one LGE church, yet they believed it had influenced the missional culture of the church. Reach Australia is a collaboration of Australian church and ministry leaders that provides church consultations,

105. Compassion, "About Us."
106. Interviews with CH2_MC, August 29, 2019; CH4_CM, May 7, 2019; CH6_CM, June 16, 2019; CH9_MC, August 29, 2019.
107. Interview with CH4_CM, May 7, 2019.
108. Interview with CH1_CM, September 26, 2019.
109. Interview with CH1_SP, August 26, 2019.
110. Interview with CH1_SP, August 26, 2019.

and hosts training events and conferences. The organization's vision is to equip church and ministry leaders with the goal of seeing "healthy, evangelistic, and multiplying churches reaching the lost across Australia."[111] As the vision of the organization indicates, there is a primary emphasis on mission within Australia through local evangelism and planting churches. One of the contributing ministries to Reach Australia is Vine Growers, which helps churches apply the approach to church ministry promoted by Colin Marshall and Tony Payne.[112] Interviewees from two churches referred to this approach which articulates the purpose of a church under the four categories of "engage, evangelize, establish, and equip."[113] This approach argues that each activity in the church should be seeking to engage or evangelize non-Christians, establish Christians in their faith, or equip them for ministry. Some activities will do a number of these things. Several interviewees spoke of the great benefit of this framework in guiding the various ministries of their church to be more intentional.[114] One of them particularly referenced the value of the Reach Australia conference in helping the church staff and lay leaders better understand and execute local church ministries.[115] He felt it had strengthened the local mission engagement of the church. However, another interviewee at this same church noted the encouragement that staff received through the conference, yet was concerned that the limited geographical scope of the missional focus may inadvertently decrease involvement in distant mission by redirecting the attention of the church members to only local needs and opportunities.[116]

These organizational connections had some impact on the mission beliefs of some of the churches examined, but they were much less apparent than the personal relational connections to mission workers. These four organizations were noted for their significance in the life and ministry of a few of these churches, but none of them were described as primary sources of cultural convictions. Interviewees emphasized the network of relationships with mission workers more than the connections to organizations. Members of MGE churches particularly emphasized their

---

111. Reach Australia, "About Us."

112. Marshall and Payne, *Trellis and the Vine*; Marshall and Payne, *Vine Project*.

113. Marshall and Payne, *Vine Project*, 241–97.

114. Interviews with CH3_SP, August 8, 2019; CH3_CM, August 23, 2019; CH1_CM, September 26, 2019.

115. Interview with CH1_CM, September 26, 2019.

116. Interview with CH1_MC, September 27, 2019.

connection to individual mission workers with whom they had long historical connections; they communicated with the mission workers more regularly, honestly, and with greater levels of mutuality, and they were more likely to speak of this connection as a partnership. These relationships were both a consequence and a cause of the high levels of distant mission involvement in MGE churches. Churches that engaged deeply with mission workers were stimulated to be more fully involved because their missiological emphases were shaped by these relationships. The dynamics of these personal relationships and their influence on church culture and climate can be best appreciated through the insights of social exchange and social capital theories.

SOCIAL EXCHANGE THEORY

Social exchange theory (SET) draws on insights from anthropology, social psychology, and sociology to explain the dynamics of interpersonal interaction.[117] SET can be simply explained as "the economic analysis of noneconomic social situations"[118] in which benefits such as status, information, support, compliments, and love are considered potential "exchange resources" alongside goods, services, and money.[119] At its most basic level SET explores the patterns of behavior that arise between two parties in which one's actions towards the other results in an appropriate response. While the responses of each party are to varying degrees rational, B. F. Meeker suggests that "reciprocity, altruism, group-gain, status consistency, and competition" also have an influence.[120] These motivations will likely shape relationships in a variety of ways, yet through repeated interactions the relationship will display more qualities of interdependence.[121] This will manifest as different expectations of how the other party will respond in the relationship.[122] In "communal" relationships, benefits are given by one party without any expectation of response or return, as in the care of a parent for an infant. By contrast, "exchange" relationships have clear expectations of reciprocation like payment for goods

---

117. Cropanzano and Mitchell, "Social Exchange Theory," 874.
118. Emerson, "Social Exchange Theory," 336.
119. Cropanzano and Mitchell, "Social Exchange Theory," 880.
120. Meeker, "Decisions and Exchange," 485.
121. Cropanzano et al., "Social Exchange Theory," 480.
122. Clark and Mills, "Theory of Communal," 232–50.

or services. Clark and Mills note that most relationships fall along the continuum between these two polarities and can be described in terms of their communal strength.[123] The communal strength of a relationship with a close friend will be higher than with a stranger, but lower than with a spouse or child. These social exchange perspectives provide valuable insights into the relationships between churches and mission workers.[124]

Before applying these insights to the church—mission worker relationship it is important to recognize the ways in which these relationships differ from those typically examined by SET. Most SET research has examined relationships in commercial settings.[125] The exchanges between employees and their superiors, and between sales assistants and customers have been the primary spheres of interest. The church—mission worker relationship differs from these relationships in several ways. Firstly, rather than being a relationship between two individuals, the church is a group of people who do not always act as a unified entity. Secondly, in most cases the church is providing financial support to the mission worker, but not as payment for goods or services. As one church's documents stated, "We see the giving of financial assistance as an integral part of the partnership—an expression of our love and commitment, and a genuine sharing with mission partners in the work."[126] The primary focus of their relationship is not each other but those that the mission worker is serving in their context. Finally, there are theological convictions that may discourage viewing the church—mission worker relationship in exchange terms. In response to the willing self-sacrifice of Jesus, Scripture exhorts Christians to "value others" above themselves (Phil 2:3) and to "be generous on every occasion" (2 Cor 9:11). These differences highlight the limitations of the social exchange construct to fully explain these relationships, nevertheless it provides some valuable insights to aid our understanding of these connections.

Social Exchange Theory and Church—Worker Relationships

David Dunaetz applied a social exchange lens to the relationship between mission workers and evangelical churches to suggest ways that workers

123. Clark and Mills, "Theory of Communal," 238.
124. Dunaetz, "Missionary's Relationship," 303–23.
125. Cropanzano et al., "Social Exchange Theory," 479–81.
126. CH4, Mission Partnership Principles, December 2013.

may strengthen the relationship.[127] Drawing on the work of Clark and Mills,[128] Dunaetz suggested that the relationship may initially display more exchange qualities in which both parties' behavior is shaped by a subconscious cost—benefit analysis. He argued that mission workers will form effective partnerships where they are aware of and able to meet the expectations of the church. As these positive reciprocal social exchanges are repeated the relational bond between the two parties is strengthened and the communal strength of the relationship increases.[129] This means both the church members and the workers become more willing to make their resources available to the other and greater levels of mutuality become evident. In cases where the mission worker was previously a member of the church, the relationship begins with higher levels of communal strength. Churches are committed to supporting their members because they have a strong relational connection with high levels of trust and commitment.[130] The longer history of the relationships with mission workers in MGE churches is therefore a contributing factor to the stronger and more mutual relational bonds that exist.

A social exchange perspective also helps to explain the significance of the communication practices between MGE churches and mission workers. One central observation of SET is that one party's action will be reciprocated by the other party in both intensity and nature.[131] When one person shows kindness to another, they are likely to be shown kindness in return, similarly one person's negative attitude or demeanor towards another is likely to be returned. In the church—worker relationship this suggests that regular personal communication from the church is likely to result in more regular personal communication from the worker. A review of the content of the communication between the churches and the mission workers suggests a preference for a more communal style contact in the MGE churches. A congregation member at one MGE church appreciated the opportunity they had to "have a conversation which was more personal and to ask questions" of a mission worker.[132] Similarly, in another MGE church a congregation member described the primary goal of a visit from the mission workers to the youth group as "really just to get

127. Dunaetz, "Missionary's Relationship."
128. Clark and Mills, "Theory of Communal."
129. Cropanzano and Mitchell, "Social Exchange Theory," 888.
130. Cropanzano et al., "Social Exchange Theory," 490–91.
131. Lyons and Scott, "Integrating Social Exchange," 66–79.
132. Interview with CH3_CM, August 23, 2019.

to know them."[133] A number of people from other MGE churches indicated that the communication with the mission workers enabled them to get beyond what is shared in a prayer letter to "personal engagement."[134] Where members demonstrate this desire for meaningful relational connection, SET suggests that the communication from the workers is likely to be more regular and personal. Consequently, the depth of the relationship will increase, and it will grow in communal strength.

In LGE churches the communication tended to be more focused on the transfer of information than on building relational connection. The pastor of one LGE church described how the information from the mission workers' prayer letters was collated by the church administrators and attached to an email sent to the Bible study leaders. Though regularly distributed, one church member queried "how many Bible study leaders open it."[135] In another LGE church a congregation member noted that, though the minister has a long friendship with the mission workers, the church members did not know them. "You know, help us to . . . love them and support them and know what's happening with them."[136] When speaking about the communication with mission workers, interviewees from LGE churches primarily spoke of sharing information about where the workers were and what they were doing.[137] In situations like this, SET predicts that both the affective benefit and the level of activity expressed in an interaction will be reflected in the other party's response.[138] Superficial communication habits will develop between the church and the mission worker resulting in a weaker relational connection. Even in churches where the relationship was initially strong the connection will progressively lose communal strength and begin to take on more exchange characteristics if communication is not maintained. Despite its limitations, social exchange theory provides valuable insights into how the history and communication practices of the church—mission worker relationship will impact the quality of that connection. The theory is consistent with the patterns of relationship that were evident between MGE

---

133. Interview with CH8_CM, May 22, 2019.

134. Interviews with CH4_SP, March 28, 2019; CH9_CM, September 10, 2019; CH6_CM, June 16, 2019.

135. Interview with CH2_MC, August 29, 2019.

136. Interview with CH1_MC, September 27, 2019.

137. Interviews with CH1_CM, September 26, 2019; CH1_MC, September 27, 2019; CH2_CM, September 2, 2019; CH5_CM, July 8, 2019; CH5_SP, June 13, 2019.

138. Cropanzano et al., "Social Exchange Theory," 500–501.

churches and distant mission workers which displayed more communal features.

SOCIAL CAPITAL THEORY

Social exchange theory provides some explanation of the patterns of relationship observed in this research, but social capital theory more fully explains the role that these relational connections play in shaping the culture and climate of mission in MGE churches. Social capital describes the benefits that flow to individuals, groups, and societies through social connections. The term was first used by L. J. Hanifan in 1916 to describe a rural school community,[139] though it was not until the latter part of the twentieth century that the concept was used more widely. Though fundamentally a sociological concept, psychologists, economists, and others have used it to explore the broader impacts of social connection. Due to the many contexts and issues the idea has been used to address, different dimensions of social capital have been emphasized and the concept has become widely contested.[140] As Saukani and Ismaili note, "what exactly constitutes social capital, the elements and components that contribute to its formation, and how to measure this intangible concept all remain unclear."[141] Various efforts have been made to disentangle the conversation, though the differences often arise from differing presuppositions. Fulkerson and Thompson analyzed the sociological literature and proposed two broad categories into which most approaches fell.[142] The "normative approach" emphasized the relational bonds which foster "norms of trust and reciprocity" among the members of a group and thereby stimulate actions which benefit all members.[143] This view is often emphasized by those concerned with societal dysfunction, particularly as it relates to development and social cohesion. By contrast, the "resource approach" builds on the work of Mark Granovetter and Pierre Bourdieu and emphasizes the nature of network connections and the benefits that flow to both individuals and groups through these relationships.[144] This approach

139. Hanifan, "Rural School Community Center," 130–38.
140. Fulkerson and Thompson, "Evolution of Contested Concept," 536–57.
141. Saukani and Ismail, "Identifying the Components," 632.
142. Fulkerson and Thompson, "Evolution of Contested Concept."
143. Fulkerson and Thompson, "Evolution of Contested Concept," 540.
144. Fulkerson and Thompson, "Evolution of Contested Concept," 553–54; Granovetter, "Strength of Weak Ties," 1360–80; Bourdieu, "Forms of Capital," 241–58.

tends to be emphasized in the analysis of inter-group connections as it highlights the benefits people gain by diversifying their web of contacts.[145] Though Fulkerson and Thompson acknowledge that these approaches are not mutually exclusive, they suggest that authors tend towards one approach or the other depending on the goal of their research.

The findings of this study suggest that the resource approach to social capital is most relevant to understanding the mission practices of Sydney evangelical churches, although normative tendencies are also at work. One definition of social capital that reflects this resource emphasis is offered by Nahapiet and Ghoshal who define social capital as "the sum of the actual and potential resources embedded within, available through, and derived from the network of relationships possessed by an individual or social unit."[146] Nahapiet and Ghoshal were primarily concerned with the impact of social capital on organizations and how relational connections provided intellectual capital in addition to the human capital highlighted by Coleman.[147] They noted that social connections aid the flow of information within and between networks such that those with high social capital can access greater knowledge and expertise.[148] Furthermore, the greater levels of trust and shared social norms that come with social capital increase the efficiency of actions and facilitate cooperation. In both these ways, organizations with high social capital can do things more easily.[149] The contribution of churches to societal social capital has been widely considered,[150] but this organizational perspective on social capital has not been applied widely to the activities of local churches. Powell and Pepper identified a relationship between social capital and innovation in Australian local churches,[151] but the connection between a church's social capital and its involvement in mission has not previously been considered.

Social capital is often described as either bonding or bridging in nature. Bonding social capital describes the connections between members

---

145. Burt, "Network Structure," 345–423.
146. Nahapiet and Ghoshal, "Social Capital," 243.
147. Coleman, "Social Capital," S95–120.
148. Kwon and Adler, "Social Capital," 417.
149. Nahapiet and Ghoshal, "Social Capital," 245; Putnam, *Bowling Alone*, 19.
150. Putnam and Campbell, *American Grace*; Beyerlein and Hipp, "From Pews to Participation," 97–117; Foley and Hoge, *Religion and New Immigrants*; Leonard and Bellamy, "Dimensions of Bonding," 1046–65.
151. Powell and Pepper, "Local Churches and Innovativeness," 278–301.

within a homogeneous group which result in high levels of trust and shared social norms.[152] Bridging social capital describes the connections that extend beyond the group, typically to people and organizations that are different to those inside the group. Research in the corporate sector has demonstrated that, while bonding capital is valuable for facilitating the flow of information and reinforcing norms of behavior within an organization, it is the bridging connections that have the greatest impact on overall performance. As Ronald Burt has shown, these external bridging connections provide access to knowledge and opportunities that cannot come from within.[153] The World Bank's work on poverty alleviation also noted the importance of bridging capital that crosses levels of socio-economic power for improving the well-being of poor communities in developing contexts.[154] Both bonding and bridging capital are therefore important. A group with high bonding capital may provide effective personal support for members, but in the absence of bridging capital, introspection and tribalism may result.[155] Geys and Murdoch have further refined these categories by differentiating between the degree of homogeneity of the people in the relationship and whether the connections extend beyond the borders of the group or not.[156] They suggested that bonding and bridging primarily refer to how similar the people are, and internal and external refer to whether the people are in the same group or not. In this study's exploration of relationships between local churches and distant mission workers, the connections are clearly external though they have elements of both bonding and bridging social capital. The shared theological and cultural heritage creates a bonding dimension, while the differences in context and experiences adds a bridging element. Both types of social capital must therefore be considered.

In addition to these different types of social capital, Nahapiet and Ghoshal highlighted three dimensions of organizational social

---

152. Woolcock and Narayan, "Social Capital," 225–49; Leonard and Bellamy, "Dimensions of Bonding," 1048–49.

153. Burt, "Network Structure," 362–73.

154. Szreter and Woolcock, "Health by Association?," 650–67. This type of social capital was termed "linking" capital.

155. Evangelical churches have been critiqued for having a tendency to exclusive bonding capital, however, there is significant evidence to show that this is not a consistent picture. Schwadel et al., "Social Networks," 305–17; Vermeer and Scheepers, "Bonding or Bridging?," 962–75.

156. Geys and Murdoch, "Measuring," 523–40.

capital—structural, relational, and cognitive.[157] The structural dimension describes the network and direction of the social connections that exist. It considers the density of both bridging and bonding connections, internally and externally, and the social and cultural boundaries that are bridged by these links.[158] The relational dimension considers the nature of the bonds that have been formed between people. For example, the connection between people that have been friends for many years is relationally very different to the bond between recent business acquaintances. In the language of social exchange theory this is the communal strength of the relationship. The third dimension of social capital considers the cognitive nature of the connection which is the dimension that has the greatest impact on intellectual capital. This includes the shared understanding or worldview which is often expressed through shared language, narrative, and goals. These three dimensions of social capital provide an analytical framework that can be used to explore the presence and influence of social capital in the relationships between local churches and mission workers in this study.

In MGE churches, the structural dimension of social capital was enhanced by the number of distant mission workers that the church was connected to. Compared to churches of a similar size, MGE churches had more connections to more diverse locations with greater communal strength. These relationships were an important source of external bonding and bridging social capital. The mission workers had often previously been members of the church providing elements of bonding social capital, but their distant location and ministry context added valuable elements of bridging social capital. This structural dimension was a notable point of difference between the MGE and LGE churches; however, it was the relational and cognitive dimensions of social capital that were most clearly enhanced. Consideration of the relational and cognitive dimensions highlights the impact they have on the church's intellectual capital which shapes the missiological emphases expressed through the culture and climate for mission involvement.

---

157. Nahapiet and Ghoshal, "Social Capital," 244–45.
158. Burt, "Network Structure," 346–48.

RELATIONAL DIMENSIONS OF SOCIAL CAPITAL IN CHURCH—WORKER RELATIONSHIPS

In their exploration of the relational dimension of social capital, Nahapiet and Ghoshal identify four key facets that are evident when this dimension is high. These are "trust and trustworthiness, norms and sanctions, obligations and expectations, and identity and identification."[159] By examining these four facets in the relationships between mission workers and MGE churches, the presence of significant social capital becomes clear. One notable source of trust and trustworthiness in the church—mission worker relationship was shared theological convictions. Interviewees often mentioned the importance of theological agreement with the mission workers they supported.[160] This was consistent across LGE and MGE churches, though in LGE churches where the relational connection to the worker was primarily mediated through a mission organization, it was the theological credentials of the organization that were most important.[161] Beyond this foundational theological level, church—mission worker relationships in MGE churches showed higher levels of trust for several reasons. As per social exchange theory, the long historical connections provided multiple positive relational exchanges over a long period of time which built trust in the relationship.[162] This was especially evident where the mission workers had been former members of staff at the church. Two of the MGE churches explicitly noted their preference to support mission workers that have "proven themselves in ministry among us."[163] As these relationships developed, communication habits further impacted the development of trust. One church specifically instructed their mission partners to communicate honestly "not neglecting to mention the things that are difficult."[164] As this honest communication was received and appropriately responded to, the trust aspect of social capital grew. This high level of trust in the relationships between MGE

---

159. Nahapiet and Ghoshal, "Social Capital," 244.

160. Interviews with CH4_SP, March 28, 2019; CH9_MC, August 29, 2019; CH10_SP, June 3, 2019; CH8, Mission Guidelines and Policies, Version 5, 2014.

161. Interview with CH5_SP, June 13, 2019; CH2_SP, June 24, 2019.

162. Cropanzano et al., "Social Exchange Theory," 489.

163. Personal communication with CH9_MC, March 18, 2020; CH8, Mission Guidelines and Policies, Version 5, 2014.

164. CH4, Mission Partnership Principles, December 2013.

churches as mission workers demonstrates a level of social capital that was not apparent in LGE churches' relationships.

Social capital was further evident between the church and the mission workers in MGE churches through shared norms of behavior. In both LGE and MGE churches, many of these behavioral norms arose from shared evangelical convictions. The emphasis on evangelization, the centrality of Scripture, and love for those in need shaped the activities of both the workers and the churches. However, through the consistent patterns of communication in MGE churches these norms were further reinforced. As noted above, regular communication was a key norm that shaped the church—mission worker relationship and further built social capital. As mission workers shared their experience in life and ministry, the church members were encouraged not only to communicate back but also to emulate their practices.[165] When requests for prayer were sent by the mission partners, norms of belief were shared thereby reinforcing the conviction that mission work is dependent on God. These active expressions of Christian faith served to bind the church members and mission workers together as they encouraged one another to continue in their practice. Another shared behavioral norm that reflected the high social capital in these relationships was the alignment of the church and mission worker's ministry goals. One MGE church supported a national mission worker in Israel because of the church's prioritization of mission to Jewish people.[166] Another MGE church particularly focused on supporting the construction of a chapel building in a developing country where its mission workers were based because they were also redeveloping their own buildings.[167] The minister of this church suggested that, though the personal relationship with mission workers was foundational to their partnership, the alignment of ministry objectives helped the relationship to flourish long-term.[168] These shared norms of practice and belief were evident to some extent in all churches, yet they were a more consistent feature that demonstrated the depth of social capital in the relationships between MGE churches and mission workers.

Shared obligations and expectations are the third facet of the relational dimension of social capital which was a strong feature in MGE church—worker relationships. Some MGE churches articulated these

---

165. Interview with CH4_SP, March 28, 2019.
166. Interview with CH9_SP, October 9, 2019.
167. Interview with CH10_MC, July 19, 2019.
168. Interview with CH10_SP, June 3, 2019.

relational expectations in policies and documents which one minister described as an expression of the "mutual commitment to each other . . . put down on paper."[169] One expectation emphasized in these policies relates to regular communication. There was an expectation that mission workers would keep the church informed about their life and ministry.[170] There was also an expectation that the church would intentionally maintain the relationship by communicating with the worker.[171] These communication obligations and expectations were often fostered through regular two-way contact between mid-week small groups and the mission workers. These connections provided a context in which the worker expected to receive prayer and encouragement from the church members, and the church members expected friendship, relationship, and encouragement from the worker.[172]

The foundational obligation of the church—mission worker relationship is the financial support that the churches provide. Mission workers were dependent upon the churches to provide the finances they needed to continue in the work they were doing. Though there was no evidence that churches considered the finances as payment for the work being done, the level of financial support given was indicative of the depth of the commitment. Two churches from which people were interviewed, one MGE and one LGE, categorized their mission partners according to the nature of their commitment. The workers in the lower category were occasionally profiled and church members were encouraged to pray for and support them, but they received little or no financial support from the church. The workers in the higher category were given more financial support and provided the focus for the church's communication and support of mission work. This substantial financial support was a clear indicator to both the worker and the church members that this was a relationship of great importance to the church. This financial commitment reflected the degree of relational interdependence which is a feature of high social capital connections.[173] When the financial dependence is absent or removed, the relationship becomes less significant. One interviewee spoke of a mission worker that the church previously supported

---

169. Interview with CH4_SP, March 28, 2019; CH4, Mission Partnership Principles, December 2013; CH8, Mission Guidelines and Policies, Version 5, 2014.
170. Interview with CH4_MC, April 4, 2019.
171. Interview with CH6_CM, June 16, 2019.
172. Interview with CH8_MC, May 30, 2019.
173. Coleman, *Foundations*, 321.

both financially and relationally, but when the worker took up a paid position doing similar work in the same place, both the financial and relational connection waned.[174] Similarly, an LGE church member noted that her church's previously high level of engagement with distant mission had reduced markedly because, over the last decade, church members sent out from the church for ministry had gone into paid church ministry elsewhere in Australia, rather than overseas mission roles requiring ongoing financial support.[175] The lack of need for financial support had translated into a lack of relationship. These financial and relational obligations and expectations are therefore a potent source of relational interdependence and social capital between MGE churches and mission workers.

The final facet of the relational dimension of social capital described by Nahapiet and Ghoshal is identity and identification.[176] This speaks to the degree to which mission workers and churches see themselves as relationally bound to one another. The shared theological convictions are a clear source of shared identity. The churches were willing to support these workers because they had the same goal of making the gospel known throughout the world.[177] In MGE churches, where the mission workers had previously been members of the church, this shared identity was even stronger.[178] When asked if the mission partners were previously members of the church, one MGE church member stated, "They're still members of the church."[179] Even for mission workers who have not been members of the church, close relational connection fostered this shared identity. When reflecting on the value of personal communication such as video calls with mission workers, one church member noted that it "helps the church to see missionaries, not as just some "super Christians" but kind of as normal."[180] Church members were thereby able to identify more closely with the mission workers they supported. This closer identification between MGE churches and the mission workers was a great

---

174. Interview with CH4_MC, April 4, 2019.

175. Interview with CH2_CM, September 2, 2019.

176. Nahapiet and Ghoshal, "Social Capital," 244.

177. CH2, Mission Committee Terms of Reference, October 7, 2019; CH4, Mission Partnership Principles, December 2013; CH5, Mission Policy, 2019; CH8, Mission Guidelines and Policies, Version 5, 2014.

178. Interviews with CH3_MC, 8 September 2019; CH4_SP, March 28, 2019.

179. Interview with CH10_CM, July 19, 2019.

180. Interview with CH9_CM, September 10, 2019.

source of social capital. The strength of these four facets of the relational dimension in these relationships demonstrates the presence of high levels of social capital and the capacity that this provides to positively impact the two parties.

COGNITIVE DIMENSIONS OF SOCIAL CAPITAL IN CHURCH—WORKER RELATIONSHIPS

In addition to the strength of the social capital evident from the relational dimension, the cognitive dimension of social capital between the MGE churches and mission workers enables the transfer of intellectual capital to the church. This cognitive dimension was evident in shared narratives, values, attitudes, and worldviews. Although it was present to some extent in LGE churches, the lack of relational connectedness between the churches and the mission workers greatly limits its impact. As with the relational dimension in MGE churches, the fact that many mission workers had previously been members of the churches increased this cognitive dimension. Church members were more open to the perspectives and insights that the workers gleaned from their missionary experience and were ready to learn from them. One mission coordinator noted that because of the relationship between the church and the worker, there was "better communication and insight, and stories back and forth, and encouragement."[181] This information transfer had a positive impact on the churches as it not only educated but also encouraged, transformed, and motivated.

The cognitive dimension of social capital in the relationships between MGE churches and mission workers shaped church members' understanding of the world, cultural differences, and mission. One church leader observed that there is a tendency for Christians living in Sydney to become "a bit myopic" in their understanding about the spread of the faith and the challenges to mission.[182] Contact with mission workers around the world helped people to appreciate the global variation and to see that "God's doing different things in different places."[183] Church members not only learned about the mission workers they were supporting, but also the ministry that was happening in that region of the world.

---

181. Interview with CH10_MC, July 19, 2019.
182. Interview with CH4_SP, March 28, 2019.
183. Interview with CH4_SP, March 28, 2019.

Interviewees noted how this helped them to "appreciate the wider scope of God's global mission" and to grow in their understanding of how they might contribute.[184] It also helped to lift "people's eyes up above their own situation," especially as they saw the ways that Christians in other places persevered in the face of persecution.[185] This was observed to strengthen church members' faith, their confidence in the gospel message, and their own ways of serving God. The connection to the mission workers became a source of motivation for church members to participate in mission themselves by providing a model of self-sacrificial service of God and commitment to mission work.[186] Several MGE church leaders noted this benefit as a reason why they supported mission workers serving in diverse contexts.[187] In one MGE church, the leadership explicitly encouraged the mission workers to seek to develop "mission mindedness" in the church members.[188] In another MGE church, the minister saw that this connection could "provoke others to think about going" and he intentionally gave opportunities for the workers to speak to church members about this.[189] However, it was not just the verbal encouragement that shaped the culture and climate of mission involvement. The most important aspects of this cognitive dimension of social capital was the intellectual capital that flowed through the relationships which shaped the core beliefs about mission.

These core beliefs shaped the missiological emphases and climate for mission involvement in these churches, though they were rarely explicitly stated. While the broad theological convictions regarding the importance of mission involvement were shared across MGE and LGE churches, there were three core beliefs influencing the involvement of churches in mission which were more evident in these MGE churches.[190] These

---

184. Interview with CH9_CM, September 10, 2019.

185. Interview with CH9_SP, October 9, 2019,

186. Interviews with CH4_SP, March 28, 2019; CH8_MC, May 30, 2019.

187. Interviews with CH3_MC, September 2, 2019; CH4_SP, March 28, 2019; CH8_MC, May 30, 2019. These observations are consistent with Ronald Burt's argument that the social capital arising from sparse relational networks, including connections to a wide range of sources, are more efficient than those with dense networks. See Burt, "Network Structure," 392–98.

188. CH8, Mission Guidelines and Policies, Version 5, 2014.

189. Interview with CH4_SP, March 28, 2019.

190. To fully analyze these core beliefs, a more comprehensive ethnographic analysis would be required, yet there is clear evidence from the differences in values and climate for mission explored in chapter 6 that these differences in belief exist. See also

beliefs were key elements of the intellectual capital these churches gained through the social capital of their deep relational connections to distant mission workers. Edgar Schein stated that an organization's "shared basic assumptions [are] learned by a group as it solved its problems of external adaption and internal integration,"[191] so these core beliefs were learned in these MGE churches as they participated in partnership with distant mission workers. These beliefs reflected the shared understanding among members of these churches about the world, themselves, and the experience of mission involvement. Regarding the world, they had different beliefs about their responsibility for distant mission; regarding themselves, they had different views about their capacity for mission; regarding the experience of mission, MGE church members saw it as a positive opportunity rather than a burden.

Responsibility for Distant Mission

The differences between interviewees in terms of their perceived responsibility for distant mission were discussed in chapter 5. As an aspect of interviewees' beliefs about the purpose of their church, those in MGE churches spoke more often about the importance of involvement in distant mission. Though church leaders in LGE churches expressed the conviction that involvement in distant mission was valuable, the members of their churches spoke more about the needs for mission in the local community. Distant mission involvement was good, but other people could do that while they were focused on their own context.[192] By contrast, interviewees from MGE churches consistently noted the responsibility that they and their churches had to contribute to distant mission. They saw distant mission participation as part of their identity as Christians and a natural extension of their local mission.[193] This extended beyond partnering with current distant mission workers to intentionally encouraging more church members to become distant mission workers in the future. Members and leaders of MGE churches had a shared belief that involvement in distant mission was a core responsibility of their church.

Schein, *Organizational Culture*, 178–83.

191. Schein, *Organizational Culture*, 17.

192. Interviews with CH1_SP, August 26, 2019; CH1_CM, September 26, 2019; CH5_MC, July 8, 2019; CH5_CM, July 8, 2019.

193. Interviews with CH4_SP, March 28, 2019; CH8_MC, May 30, 2019; CH10_MC, July 19, 2019.

This responsibility was a consequence of the intellectual capital that MGE churches gained through the social capital of relationships with distant mission workers. The pre-existing connections to these workers provided an initial impetus for involvement, but the cognitive dimension of social capital resulting from these relationships motivated ongoing involvement. Interviewees noted that observing the commitment of these workers encouraged them to be more involved.[194] They also learned about the needs and opportunities for ministry in other contexts. The differences in Christian resources between their own context and that of the workers encouraged their participation.[195] As one minister stated, "It's seeing the bigger picture of the Christian world and so I think it is helpful."[196] Previous research has shown the central importance of personal relationships with mission workers in leading people to become cross-cultural missionaries.[197] In churches with strong relational connections to mission workers there were many more opportunities for this contact. It was therefore unsurprising that this survey found that MGE churches had nearly five times more distant mission workers sent out from their church than did LGE churches (see table 6). These relational connections therefore provided intellectual capital which motivated participation in distant mission.

This global awareness also extended beyond the facts of what was needed in other places to include deeper insights into the impact of cultural difference on local mission. A congregation member expressed their appreciation for the cultural insights that a mission worker brought when they visited the church. The understanding they gained into the way cultural norms and beliefs may impede the Japanese people's belief in Jesus helped him to understand some of the challenges he was experiencing in sharing his faith with his friends in Australia.[198] Similarly, the freedom with which a mission worker in West Asia was able to speak to local people about spiritual matters was seen as an encouragement to church members in Australia who felt the opposition to spiritual conversation from their secular friends.[199] Their contact with distant mission workers was appreciated because they were able to draw on their

---

194. Interviews with CH4_SP, March 28, 2019; CH8_MC, May 30, 2019.
195. Interviews with CH8_MC, May 30, 2019; CH6_MC, June 16, 2019.
196. Interview with CH9_SP, October 9, 2019.
197. Hibbert et al., "Journey towards Long-Term."
198. Interview with CH6_CM, June 16, 2019.
199. Interview with CH4_SP, March 28, 2019.

experiences of living as a Christian in a vastly different context.[200] This cultural understanding enhanced church members' motivation to engage in mission both locally and at a distance. They saw the global needs and opportunities that they could contribute to, and they were both encouraged and equipped to engage locally.

Capacity for Mission

A second aspect of the intellectual capital that MGE churches gained through their relationships with distant mission workers related to beliefs about the church's capacity for mission involvement. Interviewees' beliefs about their church's resources and consequent ability to make a meaningful contribution to distant mission evidentially shaped the church's culture of mission involvement. Those from MGE churches expressed the view that their church had adequate resources, while the members of LGE churches felt their capacity was limited and other needs were more pressing. These perspectives on capacity were not only shaped by people's opinion on the total number of resources; there was also a difference in the kinds of resources that were considered. In LGE churches, where interviewees noted the limitation of resources, it was primarily financial resources that were discussed. By contrast, interviewees from MGE churches referred to a range of resources that they saw as contributing to the church's involvement in distant mission. These differing perspectives on the church's capacity had a powerful effect on the group's willingness to be involved.

Interviewees in MGE churches spoke in various ways about how the wealth of the church facilitated involvement in mission. This concept of wealth was not limited to financial resources. It also referred to the experience, knowledge, and wisdom of the people in the church. The minister of one MGE church noted the number of "very well-trained, well-taught Christians" and suggested that it was incumbent upon the church to share their "riches" with people in other places.[201] Similarly, a congregation member from another MGE church described it as "gospel rich and resources rich" suggesting that it therefore had a responsibility to use this wealth well for distant mission purposes.[202] In both cases the interviewees believed that the church had a lot to offer and that this

---

200. Interview with CH10_CM, July 19, 2019.
201. Interview with CH4_SP, March 28, 2019.
202. Interview with CH3_CM, August 23, 2019.

capacity motivated their action. The mission coordinator of a third MGE church noted that it was a "wealthy church" made up of people from a "wealthy demographic."[203] Though encouraged by the generosity of many church members, she believed that there were significant untapped resources and that the church could be "more sacrificial."[204] By contrast, the minister from CH8 reported his surprise at the level of generosity towards distant mission when he first joined the church, "Initially, when I came on board, I thought, how is the church doing this? This is crazy high."[205] However, he came to understand that the church had a number of wealthy members and a long history of generous support for distant mission. The mission coordinator in this church stated that members of the mission committee consistently say, "If we need to send more missionaries, God will provide the money. Don't worry about it."[206] This confidence that the church will not be limited by its financial resources reflects a core belief about the church's capacity for mission involvement which had been reinforced through years of participation. This interviewee spoke about the how the church had increased the number of mission workers it supported and the amount of money that it sent, but that it had continued to meet budget.[207] Similarly, as people went out from the church for the purpose of mission, the church's ministry continued to thrive. These experiences had reinforced the belief that the church had the capacity, in both money and people, to be actively involved in distant mission.

Though interviewees from some of the MGE churches noted both the financial and human wealth of their church, others focused only on non-financial capacity. All three interviewees from one MGE church highlighted the large number of church members with significant past experience in Christian ministry.[208] They described this as a valuable "resource" which helped to drive the church's ongoing involvement in mission.[209] In a similar way, a congregation member from CH6 noted

203. Interview with CH9_MC, August 29, 2019.
204. Interview with CH9_MC, August 29, 2019.
205. Interview with CH8_SP, April 11, 2019.
206. Interview with CH8_MC, May 30, 2019.
207. Interview with CH8_MC, May 30, 2019.
208. Interviews with CH10_SP, June 3, 2019; CH10_CM, July 19, 2019; CH10_MC, July 19, 2019.
209. Though the description of people as "resources" is problematic, it is a common way to speak of a church's capacity for impact. See Inkson, "Are Humans Resources?," 270–79.

that while people may not be able to contribute more financially, "there can always be more done in terms of prayer and communication."[210] These perspectives on capacity had been reinforced by past experiences of encouraging and supporting people while they were serving in distant mission. The minister of one of these churches spoke of the opportunity that many of the church members with expertise in education had in supporting a mission school in a developing nation.[211] Similarly, the positive feedback that church members received when the mission partners visited encouraged their own involvement in distant mission. The high levels of participation of MGE church members in distant mission helped them to recognize the variety of ways in which they could contribute and the resources that they had to do that. This awareness of their capacity further stimulated their involvement.

By contrast, members of LGE churches often expressed the belief that their church's mission involvement was limited by their capacity, especially financially. Interviewees from two of the LGE churches mentioned significant financial difficulties they had experienced in the recent past. The minister of one LGE church shared how he had arrived at the church several years before, when the church was in serious decline.[212] Since he arrived the church had grown numerically and, to a lesser extent, in financial support for distant mission, though the minister expressed a desire to see this increase further.[213] One of the members of this church felt that there were more opportunities for mission involvement both locally and further afield, but that the church was restricted by limited human capital and financial resources.[214] Another LGE church also had financial difficulties prior to the current minister arriving. He described the church as "basically insolvent" when he arrived.[215] A member of the mission committee expressed the view that these financial difficulties had limited the church's support for distant mission workers.[216] Though the church's attendance and financial situation had improved, the minister

210. Interview with CH6_CM, June 16, 2019.
211. Interview with CH10_SP, June 3, 2019.
212. Interview with CH5_SP, June 13, 2019.
213. Interview with CH5_SP, June 13, 2019.
214. Interview with CH5_CM, July 8, 2019.
215. Interview with CH2_SP, June 24, 2019. Median personal weekly income in this suburb was 23 percent higher than the Australian median. Australian Bureau of Statistics, *2016 Census*.
216. Interview with CH2_MC, August 29, 2019.

believed there was a lack of generosity towards mission which hampered the church's capacity to be involved.[217] In a similar way, interviewees from the third LGE church stated that, even though church members had ample financial resources, there was a lack of personal engagement. The church was located in a wealthy suburb and as the minister stated, "to live here you've got to earn a lot of money."[218] One congregation member described the church as "richly resourced."[219] Another said, "I think we have the financial resources," yet he noted, "[mission is] something that [the church members] want to do, but it's not a priority for them."[220] Similarly, the minister wondered if "we've been so focused on trying to build things up here, can we spare anything?"[221] Here the root cause of the limitation in capacity was not financial, but spiritual and motivational. Therefore, in each LGE church interviewees noted a limitation in their church's capacity for engagement with mission. In some cases, this limitation was financial, yet other underlying constraints were also noted. Unlike the MGE churches, the limited nature of the church's involvement in distant mission meant this belief was not challenged.

This difference between interviewees in MGE and LGE churches suggests that there is a core belief regarding the church's capacity for mission which shapes their involvement. This view of their capacity may be influenced by the financial situation of the church, though it impacts more than the level of financial support. Interviewees from MGE churches noted the variety of resources that were available for the task of mission which motivated greater participation, while interviewees from LGE churches were more likely to highlight the financial limitations. In LGE churches there is an apparent assumption that there needs to be some change in the church's circumstances before it can be more fully involved in distant mission activities. However, the relational connection to distant mission workers experienced by interviewees in MGE churches provided the intellectual capital that helped people appreciate the capacity they had to participate. By being involved they realized that they did have the capacity and were thus encouraged to continue. This was not the experience of interviewees from LGE churches.

217. Interview with CH2_SP, June 24, 2019.
218. Interview with CH1_SP, August 26, 2019.
219. Interview with CH1_MC, September 27, 2019.
220. Interview with CH1_CM, September 26, 2019.
221. Interview with CH1_SP, August 26, 2019.

Mission as an Opportunity

The third aspect of intellectual capital that flowed through the cognitive dimension of social capital relates to the perception that involvement in distant mission activities is worth embracing. Interviewees in MGE churches were very positive about the value of distant mission involvement, seeing it as a privilege and opportunity to be grasped. This was especially true among church leaders who noted the cognitive benefits that flowed through significant relationships with mission workers. Several church leaders in MGE churches observed how mission workers provided a lived example of personal commitment to God.[222] One minister described workers as "a great model for us in just thinking about our commitment to Jesus and his work."[223] One church member spoke fondly of the first mission worker that had gone out from his church, noting how this mission worker's perseverance had a profound effect on the church members, "what made an impact was . . . how she sacrificially lived her life, to give to others, to help others . . . I think she was an encouragement, as much as a challenge."[224] Furthermore, misconceptions about the requirements for mission workers were removed as church members saw that they were not "super Christians."[225] This exposure to mission workers provided a positive challenge for church members to consider their own future and how they might participate in mission.[226] In the words of one church leader, this helped people to "lift their eyes above their own situation" and consider what it looks like for them to live as faithful followers of Jesus in their own context.[227] Short-term mission trips were particularly noted to provide this benefit as church members experienced the context, life, and work of a mission worker.[228] Those who participated in these trips not only benefitted from these experiences, but they were also able to provide education to the whole church.[229] This cognitive impact supported the efforts of church leaders who saw raising up new mission workers as part of their ministry. The intellectual capital that came through these

---

222. Interviews with CH8_SP, April 11, 2019; CH9_SP, October 9, 2019.
223. Interview with CH4_SP, March 28, 2019.
224. Interview with CH8_MC, May 30, 2019.
225. Interview with CH9_CM, September 10, 2019.
226. Interview with CH8_MC, May 30, 2019.
227. Interview with CH9_SP, October 9, 2019.
228. Interview with CH6_SP, May 2, 2019.
229. CH8, Mission Guidelines and Policies, Version 5, 2014.

connections gave all the church members a clearer understanding of how they could be involved in mission.

The belief that involvement in a distant mission is a beneficial activity was also evident among MGE church members as they expressed their own encouragement from these relational connections. The opportunity to be involved in the spread of the Christian message in distant places greatly inspired church members. One interviewee recalled the regular encouragement that the members of his church received as their mission partners reminded them that they were involved in all of God's work in the place where the worker served. He said, "They don't just share about their own ministry, they share about the ministry of their whole field. And that grows the vision."[230] Another interviewee noted the positive impact as the church members heard the stories of workers who were encouraged through their support, and of non-Christian people responding to the gospel.[231] Interviewees from one MGE church spoke about the joy they had as they helped to fund the construction of a chapel building at a mission hospital in a developing country at the same time as they were renovating and extending their own church building. Through their relational networks, they were able to join in the celebrations at the start and completion of the chapel construction. This gave the church members a deep sense of satisfaction in being able to partner with mission work overseas in ways that reflected their own ministry efforts.[232] The mission coordinator at another MGE church similarly noted the positive impact on church members when they received a response to the gifts they had sent to distant mission workers, "it just brings [the mission worker] joy, and brings the Lord joy, and it brings the person praying for them joy."[233] As one church member remarked, "[God] incredibly invites us to participate in his mission for the world."[234] One MGE church leader described this as not only a temporal encouragement, but also the "eternal reward" of being in heaven with people who became Christians through the ministry of the mission workers that the church had supported.[235] The relational connections between MGE churches and distant mission workers therefore strengthened the belief among church members that

230. Interview with CH8_MC, May 30, 2019.
231. Interview with CH9_MC, August 29, 2019.
232. Interview with CH10_MC, July 19, 2019.
233. Interview with CH9_MC, August 29, 2019.
234. Interview with CH10_MC, July 19, 2019.
235. Interview with CH9_SP, October 9, 2019.

involvement in distant mission was something to be embraced with joy. This was another valuable dimension of the intellectual capital that resulted from the social capital of these rich relational networks.

These perspectives on involvement in distant mission were not completely absent from the interviews with people in LGE churches, though they were noted by church leaders as hopes for the impact of mission involvement in the future. The minister at CH2 spoke of meaningful engagement with distant mission workers as one way to expand the church members' sphere of concern.

> We're trying to say to people, "Stop thinking about your own self. And think at least about something outside of you." . . . It's really hard in our consumer society and so there has to be a massive change of heart in the church in general. That's how I feel.[236]

For this reason, this minister had recently sought to establish "a real mutually beneficial relationship" with a new mission partner.[237] Similarly, the minister of CH1 spoke of a recent effort to connect the church to a group of churches in a developing country. In speaking of the impact of this venture they said, "I'm hoping that'll really lift our vision on mission," helping church members to think beyond "our little local bubble."[238] But these benefits of involvement in distant mission were not present realities and were not mentioned by the members of these churches. By contrast, these members saw distant mission as something that was good to support, but which was not their primary concern.[239] The perceived privilege of involvement through these connections with distant mission workers was not expressed by LGE church members.

In each church, these beliefs about the opportunity for distant mission involvement worked together with beliefs about the church's responsibility and capacity for mission involvement to shape the extent to which participation was encouraged. These cultural beliefs regarding the place of the local church in distant mission had shaped the climate for mission. In MGE churches people saw participation in distant mission as a core activity of the church because they felt a strong responsibility for the task, they believed they had the capacity to make a meaningful contribution,

---

236. Interview with CH2_SP, June 24, 2019.
237. Interview with CH2_SP, June 24, 2019.
238. Interview with CH1_SP, August 26, 2019.
239. Interviews with CH1_CM, September 26, 2019; CH5_CM, July 8, 2019; CH5_MC, July 8, 2019.

and they viewed participation as a privilege and opportunity to be embraced. These beliefs were a consequence of the intellectual capital that resulted from the social capital of their relationships with distant mission workers. As Jo Anne Schneider's research into non-profit organizations notes "bridging capital . . . can change organizational cultures as well as shift the values of their participants."[240] By contrast, in LGE churches with minimal relational connections, these beliefs were weak or absent, resulting in a weak culture and climate for distant mission involvement. Even where leaders stated that distant mission was a priority, the church's beliefs about their limited responsibility, capacity, and the burdensome nature of involvement shaped the culture of the church. There were a few individuals who were enthusiastic about distant mission involvement, but across the church these beliefs shaped the missiological emphasis on local mission. Concern for distant mission was not integrated into the life of the church and was not evident in the climate for mission.

ADDITIONAL BENEFITS OF SOCIAL CAPITAL IN CHURCH—WORKER RELATIONSHIPS

This consideration of the structural, relational, and cognitive dimensions of social capital between MGE churches and their mission workers has demonstrated the richness of these relationships and their impact on church involvement in mission. Churches with rich networks of external social capital gain intellectual capital that influences the ways they engage in mission. Not only was the social capital a consequence of the higher levels of involvement in distant mission, it also facilitated this involvement by improving the efficiency of the church's distant mission activities and by increasing the bonding social capital of the church.

Increased efficiency of action was a key benefit of social capital that MGE churches enjoyed due to their relationships with distant mission workers. The members of these churches were more able to meaningfully participate in mission activities outside of their immediate context through these relationships. This was noted in the examples above of helping to build a chapel in a developing nation, and by facilitating the spread of the gospel message in distant lands. The opportunities these relationships provided for short-term mission trips was another example of this efficiency of action. The trust that existed between a church and

---

240. Schneider, "Organizational Social Capital," 653–54.

the mission workers provided an opportunity for church members to experience life and ministry in another context with a known guide. By partnering with mission workers who knew the context and culture, the trips were well coordinated and were more likely to provide a positive experience for those who went.[241] The members of one MGE church had been involved in several short-term mission trips, some of which visited mission partners overseas. The pastor viewed these trips as a key dimension of the mission involvement of many of the church's members.[242] As they visited the mission workers, they had the opportunity to strengthen the bond between the congregation and the worker. As one interviewee from this church noted regarding those who participate in these trips, "When they come back, they can explain the gospel work that is happening there with missionaries."[243] Another MGE church's mission coordinator similarly noted the benefit of involvement in short-term mission trips. He spoke of the ways that it helped those who went on the trips to "open their eyes to God's bigger world."[244] These trips had led many church members to become more actively involved in the church's support of mission workers generally. These benefits flowed from the increased efficiency of action that comes through the social capital of highly engaged mission churches.

A final benefit of the high bridging social capital in MGE churches was its capacity to enhance the bonding capital of the church. Leonard and Bellamy found that one of the primary contributing factors to the bonding capital of Australian local churches was "collective agency."[245] That is, churches with a clear vision and the capacity to see that vision realized had higher levels of bonding capital. For MGE churches, the support of distant mission was seen to be a core dimension of the church's purpose which was expressed through these relational connections. As these relationships developed, the church members were encouraged to have meaningful participation in this distant work through their prayers, finances, and intentional relational connection. This was typically only one component of the churches vision, but it enhanced the collective agency of these churches. One church leader expressed this conviction noting that the church's involvement in distant mission has "unified the

241. Zehner, "Rhetoric of Short-Term," 185–207.
242. Interview with CH6_SP, May 2, 2019.
243. Interview with CH6_CM, June 16, 2019.
244. Interview with CH8_MC, May 30, 2019.
245. Leonard and Bellamy, "Dimensions of Bonding," 1050.

church."[246] This higher bonding capital further enables the church to work together in their support of distant mission which in turn enhances the bridging capital.

SUMMARY OF RELATIONAL NETWORK SIGNIFICANCE

As this chapter has demonstrated, the most important difference between MGE and LGE churches noted in this study was the relational networks between the churches and distant mission workers. This chapter has examined these relational networks and used the insights of social exchange and social capital theories to explain their impact on the churches' culture and climate. When asked about their involvement in distant mission, all interviewees spoke about the mission agents that they were associated with. There were a small number of interviewees from MGE churches that highlighted the recipients of mission in these distant locations, yet most emphasized the agents. However, there was an apparent difference between MGE and LGE churches in both the agents they spoke of and the nature of their association with them. Interviewees from LGE churches were more likely to emphasize the organizations that they supported, and they were less likely to use the language of partnership or to speak of the benefits of these connections. They acknowledged the importance of distant mission, but they demonstrated their willingness to delegate the task to those organizations that they perceived to be better equipped for the task. By contrast, interviewees from MGE churches described rich relational networks with multiple distant mission workers. These workers were usually connected to mission organizations, but the emphasis was on the individuals who were spoken of as partners in the distant mission task. They typically had long historical connections to the churches that had been maintained through well-developed communication practices. These relationships showed high levels of mutuality such that both the workers and the churches benefitted from the relationship. Interviewees at all churches spoke of their connections to different mission organizations, but those that emphasized relational connection to individual workers had the greatest positive impact.

The perspectives of social exchange and social capital theories explain the mechanisms by which these relationships impact the missional culture and climate in MGE churches. Social exchange theory describes

246. Interview with CH8_SP, April 11, 2019.

how relationships grow in communal strength over time and why the long historical associations between MGE churches and mission workers create rich relational networks. Social capital explains the multiple benefits that flow to the MGE churches through these networks. It was shown how members of MGE churches enjoyed levels of trust, shared norms, agreed expectations, and a shared identity with these distant mission workers which led them to be more engaged and committed to mission both locally and at a distance. Their missional beliefs were also shaped by the intellectual capital that came through this social capital. This gave them a greater sense of responsibility for distant mission, a belief that they had the capacity to make a meaningful contribution, and the conviction that participation in distant mission is a privileged opportunity. These beliefs were less evident in LGE churches which was consistent with their weaker climate of distant mission participation. These relational networks were rich sources of social capital for the MGE church members which provided positive feedback to encourage greater levels of involvement. The increased social capital also made future involvement easier and strengthened the internal bonding capital of the church which helped to unite them around a common vision. From the perspective of social capital theory, the rich relational networks between MGE churches and their distant mission workers were both a consequence and a cause of the higher levels of mission involvement as they shaped the missiological emphasis on both local and distant mission.

8

Participatory, Delegatory, and Bifurcated Mission

MISSION ENGAGEMENT MATRIX

This research has explored the patterns of mission involvement among conservative evangelical churches in the greater Sydney region of Australia. A survey of 242 church leaders provided data on the mission practices of 205 churches that self-identified as evangelical. Church size was found to influence the level of both local and distant mission activity with larger churches displaying more activity than smaller churches. However, the diverse patterns of involvement suggested a variety of other influential factors. Analysis of the survey findings revealed a relationship between a local church's level of involvement in distant mission activities and its level of involvement in local mission activities. Churches that engaged in higher levels of mission activity in their local community were more likely to identify as missional, yet they were not more likely to show high levels of involvement in distant mission than the average church. By contrast, churches that reported higher levels of involvement in distant mission were more likely to be highly engaged in local mission activities than average. Semi-structured interviews were performed with thirty people from ten Sydney evangelical churches, including clergy and lay members from each church. These churches all displayed higher than average levels of involvement in local mission. Seven of them also displayed higher than average levels of involvement in distant mission and were designated as more globally engaged (MGE) churches. The other three showed lower than average levels of involvement in distant mission and were designated less globally engaged (LGE) churches. A grounded theory analysis of these interviews revealed two missiological approaches to local church mission involvement. These represent two of the four approaches outlined in the church mission engagement matrix (see figure 9).

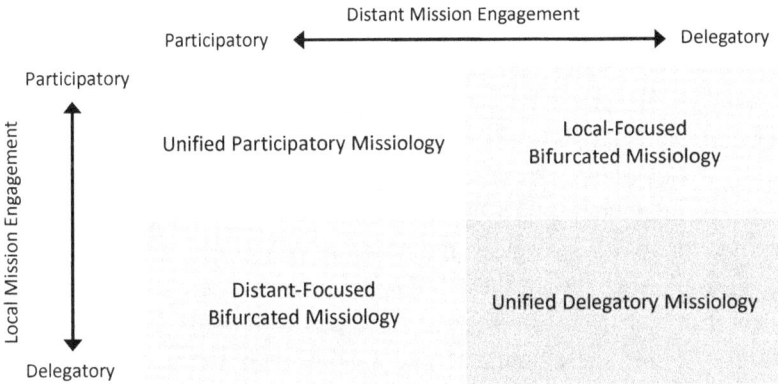

Figure 9. Two-by-Two Matrix of Church Mission Engagement

This matrix recognizes that engagement in local and distant mission can each be described along a continuum from a participatory approach at one end to a delegatory approach at the other. While a participatory approach stimulates high levels of engagement in mission, a delegatory approach affirms the value of mission but supports other people to do it. The engagement matrix combines the two spectra to describe four approaches to mission engagement. MGE churches displayed a "unified participatory missiology" which encouraged the involvement of all church members in both local and distant mission activities. By contrast, LGE churches displayed a "local-focused bifurcated missiology" which encouraged high participation in local mission activities but a delegatory approach to distant mission. This delegatory approach recognized the value of distant mission but entrusted fulfilment of the task to others. As this research only interviewed people from churches that showed high levels of involvement in local mission, there were no examples of churches that displayed either of the other two patterns of engagement. According to the matrix, a unified delegatory missiology would not encourage church members to personally participate in mission activities but would rather delegate both the local and distant tasks to others. This may involve supporting local evangelists and overseas mission workers but not personally engaging in either sphere. A distant-focused bifurcated missiology displaying a participatory approach to distant mission but a delegatory approach to local mission is conceivable, however, the results of the survey indicated that this was less common than the other pattern of bifurcation. This was further reinforced by the interview evidence which suggested that the social capital benefits of a participatory approach to distant mission stimulate participation in local mission as well.

The most significant difference between the unified participatory missiology and the bifurcated missiologies was the separation between local mission and distant mission. Rather than holding the two together as equal expressions of the same Christian practice, churches with a bifurcated missiology approached each aspect differently. In terms of the foundational ecclesiological and missiological convictions, there was great similarity between these two approaches. All people expressed the view that their churches were autonomous communities of Christians who were spiritually bound to one another with a shared responsibility for mission. The beliefs about the nature, goal, and location of mission were also essentially the same. The difference was in the perceived purpose of the local church and the missiological emphasis on local and distant contexts. While the importance of mission to non-Christians was affirmed by members of all churches, those with a unified participatory missiology placed an equal emphasis on local and distant mission, but those with a bifurcated missiology did not. The former displayed a meaningful commitment to mission in distant contexts and a desire to prepare and send church members out on mission, but the latter delegated that task to others while focusing themselves on local mission needs. Those with a unified participatory missiology were more aware of and concerned about spiritual needs in distant places. They emphasized the direct agency of God in mission and viewed participation as a privilege rather than a burden. By contrast, those with a local-focused bifurcated missiology gave less consideration to distant spiritual needs or the agency of God in mission. The primary cause of these differences was not divergent understandings of the nature of the church or the definition of mission, rather they were consequences of the organizational culture and missional beliefs that were shaped by the relational networks of these churches. These missiological categories describe the patterns of mission engagement evident in the sample of churches in this study but may serve as a heuristic device in future church evaluation. Further investigation and refinement are needed, yet, if evidenced more widely, the mission engagement matrix may be employed to interpret and guide church practice.

RELATIONAL NETWORKS AND MISSIONAL BELIEFS

The primary feature of churches with a unified participatory missiology was a relational network of mutual connections with distant mission workers. In churches with a delegatory approach to distant mission, the number of distant contacts was limited, or the connections were restricted to key members of the church with an interest in global mission. By contrast, a unified participatory approach engaged people throughout the church. These relational connections were encouraged by the regularity of communication between the church and distant workers as well as regular opportunities to maintain and develop the relationships. In many cases the richness of the relationship derived from the long history of association between the church and the mission worker which predated the worker's distant ministry. When distant mission workers had previously been attendees, or even staff, at a church, the relational connection was more easily maintained. This suggests that a unified participatory missiology is more likely to be evident in churches that have sent out their own members. Where multiple members of the church regularly engaged in personal communication with distant mission workers, the relational connections thrived, and the participatory approach was encouraged.

A key feature of these relationships was an emphasis on mutuality which was not evident with a delegatory approach. While a delegatory approach emphasized a unidirectional support model of engagement, a participatory missiology facilitated multidirectional partnership. These relationships moved beyond exchange patterns to display communal characteristics. Church members were motivated to engage with distant mission workers and make a meaningful contribution in whatever way they could. This facilitated the flow of a variety of resources from the church to the mission workers, such as technical skills, physical resources, and psychological care. The mission workers were also more likely to contribute to the church. By engaging personally with the members, they shared their wisdom, experience, and knowledge. These benefits experienced by the churches were examples of external social capital.

Drawing on the experiences of these MGE churches, it is possible to describe the ways in which these social capital benefits would be evident in churches displaying a unified participatory missiology. These benefits are understood in terms of structural, relational, and cognitive dimensions. The structural social capital provides many ways that church members can be involved in distant mission. Through connections with people serving in a variety of ways and places, church members' involvement in mission can take many forms. Participation is easier because of these relational connections. The relational social capital means that church members are personally shaped by the relational connection. Honest communication with mission workers builds trust and authenticity which stimulates engagement. Norms of behavior and purpose are shared between the distant mission workers and church members thus providing a model for self-sacrificial Christian ministry. This may extend to a shared identity in which local church members recognize their own missional capacity. These social capital benefits bring increased efficiency of action, enhanced flow of information about the world, and an increased sense of "collective agency."[1] Church members are not only inspired for participation in distant mission, they are also motivated for involvement in local mission. As Pam Arlund notes,

> As a part of this global family of God, we have joy when we are connected globally. Local bodies praying for those who do not know Jesus, giving finances, personnel, and resources to the other side of the world and establishing friendships globally will not weaken the church and will not damage local outreach. In fact, calling people to global purposes and awakening them to the purpose of the family of Abraham will also awaken people to local outreach.[2]

This highlights the intellectual capital that flows through the cognitive dimension of social capital and complements the structural and relational impacts of a participatory missiology. Churches that display these deep relational networks will have their missional beliefs shaped by the experience. Though the foundational missiological convictions about the nature, goal, and location of mission are not changed, beliefs regarding the church's capacity, responsibility, and attitude to distant mission are changed. The members of these churches realize that they have the

---

1. Nahapiet and Ghoshal, "Social Capital," 243; Leonard and Bellamy, "Dimensions of Bonding," 1050.

2. Arlund, "Acts 1:8," 55.

capacity for involvement because their distant relationships facilitate a multidimensional partnership. They can personally contribute to distant mission through financial, emotional, practical, and spiritual means. They experience God's abundance as they see him provide for both them and the mission workers. These relationships also serve to heighten the church members' appreciation of their responsibility for distant mission as they gain an accurate understanding of the needs and opportunities for mission in distant contexts. They will see the significant disparity in access to Christian resources in different contexts and better appreciate the need they have to contribute. Thirdly, these relational connections bring joy as members see Christian mission taking place and they recognize the privilege of being involved. This experiential knowledge stimulates further mission involvement to create a positive feedback loop (see figure 10). The rich relational networks with distant mission workers shape the church members' missional beliefs regarding their capacity, responsibility, and opportunity for mission. This forms a missional culture which is expressed through priorities, processes, and practices within a church which creates a strong organizational climate for both distant and local mission involvement. This culture and climate mean that church members see participation in distant mission activities as the expected behavior leading to the ongoing development of richer relational networks with distant mission workers.

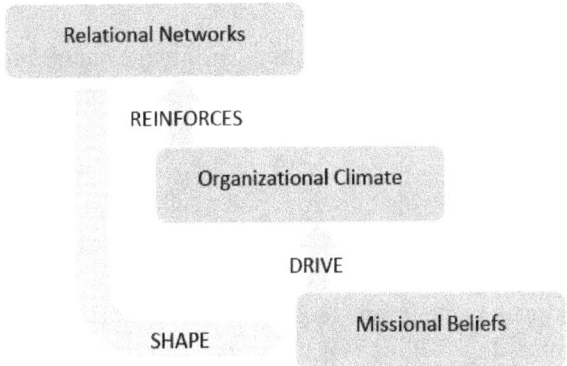

Figure 10. The Positive Feedback of a Unified Participatory Missiology

A local church with a local-focused bifurcated missiology is unlikely to experience these benefits because the relational networks that drive the system are not sufficiently developed. Even where distant mission is supported by the church, the relationships are fewer in number and more transactional in nature. Distant mission workers receive financial and prayer support to do mission activities on the church's behalf, but the members are not meaningfully engaged. In some cases, a delegatory approach could involve the church sending significant financial resources, yet where the relational connection is limited the social capital benefits and positive feedback are missed. If the workers only connect with the church leadership or a small group of members who are enthusiastic about mission, the rest of the church will miss out. The relational stimulus to engagement in mission is lost and the core missional beliefs regarding the church's capacity and responsibility for mission involvement are not challenged. They are also more likely to perceive distant mission as a necessary burden rather than a privileged opportunity to be embraced. The organizational culture that drives a climate of mission involvement is therefore missing. Efforts to stimulate a change in distant mission practice by introducing new processes or practices will have limited lasting impact because the beliefs that underpin a delegatory approach persist. The influence of the relational networks is needed to shape the organizational culture of the church and to align the three core missional beliefs to a unified participatory missiology.

MISSIONAL BELIEFS AND THE LOCAL CHURCH

As discussed in chapter 5, convictions regarding the nature, goal, and location of mission did not differ markedly between a unified participatory missiology and a delegatory approach to distant mission. In both cases, the primary concern for other people's spiritual needs was complemented by the view that Christians must love holistically and seek to address all human needs. Similarly, there was a consistent emphasis in the missionary task on proclamation of the gospel message together with a realization that Christian actions and lifestyle are essential elements of faithful mission. Both participatory and bifurcated approaches recognize that mission is needed in all contexts, but the latter places a different emphasis on local and distant, and engages in each differently. This highlights the different missional beliefs between the two approaches which concern the church's capacity, responsibility, and attitude toward distant mission involvement. These three missional beliefs are the primary differences between a unified participatory missiology and a bifurcated missiology and therefore warrant deeper consideration.

Perceived Capacity for Mission Involvement

A person's perception of their church's capacity for distant mission involvement is likely to be consistent with the missiological approach of their church. People in churches displaying a delegatory approach to distant mission are more likely to focus on the limited nature of the church's resources with a greater emphasis on finances. They stress the need to wisely apportion resources to address the most pressing concerns and assume that there will be some worthy activities that cannot be supported. By contrast, people from churches with a unified participatory missiology are more likely to see financial resources as just one aspect of their capacity. Together with the financial and physical resources of the church, the wisdom, knowledge, experience, abilities, and spirituality of the church's members are seen to enable the church to be involved in distant mission in a variety of ways. This difference in the scope of resources considered shows that these beliefs are not dependent on the objective capacity of the church. Though financial difficulties may strengthen the perception of limited capacity, members of a small church with relatively limited resources but displaying a unified participatory missiology are more likely to be aware of the variety of ways in which they can engage. Therefore, it is not the actual resources but the perceived resources which are likely to determine the approach to mission engagement.

The impact of a person's perceived capacity of available resources has previously been recognized for its influence on mission participation. A recent examination of Ethiopian diaspora churches in the United States noted that they were variously involved in local mission, but that their international efforts were "restricted only to Ethiopians."[3] In exploring the causes of this limitation, the author noted the influence of ethnocentrism and a belief that Ethiopians are recipients rather than agents of mission, yet another notable factor was the belief that international mission was "too expensive" and that the churches lacked the financial capacity to be involved.[4] The author concluded that, among these churches, "mis-

---

3. Korcho, "Case for Missions," 247.
4. Korcho, "Case for Missions," 247.

sion is wrongly associated with the "haves" and "have-nots" mentality."[5] This issue was explicitly addressed through a global consultation on the involvement of Christians from less wealthy contexts in the funding of Bible translation.[6] The desire to facilitate true global partnership led the members of the Wycliffe Global Alliance to wrestle with this disparity of wealth. The consultation affirmed that financial capacity should not be a determinant of involvement, but rather "everyone can give because everyone has something to contribute."[7] Theologically, they affirmed the belief that "God creatively provides for [God's] mission through a diversity of people, means, and resources [and] . . . each person can joyfully and generously give according to the blessings God has given."[8] This highlights the fact that there is a myriad of ways that churches can contribute to global mission regardless of their financial resources. As Kenyan mission leader, Dennis Tongoi observes, "a generous life is not based on how much one has or does not have; it is not only for those who have a surplus . . . [It is a] giving of oneself, not just of one's possessions."[9] This is equally true in an Australian context where churches can show high levels of involvement in mission regardless of their financial capacity. However, in churches with a delegatory approach to distant mission the perception of capacity is more likely to limit participation in distant contexts.

The significance of social contexts for shaping this perception of capacity has previously been identified in people's approach to charitable giving. Sociologist Robert Wuthnow examined the history of Christian giving in America and noted that theology plays a role but that generosity was also "an aspect of social life that is embedded in social institutions."[10] Wuthnow's research found four key factors that increased the amount of money people gave to Christian entities: a religious upbringing, personal devotional practices as an adult, conservative Christian beliefs, and social connection through volunteering or church-based friendships.[11] He concluded that personal beliefs and social connections work together to

5. Korcho, "Case for Missions," 247.
6. Franklin and Niemandt, "Funding God's Mission," 384–409.
7. Franklin and Niemandt, "Funding God's Mission," 393. They also noted the problems of dependency and paternalism that have been perpetuated by Western missionary affluence. See Bonk, *Missions and Money*.
8. Franklin and Niemandt, "Funding God's Mission," 401.
9. Tongoi, "Living Generously," Part III.
10. Wuthnow, *Faith and Giving*, 3.
11. Wuthnow, *All in Sync*, 18–19.

shape a person's approach to giving. This is consistent with the findings of this study as people in churches with a delegatory approach to distant mission had a shared belief that their capacity is limited which limited their involvement. By contrast, people in churches with a participatory missiology had a culture of engagement in mission which was not impacted by their capacity.

These differing perceptions may reflect deeper beliefs about God's provision and the economic assumptions that shape worldview. Max Weber famously argued that the Calvinist belief in an earthly vocation provided the foundation for capitalism and the Western market economy.[12] However, it is widely recognized that these economic assumptions now hold greater sway over the global population than any Calvinist convictions. David Loy has described market capitalism as the world's dominant religion, suggesting that it is "the most successful religion of all time, winning more converts more quickly than any previous belief system or value-system in human history."[13] Lesslie Newbigin went one step further and described the "ideology of the free market" as "a form of idolatry."[14] Similarly, Walter Brueggemann suggested that "consumerism . . . has become a demonic spiritual force among us."[15] He argued that it is founded on the "myth of scarcity" but "God's abundance transcends the market economy."[16] Tracing the "liturgy of abundance" through the Bible, Brueggemann notes its presence in the creation account, the Exodus narrative, and particularly in the ministry and teachings of Jesus.[17]

Churches that display a unified participatory missiology live out the conviction that God will provide for them and the ministries that they support. By contrast, a delegatory approach is often shaped by the assumption that resources are scarce, and it would be unwise to invest too heavily in distant needs. Christians that follow a delegatory approach to distant mission are unlikely to explicitly state that God's lack of provision limits their global mission involvement. Yet, as Patrick Kuwana observes, "the very worldview of scarcity is one that questions the goodness of

---

12. Weber, *Protestant Work Ethic*.
13. Loy, "Religion of the Market," 276.
14. Newbigin, *Open Secret*, 95.
15. Brueggemann, "Liturgy of Abundance," 342.
16. Brueggemann, "Liturgy of Abundance," 343; Barram, *Missional Economics*, expands Brueggemann's biblical survey highlighting the significance of God's abundant generosity to the formation of Christians.
17. Brueggemann, "Liturgy of Abundance," 342–47.

God."[18] A delegatory approach may therefore indicate that the economic assumptions of the free market are having a greater influence on the church's approach to mission than their stated beliefs of God's provision. A participatory missiology does not make people immune to the pervasive economic context, but the formation that comes through the relational networks and generous involvement in distant mission facilitates a theological recalibration. As R. Scott Rodin suggests, "generosity is an act of trust" in which Christians show that they "worship a God of abundance."[19]

Christian generosity is a practice which has been noted to have deep biblical roots. Craig Blomberg's survey of the biblical teaching on wealth and generosity concludes that Christians are to be stewards of God's resources which he provides for them to be generous.[20] Blomberg notes that the Scriptures praise people for their generosity (Acts 28:7; 2 Cor 8:2; 9:5, 11, 13) and even command them to be generous (Luke 11:41; 1 Tim 6:18). Miroslav Volf's theological perspective suggests that generosity is one way that Christians become like God.[21] Through creation and providence, God has given freely to all people and Christians should do likewise.[22] This is more than good stewardship, Volf suggests that the trinitarian nature of God means that giving is intrinsic to his being. Through a social understanding of the trinity, Volf notes that the Father, Son, and Holy Spirit delight to give to and receive from one another. "Each divine person gives, receives, and returns. Each loves and glorifies the other two, and each receives love and glory from them."[23] This divine reciprocity is an expression of equality and generosity within the Godhead. As those who are "in Christ" (Rom 6:11, 23; 8:1, 39; 12:5), Christians experience this love and generosity of God and are drawn into relationships with other Christians in which that same generosity can be shown. Generous reciprocal relationships are therefore a core expression of God's character among Christians. Partnership with distant mission workers is a concrete example of these reciprocal relationships. In the context of a local church, they may serve to counteract the economic assumptions of the free market. Rather than a perception of limited

---

18. Kuwana, "Freedom to Live," Part IV.
19. Rodin, "Generous Life," Part I.
20. Blomberg, *Christians*.
21. Volf, "Being as God Is," 7.
22. Volf, "Being as God Is," 7–8.
23. Volf, "Being as God Is," 9.

resources inhibiting church involvement in mission, the intentional development of generous reciprocal relationships may help church members to recognize the abundance of God's provision.

Perceived Responsibility for Mission Involvement

The second missional belief that is likely to differ between churches with a unified participatory missiology and a local-focused bifurcated missiology is the perceived responsibility for distant mission. In both approaches the need for Christians to be involved in mission is recognized. A unified participatory missiology holds together the need for involvement in local and distant mission. People are encouraged to be actively engaged in both by sharing their faith locally and developing relational connections to distant mission workers. By contrast, a bifurcated missiology separates the local and the distant. With a delegatory approach to distant mission, it sees distant activities as the primary responsibility of others while the local church focuses on local needs. This difference of perceived responsibility for distant mission has long been a concern among evangelical mission leaders. In 1902, Andrew Murray stated that one "key to the missionary problem" was that many pastors did not "believe that the great aim of the existence of their congregations [was] to make Christ known to every creature."[24] In 1958, Lesslie Newbigin observed that, "the church's mission is concerned with the ends of the earth. When that dimension is forgotten, the heart goes out of the whole business."[25] And in 2000, James Engel and William Dyrness suggested that the "displacement of the local church in world outreach" was one of the key causes of weakness in global mission.[26]

Changing definitions of mission has often been blamed as the cause of waning concern for distant mission in local churches. Through the eighteenth and nineteenth centuries, the language of mission among Protestants primarily referred to Christian "encounter with the world beyond Europe and America."[27] Through the twentieth century, conversations in the ecumenical movement and the growth of the majority world church broadened the definition of mission to include "everything the

24. Murray, *Missionary Problem*, 17.
25. Newbigin, *One Body*, 27.
26. Engel and Dyrness, *Changing the Mind*, 74.
27. Stroope, *Transcending Mission*, 322.

church is sent into the world to do."[28] This meant that mission equally referred to a local church's efforts to evangelize people in their immediate context, and the work of a missionary in a distant nation with no Christian presence. Lesslie Newbigin responded by highlighting the difference between "mission" and "missions," with the latter reflecting "the concern that in the places where there are no Christians there should be Christians."[29] However, the broader definition has received widespread acceptance and is blamed by some for the lack of evangelical involvement in distant mission.[30] As noted earlier, the missional church movement has been accused of perpetuating this neglect as it has challenged Christians to recognize their own communities as contexts for mission.[31] Ed Stetzer suggested that the missional church movement has failed to see the "church's mandate to be a global presence with a global mission."[32] However, this study found that churches that identified as missional were neither more nor less involved in distant mission than other churches. Similarly, the churches that displayed a delegatory approach to distant mission did not define mission differently to those with a participatory approach. Therefore, a difference in the way mission is defined was not the cause of different levels of responsibility for distant mission among Sydney evangelical churches.

A more likely cause was the difference in perceived spiritual need in distant contexts between churches with a participatory missiology and those with a delegatory approach to distant mission. Members of churches with a unified participatory missiology often noted the unequal access to Christian resources around the world and the resulting needs for Christian ministry in distant contexts. By contrast, members of churches with a delegatory approach to distant mission often noted the growth of the church in the majority world while highlighting the spiritual needs in their local communities. As one church leader said,

---

28. Stott, *Christian Mission*, 30.

29. Newbigin, "Mission and Missions," 23. This comment appears to be a response to Stephen Neill's statement that, "If everything that the Church does is to be classed as 'mission' we shall have to find another term for the Church's particular responsibility for 'the heathen,' those who have never heard the Name of Christ." Neill, *Creative Tension*, 81.

30. Corwin, "MissionS," 4–5; Spitters and Ellison, *When Everything Is Missions*; Spitters and Ellison, *Conversations*; Horner, *When Missions Shapes*.

31. Goheen, *Introducing Christian Mission*, 404.

32. Stetzer, "Missional and Missions," 40–41.

> It can be discouraging sometimes when you try and share Jesus with your family and you don't always see a lot of ground. But then to witness places in the world where people are just flocking to Jesus. It just gives you a renewed hope for the gospel.³³

This belief that Christianity is thriving in other countries but needs greater support locally is consistent with a shift in perspectives on global Christianity discussed by Robert Wuthnow.³⁴ Wuthnow examined the transnational and transcultural activities of US churches and suggested that the "global Christianity paradigm," which highlights the shift of Christianity's center of gravity to the majority world, fails to appreciate the important role American churches play globally.³⁵ He argued that this narrative discouraged the participation of American Christians in global mission.

> A US reader learning that Christianity is flourishing so well on its own in the global South could reasonably conclude that US churches should mind their own business . . . If anything, he or she might conclude that the mission of US churches should be to their own communities, given the demise of Christianity in the global North."³⁶

This dynamic appears to be a feature of the local-focused bifurcated missiology. Though involvement in mission is valued theologically, the belief that the Christian faith is vibrant in distant nations and weak in Australia supports the separation of the local and distant mission and weakens the sense of responsibility for involvement in distant contexts.

These beliefs are potentially being reinforced by ministry resources that highlight the spiritual needs in Australia but make little reference to needs elsewhere. One interviewee expressed the concern that attendance at a Reach Australia conference inspired her church's leaders to be more actively involved in local mission activities but not in distant mission.³⁷ One of the contributing ministries to Reach Australia is Vine Growers,

---

33. Interview with CH1_SP, August 26, 2019. This person was referring to Indonesia, a country where 3.5 percent of the population are evangelical Christians. See Johnson and Zurlo, *World Christian Encyclopedia*, 394.

34. Wuthnow, *Boundless Faith*.

35. Wuthnow associates the "global Christian paradigm" with Philip Jenkins, Andrew Walls, David Bosch, Kwame Bediako, Samuel Escobar, and Lamin Sanneh among others. *Boundless* Faith, 32–61.

36. Wuthnow, *Boundless Faith*, 60.

37. Interview with CH1_MC, September 27, 2019.

which helps churches apply the approach to church ministry developed by Colin Marshall and Tony Payne.[38] Marshall and Payne's resources focus local church mission on the task of making disciples as commanded in Matthew 28:18–20. They are at pains to note that the reference to "all nations" in this passage is not limited to overseas locations.

> The where of making disciples is everywhere from the family dinner table to the proverbial mission fields of deepest, darkest Africa (a place, incidentally, where one is more likely these days to find a learner of Jesus than in the middle-class suburb of the "Christian" West).[39]

Though Marshall and Payne are seeking to emphasize the fact that local and distant mission are the same, the parenthetical remark reflects the belief that Christianity shows greater vitality in distant contexts than it does in Australia. This serves to distinguish local from distant mission and supports the lack of responsibility for distant mission that is evident with a delegatory approach.

The last century has seen a dramatic shift in the global distribution of evangelical Christians, but there remains a significant need for distant mission. According to the World Christian Encyclopedia, in 1900 only 7.8 percent of all evangelicals lived in the nations of the Global South, yet by 2020, this was 77.5 percent.[40] Christianity is indeed thriving in some overseas contexts. As Zurlo, Johnson, and Crossing note, "The decline of Christianity in the Global North is now being outpaced by the rise of Christianity in the Global South."[41] Yet, as the data shows, this is only part of the story. A core concern of evangelicals is that all people on earth would have the opportunity to hear and respond to the gospel message. Despite the growth of Christianity in the majority world, 28.3 percent of the global population remained unevangelized in 2020; that equates to over 2.2 billion people.[42] Even beyond the task of evangelism, it is widely

---

38. Marshall and Payne, *Trellis*; Marshall and Payne, *Vine Project*. See https://www.vinegrowers.com.

39. Marshall and Payne, *Vine Project*, 130.

40. Johnson and Zurlo, *World Christian Encyclopaedia*, 25, uses the term "global south" to refer to the majority world.

41. Zurlo et al., "World Christianity," 9.

42. Zurlo et al., "World Christianity," 17. Other global databases, such as the Joshua Project (https://joshuaproject.net) and IMB Global Research (https://grd.imb.org), agree that over two billion people still require access to the Christian gospel even though their definitions vary.

recognized that Christians from the Global North continue to have an important role in global mission even if that role has changed.[43] Therefore, the belief that churches in Australia do not have a responsibility for distant mission reflects a naive understanding of global Christianity. There are more Christians in the majority world than previously and even more than in the Global North, but by any evangelical understanding of missionary need, there is an ongoing need for Christians from the Global North to be actively engaged beyond their context. Members of churches with a delegatory approach to distant mission are more likely to have a limited understanding of these global needs. However, the rich relational networks with people in distant contexts encouraged by a participatory missiology provide a deeper level of global awareness that highlights the ongoing need for distant mission involvement. With greater global awareness, a participatory missiology strengthens the perceived responsibility to be involved in distant mission.

Perceived Privilege of Mission Involvement

The third difference in missional belief between a unified participatory missiology and a local-focused bifurcated missiology relates to the way involvement in distant mission is viewed. Those with a participatory missiology described involvement in positive terms seeing it as a privilege to be embraced. Those with a delegatory approach to distant mission viewed it more negatively, as an important task but one they were not enthused about. One indicator of this difference was the verbs that were commonly used to describe the connections with distant mission workers. People from churches with a delegatory approach were more likely to speak about *supporting* mission workers while those with a participatory missiology prefer the language of *partnership*.

These differences have previously been explored by Bruce Camp who described churches as following either a "supporting," a "sending," or a "synergistic" paradigm of mission involvement.[44] In the supporting paradigm, churches are dependent upon mission organizations. They view

---

43. Borthwick, *Western Christians*; Morgan, "Global Trends," 325–38; Young, *World Christianity*. These authors all recognize that the role Christians from the Global North fulfill in world evangelization has changed, with a growing emphasis on partnership with majority world Christians, but the task remains.

44. Camp, "Major Paradigm," 133–38. Camp notes, "In reality, these paradigms represent a continuum of missions activities."

the organization as the expert, and they delegate responsibility to them. These churches provide financial support and occasional prayer support but "they are only superficially involved in the life of the missionary and his or her ministries."[45] This reflects the delegatory approach to distant mission observed in this study. The sending paradigm is a complete reversal of the supporting approach in which the church acts independently of mission agencies by dictating every dimension of their involvement. This pattern was not evident in any of the churches in this study. The synergistic paradigm is a "partnership model" in which the church works interdependently with mission workers and mission organizations seeking to be as involved as they can.[46] This is consistent with the pattern observed in churches displaying a unified participatory missiology. Camp suggests that "churches should strive for interdependence as opposed to dependent or independent paradigms." Stephen Carne argues more strongly that the support paradigm reflects a "distorted ecclesiology," and that partnership is the biblical model for local church mission involvement.[47] This pattern of partnership is often associated with the relationship between the apostle Paul and the Philippian church where it is noted to be a source of joy for both (Phil 1:4, 25; 2:2, 29; 4:1).[48] A delegatory approach to distant mission, with its emphasis on support, expects the church to provide resources and energy yet without being directly engaged. By contrast, a participatory missiology emphasizes partnership and mutuality whereby the church is actively engaged in the mission endeavor. A church that sees its task as supporting is always giving, while a church that sees its task as partnership is both giving and receiving. This has an emotional impact on the members of the church such that they perceive mission involvement as either a privilege or a burden.

This perception that mission involvement is a privilege is one of the social capital benefits that comes through the relational networks of a participatory missiology. Church members gain an increased awareness of the needs and opportunities for mission involvement, and through their connection with the mission workers they seek to address these needs. By partnering with the worker relationally, spiritually, and financially

---

45. Camp, "Major Paradigm," 134.

46. Camp, "Major Paradigm," 135. Camp saw the shift towards a synergistic paradigm as consequential of the rise of the Baby Boomer generation.

47. Carne, "Koinōnia for the Nations."

48. Bush, "True Christian Partnership," 3–15; O'Brien, "Fellowship Theme"; Sampley, *Pauline Partnership*; Schnabel, *Early Christian Mission*, 1460–63.

church members feel that they are having an impact. This also facilitates the spiritual formation of church members, as distant mission workers serve as examples of self-sacrificial devotion to God which church members are encouraged to emulate in their own context and ministry. They may even learn from the mission workers how to participate more effectively in local mission. These benefits are a source of encouragement and joy for church members that inspire them to continue.

Kirsteen Kim has previously explored the local impact of a church's participation in global mission activities by considering what can be learned from non-western expressions of Christianity around the world. As Christians seek to reach the multi-cultural, secular, and consumerist context of the West, Kim argues that they must engage with the theology and practice of non-western churches. Without "worldwide vision and global links" the church is "inclined to forget that [they] are not the whole church but only part of the much wider movement of God's grace."[49] This study's findings support Kim's assertion while noting the importance of individuals to provide these global links. For a local church in Australia to understand their relationship to mission in different places they need strong relational bonds to people who are serving in these contexts, typically people who have been sent out from their own church. These links will strengthen local mission engagement as church members see how mission is progressing in distant contexts and realize that they too are involved in God's wider mission.

In this way, a unified participatory missiology also emphasizes the *missio Dei* as it views involvement in distant mission as "joining in with the Spirit."[50] Through their relational connections to mission in distant places, church members see God providing for and enabling mission to take place around the world. These experiences of God's sovereign involvement in mission alleviates the burden of participation because the outcome is seen to be dependent on him. Believers view God as the one who does the work, and they are invited to participate through their partnership with the distant mission worker. This shifts mission involvement beyond the fulfilment of an obligation to being an expression of the church's relationship with God. This connection with God is a source of joy in the same way that worship or prayer might be. As Evelyne Reisacher notes, "If we believe that mission is first and foremost the mission

---

49. Kim, *Joining*, 283.
50. Kim, *Joining*, 1.

of God (*missio Dei*), we must anticipate that joy will characterize his mission."[51] Sebastian and Kirsteen Kim argue that this is clearly the case in the vital Korean mission movement where joy rather than obligation is the primary motivation.[52]

The place of joy in mission has gained significant attention in recent missiology.[53] John Flett's analysis of Karl Barth's theology of the Trinity, the *missio Dei*, and the church, concluded that "joy is the wellspring of the missionary act . . . [and] mission is the abundant fellowship of active participation in the very glory that is the life of God from and to all eternity."[54] Reisacher has articulated a "joy-centric mission" by drawing from several biblical texts including the Aaronic blessing of Numbers 6 as echoed in Psalm 67.[55] She suggests that the joy that comes through a relational connection to God is worked out through mission. As the gospel is a message of "great joy for all the people" (Luke 2:10), "joy splashes in all directions" when it is shared.[56] This foundation of joy provides a motivation for mission that echoes through a participatory missiology, while a delegatory approach to distant mission may more closely reflect the position described by Lesslie Newbigin.

> There has been a long tradition which sees the mission of the Church primarily as obedience to a command. It has been customary to speak of "the missionary mandate." This way of putting the matter is certainly not without justification, and yet it seems to me that it misses the point. It tends to make mission a burden rather than a joy, to make it part of the law rather than part of the gospel. If one looks at the New Testament evidence one gets another impression. Mission begins with a kind of explosion of joy. The news that the rejected and crucified Jesus is alive is something that cannot possibly be suppressed.[57]

This is a profound theological distinction. Members of churches with a participatory missiology see the privilege and joy that it is to

51. Reisacher, *Joyful Witness*, 19.

52. Kim and Kim, "Korean Missions," 279–88.

53. Yale School of Divinity engaged in a three-year project exploring the theology of joy under the leadership of Miroslav Volf with input from Jürgen Moltmann, Jonathan Sacks, N. T. Wright, and Nicholas Wolterstorff. This discussed a range of issues including the place of joy in mission. See Yale Center for Faith & Culture, "Theology of Joy."

54. Flett, *Witness of God*, 295–96.

55. Reisacher, *Joyful Witness*, 19.

56. Reisacher, *Joyful Witness*, 22–23.

57. Newbigin, *Gospel*, 116.

engage in distant mission activities because of their relational connections to mission workers. Yet the emphasis on the *missio Dei* indicates it is also an expression of their personal relationship with God. They are engaging more deeply with God as they engage in that which he is doing at a distance. It therefore serves to strengthen their faith. Those in churches with a delegatory approach to distant mission may be missing this joy because they focus on obligation as the motivating grounds for distant mission involvement. Together with beliefs about the church's capacity and responsibility for distant mission, these beliefs distinguish the culture of a church with a unified participatory missiology from one with a local-focused bifurcated missiology that delegates distant mission involvement to others.

ORGANIZATIONAL CULTURE AND CLIMATE FOR MISSION

These three missional beliefs were the fundamental factors found to shape the organizational culture and resulting climate for mission involvement in the local churches examined in this study. These missional beliefs encouraged either participation or delegation of distant mission and were expressed through the priorities and practices of the local church. Drawing on this analysis, it is possible to describe the likely organizational qualities in churches displaying either a unified participatory missiology or a bifurcated delegatory missiology. A church with a unified participatory missiology will have practices, processes, and systems that lead members to see personal participation in both local and distant mission as the normal expected behavior. This provides a strong climate for global mission engagement. By contrast, a church with a local-focused bifurcated missiology is likely to display practices, processes, and systems that lead members to see participation in local mission as the expected behavior, but involvement in distant mission as optional. This is a weak climate for global mission engagement. These different climates are likely to be expressed through the practices of prayer, finance, mobilization, and leadership.

Churches with a delegatory approach to distant mission may have some similarities of mission practice to those with a participatory approach, yet with less stimulus for personal engagement. Prayer for distant mission is a common practice in all churches, but with a delegatory approach, prayers may be perfunctory and irregular. Prayer information is often made available but, in the absence of meaningful relational connection, the church members are less motivated to pray. Prayer for distant mission is a less consistent feature of church gatherings and is not encouraged by the climate of the church. Financial support for distant mission is approached similarly. Though the models for collecting or disseminating funds may be the same in churches with a participatory or delegatory approach, the value placed on the practice is lessened with a local-focused bifurcated missiology. The lack of relational connection demotivates participation. The structures for financial support exist, but the limitation of resources is highlighted as the local needs are more keenly observed. Finally, a church displaying a delegatory approach to distant mission may have processes to stimulate engagement in local mission but does not have the same structural support for distant mission involvement. The processes to encourage relational connection with mission workers and facilitate church member participation in distant mission are not evident as the missional leadership is primarily focused on local mission activities. The structures therefore reinforce the missional beliefs.

By contrast, churches with a unified participatory missiology have a culture and climate of mission engagement that transforms these mission practices. Participation is regularly encouraged through communal prayer and communication. There is prayer for distant mission workers and global needs when members meet for church services, prayer meetings, or small group gatherings. This prayer is informed by regular communication with mission workers and, when possible, mission workers are given extended opportunities to share directly with the church. This rich climate for missionary prayer extends to private prayer practices because of the relational connection. Various systems for financial support of distant mission are employed, but they are approached more positively in participatory churches. Money is viewed as part of the wider partnership with mission workers that the church members know personally. Church members therefore see giving funds as part of an integrated church involvement in which their contribution is valued. The amount of money given is likely to be greater, but more important than the amount given is the personal engagement expressed through the gift. This participatory missiology may employ similar methods of prayer and financial giving, but the church member engagement is higher.

The church practices which are likely to display the most notable differences between a participatory and a delegatory approach are in the areas of leadership and mobilization. A participatory missiology will be expressed through leadership structures and processes that intentionally facilitate whole church involvement in global mission. This extends beyond involvement in church-based activities to encourage members to be directly involved from their home or even to consider whether they might serve in distant mission themselves. These practices create a local church's climate for global mission engagement which encourages participation in local mission activities and relational connections with distant mission workers. This in turn strengthens the missional beliefs which provides further positive feedback (see figure 6). Therefore, while the missional beliefs influence church practice it is not a unidirectional relationship, they both shape and are shaped by organizational practices.

Despite this capacity for structural features to stimulate a richer engagement in global mission, their presence alone is not reliable evidence of a unified participatory missiology. Some churches with a delegatory approach to distant mission show practices and processes of prayer or financial support that are like those in churches with a participatory approach. Church leaders may encourage these practices to strengthen the church's global engagement; however, in isolation these practices have limited capacity to change church culture. To produce the positive feedback of a participatory missiology, a rich relational network is needed to shape the missional beliefs which drive the climate of global mission involvement. As the delegatory approach often lacks these relational connections, the practices are less able to bring the transformation of missional beliefs that a strong culture of mission requires.

Churches displaying a delegatory approach to distant mission may have similar stated priorities to those with a participatory approach but lack the cultural integration. Evangelical convictions are often expressed through an espoused commitment to global mission and leaders of churches with a local-focused bifurcated missiology may speak of the importance of involvement in global mission, but the culture of distant mission engagement is not present. This often results from a misalignment between the espoused priorities and the shared beliefs regarding the church's capacity, responsibility, and attitude towards global mission. Some members of the church may be actively involved but there is a lack of cultural integration such that the cultural norms around distant mission involvement are not clear and the climate for participation is weak.[58] If the relational networks and missional beliefs are lacking, efforts

---

58. Martin, *Organizational Culture*, 120–21.

to stimulate change by instituting new processes may result in cultural fragmentation or differentiation. The structural features that result from a participatory missiology can strengthen the mission culture by facilitating relational engagement, yet without the rich networks and the social capital that results, introducing *structural* change is unlikely to bring *cultural* change. In the churches examined in this research the cultural integration and shared missional beliefs of the unified participatory missiology were dependent upon a rich network of relational connections with distant mission workers.

CONCLUSION

This study's analysis of MGE and LGE churches has identified several core factors that explain the differences in their patterns of mission engagement. This diversity is not due to varying ecclesiological convictions or beliefs about the nature, goal, or location of mission but reflect two missiological approaches to church involvement in mission. MGE churches displayed a unified participatory missiology which encouraged equal engagement in local and distant mission, while LGE churches displayed a bifurcated missiology that encouraged active participation in local mission while delegating responsibility for distant mission to others. The most important factor shaping a participatory missiology was the rich relational network between distant mission workers and the members of the church. This network was a source of external social capital which brought multiple structural, relational, and cognitive benefits that transformed the missional beliefs and practices of the church. Members of these churches believed they had the capacity and responsibility for involvement in mission globally, and they considered it a privilege to be embraced. This not only shaped their involvement in distant mission, as their approach to mission and what they learned through relationships with distant mission partners also stimulated local mission engagement. By contrast, members of churches with a local-focused bifurcated missiology had little relational connection with distant mission workers. They viewed distant mission as a valuable activity but considered it as primarily the responsibility others. Prayer and financial support were often given, but personal involvement was limited. People in these churches were less convinced of their capacity or responsibility for distant mission, and they were more likely to view it as a burden. These missional beliefs shaped the culture and climate of mission engagement, but it was the relational connections that determined these beliefs.

Conservative evangelical churches that display high levels of engagement in both local and distant mission are likely to be shaped by a unified participatory missiology. This missiology is founded on the beliefs that the church is responsible for distant mission, it has the capacity to participate in distant mission, and this participation is a privileged opportunity to join God in his mission. These beliefs are strengthened by the mutual relational network that these churches have with distant mission workers. Through these relationships, church members become engaged in distant mission and the church develops processes to encourage prayer, financial partnership, and fuller participation in local and distant mission. Though some of these processes may be evident in churches with low levels of engagement in distant mission, the absence of the relational networks and missional beliefs mean that the culture and climate of mission engagement is weak; whereas in churches with a unified participatory missiology, these structural features stimulate deeper relational engagement which further reinforce the missional beliefs. Therefore, with a participatory missiology, the network of relationships shapes missional beliefs which drive organizational practices that further stimulate global mission engagement through a positive feedback loop.

9

Implications for Local Churches and Mission

Evangelical churches in Australia have a long history of involvement in mission but, as this study has shown, patterns of participation vary markedly from church to church. Evangelical church leaders continue to affirm the importance of global mission activity, but this is expressed in many ways. A review of the literature found evidence of a shifting emphasis among local churches from a global mission concern to one that prioritizes local needs only. Anecdotally, this has resulted in great diversity in the way that local churches participate in mission with some only focused on their local context, others only distant contexts, and others committed to both. This variety has been attributed to several possible causes. The twentieth century saw significant change in the theology of mission, particularly as it related to ecclesiology. The nature and goal of mission was disputed as people responded to liberal theology and the dramatic growth in Christianity in the majority world. A growing emphasis on the *missio Dei* also stimulated a re-examination of the place of local churches in mission and the place of mission in the local church. Previous research examining the practice of local churches in other contexts identified various factors that shape mission practice, but very little research has considered the Australian context. This study addresses this need by exploring the nature, extent, and cause of the diversity of local church involvement in mission among conservative Australian evangelical churches.

This exploration examined the factors influencing patterns of mission involvement in evangelical churches in NSW and the ACT with a particular focus on Sydney. A survey of 205 evangelical churches revealed varying levels of local and overseas mission involvement. Larger churches reported higher levels of activity than smaller churches in both local and overseas mission, but by controlling for church size, comparisons were able to be made and relationships between different factors explored. Churches that identified as missional were more likely to show higher levels of involvement in local mission but not more likely to show higher levels of involvement in overseas mission. Similarly, although there was a relationship between involvement in local and overseas mission, it appeared to be unidirectional. Churches with high levels of involvement in overseas mission were more likely to show higher levels of involvement in local mission. However, churches with high levels of local mission involvement were equivalent to all other churches in terms of their involvement in overseas mission. These findings demonstrate the positive impact that overseas mission involvement has on the mission practices of a local church. Participation in overseas mission activities stimulates local mission involvement, but local mission involvement does not stimulate overseas mission participation.

This relationship and the factors shaping overseas mission involvement were examined through a grounded theory analysis of semi-structured interviews with church members and leaders from ten evangelical churches across Sydney. All these churches displayed high levels of involvement in local mission with either high or low levels of involvement in distant mission. Those with high levels of involvement in both spheres were termed more globally engaged (MGE) while those that showed high local but low distant mission engagement were termed less globally engaged (LGE). Despite the denominational diversity among the churches, the differences in practice were not due to foundational theological differences. The ecclesiological convictions of interviewees were largely the same with similar church metaphors employed to emphasize either the internal ministries of the church or the mission of the church to the local community. Interviewees from all churches also had similar understandings of the purpose of the church, highlighting the ministry to church members, mission to the local community, and mission elsewhere. The approach to local mission varied between the churches depending on the needs of the local community, but one notable difference between MGE and LGE churches was in the emphasis interviewees gave to distant mission. Members of MGE churches emphasized local and distant mission needs, while LGE church members primarily spoke of local mission.

Foundational missiological convictions were also very similar among all interviewees. The primacy of meeting people's spiritual needs through the proclamation of the gospel was evident in all churches. The importance of holistic care and the actions of Christians to complement the message was noted, but not emphasized in either LGE or MGE churches. The most notable theological difference between interviewees regarded the agency of God in mission. Interviewees from LGE churches made very little reference to the *missio Dei*, while interviewees from MGE churches spoke more regularly of God's sovereignty over, and involvement in, mission globally. This contributed to greater motivation to be involved in mission activities locally and at a distance. Rather than seeing mission as a burdensome task that they must fulfill, members of MGE churches spoke of the privilege of being involved in God's work in the world. There was greater motivation towards participation in mission, even though the foundational missiological beliefs were largely similar.

Given this theological similarity, analysis of the organizational features of churches provided a greater insight into the factors shaping their approach to mission involvement. Interviewees highlighted differences in organizational culture and climate for distant mission between MGE and LGE churches. These differences were evident in a range of practices related to prayer and finances for mission, encouragement and equipping for involvement in mission, and missional leadership structures in the church. Practices related to prayer and finances were procedurally very similar; however, in MGE churches, there was greater intentionality and members expressed a sense of personal ownership of the tasks. MGE churches also had clear processes to encourage and equip people to be involved in both local and distant mission and to send people out from the church for the purposes of mission. LGE churches equipped people for local mission but did not have the same focus on sending members out. Similarly, MGE churches had clear mission leadership structures that facilitated church member involvement, whereas LGE churches did not. These differences reflected a climate for mission involvement in MGE churches that led church members to see personal participation in distant mission as the normal and expected behavior. Participation was not discouraged in LGE churches, but distant mission was considered an optional activity that people and organizations outside the church were primarily responsible for.

These different patterns of mission involvement can be described using a mission engagement matrix which integrates participation in local and distant mission. Churches that show a participatory approach to both local and distant mission can be described as having a unified participatory missiology, whereas those that have a participatory approach to mission in one sphere and a delegatory approach to mission in another have a bifurcated missiology. The core feature of the churches in this study with a unified participatory missiology was a rich network of relational connections between the church members and distant mission workers. These relationships were mutual partnerships in which the church members joined in the mission task in various ways. These connections were a rich source of external bridging social capital for the church that had structural, relational, and cognitive dimensions. Personal involvement in distant mission was easier for church members because of these relationships, but it was the free flow of information and the cognitive dimensions of this social capital that had the greatest impact. Members of churches with a unified participatory missiology gained insight and experiential knowledge which shaped their missional beliefs. Though their foundational missiological convictions were not changed, their beliefs about their church's responsibility to be involved in distant mission and their capacity to make a meaningful contribution were strengthened. They also viewed participation in mission as a privilege to be embraced as they joined God in his mission. These shared beliefs stimulated the climate for mission involvement which encouraged mission participation both locally and at a distance. Therefore, a unified participatory missiology creates a culture of global mission engagement by drawing on the social capital that flows through the rich relational network with distant mission workers.

A secondary benefit of this participatory approach to distant mission was the positive feedback from this network of relationships that stimulated further engagement. The benefits that people experienced in terms of knowledge and transformed missional beliefs encouraged an organizational climate of mission in which the church's practices, processes, and systems strengthened participation. Church members were motivated to be involved because it was perceived to be the expected behavior. This participation further strengthened the relationships with distant mission workers which enhanced the social capital benefits. The foundational element of this cycle was these relationships, and though some intentionality is required from leaders to maintain the structural features and encourage missional beliefs, the culture of global mission engagement that results is to some extent self-reinforcing.

By contrast, churches that displayed a local-focused bifurcated missiology did not have well-developed relational connections beyond the church and primarily emphasized the local mission needs. The distant mission connections that did exist often prioritized organizations rather than individuals and were approached in unidirectional ways with the church contributing but not receiving. There was shared recognition that distant mission is important, and financial and prayer support was offered, but the emphasis was on supporting the work rather than partnering in it. Due to this lack of relational engagement, the social capital benefits that result from a unified participatory missiology were missed. Members of these churches were more likely to emphasize their limited capacity and consequent inability to be more involved in distant mission. They highlighted the great needs for mission in their local context and the responsibility that they had to address them, but they did not express a clear responsibility for distant mission. Finally, there was a greater tendency for members of these churches to see involvement in distant mission as an important, but potentially burdensome task. These beliefs were influenced by a limited understanding of the global spread of Christianity, the economic assumptions of the market economy, and a theology of mission which emphasized the obligation, rather than the joy, of mission involvement. The church's climate of mission which resulted from these convictions was one in which distant mission involvement was seen as an optional activity. Some personal contribution was warranted, but the task was primarily delegated to others.

METHODOLOGICAL REFLECTIONS

This study has shown the value of a mixed method grounded theory methodology to understand the factors shaping local church activity. The survey provided an insight into the landscape of church behavior and highlighted key factors that warranted closer consideration through the qualitative analysis. It also facilitated the purposive sampling by identifying churches that displayed the patterns of mission involvement of greatest interest to this study. This was invaluable groundwork, but as the qualitative data was analyzed the limitations of the survey tool became evident. The checkbox nature of the questions limited the richness of the data that could be collected and on questions that invited respondents to select a range of values, asking for approximate numbers would have been more accurate. Restricting the survey respondents to church leaders also limited the data that was gained. A survey of church membership exploring not only the activities but also the extent to which people felt encouraged to participate in various ways would provide greater insight into the climate for participation. This limitation was ameliorated by the secondary qualitative element to the mixed method approach which gave access to the opinions and perspectives of church members. These people are the primary actors in a local church community and their experiences, motivations, and convictions ultimately shape the actions of the church. Leaders have a significant effect on the direction and activities of a local church, and it was important to hear their perspectives, but the agency of the church members and the plethora of influences which shape their behavior is duly respected through this approach. A fuller anthropological approach that included participant observation and interviews of more church members would provide an even greater understanding of the cultural norms and values within each church. However, the methodology employed was a valuable approach which resisted the tendency to theoretical abstractions by preferencing non-expert voices where possible.

The sampling strategies of this project focused the research on a specific subsection of Australian evangelicalism. The use of evangelical mission agencies to identify potential respondents for the survey inclined the sample towards churches within the Anglican, Baptist, and Presbyterian denominations in Sydney, NSW, and the ACT. This constraint was appropriate given the emphasis on the conservative stream within Australian evangelicalism in this study, however, it limits the generalizability of the conclusions to Pentecostal or progressive evangelical churches within Sydney, or evangelical churches elsewhere in Australia. Given the many similarities that exist between these traditions, these findings may be applicable, but further research is needed for this to be determined. Expanding the number and type of churches included in the survey would have enhanced the generalizability of the findings. The use of theoretical sampling might also have guaranteed category saturation in the analysis and further enhanced the accuracy of the findings. However, despite these sampling limitations, this research has provided a valid insight into the factors shaping mission involvement of Sydney evangelical churches and the testing of these conclusions in other contexts would provide further understanding.

This research was completed by a member of the Sydney evangelical church population being examined which has provided both opportunities and limitations. Being on staff at a theological college with numerous connections to Sydney evangelical churches provided access to the population that is not generally available. Connections to the mission organizations that these churches partner with, including being a board member of one of the organizations, also provided an understanding of these churches' mission practices before the research began. This prior experience inevitably shaped the researcher's perceptions and interpretation of the data, but it gave access to data that may not have been available to others. The response rate for the survey was probably strengthened by the identity of the researcher as an insider to the culture. People were willing to share their perspectives with someone from a known institution. Similarly, church leaders were willing to be interviewed and to have members of their church interviewed. However, the identity of the researcher also influences the participants' responses. The motivation to express perspectives that they believe the researcher values will have shaped the construction of responses. The person's knowledge of the researcher and the institution he worked for would have influenced this. Similarly, interviewees who wanted to highlight the positive aspects of their church would have responded differently to those who were feeling disgruntled. These influences on the data for a project like this are unavoidable. An effort was made to limit their impact by interviewing multiple members with different roles and expertise from each church. Further aspects of triangulation through the collection of data from people external to the churches, such as mission organization leaders or mission workers, or by deeper engagement with local church historical archives would have further minimized these influences.

The complementary insights of theological perspectives and organizational theories facilitated the depth of analysis that came through the grounded theory process. Theological convictions are fundamental to the ways Christians engage with each other and the world; however, there is a tendency in evangelicalism to elevate the normative influence of theology without giving due consideration to how theological convictions are shaped by context and experience. A practical theological approach gives space for these factors as it explores the interactions between beliefs and practice. Other theoretical frameworks complement theological analysis to illuminate key issues for consideration. In this study, the theological differences between interviewees were minimal, yet organizational differences in culture and climate provided valuable insights which enriched the understanding of church behavior. Culture studies have been popular in the study of churches for many years, but the inclusion of organizational climate gave due consideration to the ways practices, processes, and policies shape behavior. By asking church members which activities they believed were expected of them, the beliefs and values shaping church culture become evident. Organizational culture and organizational climate studies are a valuable inclusion in the analysis of local congregations, but organizational studies is a vast field of research that draws on several disciplines including psychology, sociology, leadership studies, management, and others. This research interacted with a small field within organizational studies, and wider engagement would further enhance this approach for future research.

One of the key factors that an organizational perspective illuminated in this study was the impact of social capital. By considering the various dimensions of social capital in the experience of church members, the influence of relational networks on church practice became evident. Though the consideration of social capital in congregational studies is not new, it has typically employed a normative approach concerned with internal bonding capital and its contribution to wider social capital. This study has highlighted the value of a resource approach that considers the role of external social capital on local church behavior. This is of great significance as churches have increasing opportunities to engage with people from diverse contexts in a globalized world. The COVID-19 pandemic greatly stimulated local church use of digital technologies. Engaging with people around the world is now within the reach of most churches and mission workers. As churches engage these opportunities, the impact of external bridging social capital will increase. Ongoing attention to this is therefore important as the actions of local churches are considered in the future.

Finally, this research has highlighted the impact of organizational cultural beliefs on the expression of foundational theological convictions. The churches in this study displayed very similar ecclesiological and missiological convictions. Though these foundational beliefs are central in determining the actions of local churches, they could not explain the different patterns of behavior that were observed. However, there were differences in secondary beliefs that had a role in shaping these diverse actions. People's beliefs about the world, particularly the spread of Christianity and the access to Christian resources, shaped their convictions about the places that needed missional engagement. Their beliefs about their own access to resources and the ways they could make a meaningful contribution shaped their understanding of their own role in the mission endeavor. Finally, their beliefs about God's involvement in mission and the personal consequences of their own participation shaped their motivation to be involved. In all these cases, people's experience of the world and mission profoundly impacted their expression of foundational Christian beliefs. Though they agreed about the nature and purpose of the church, and the nature, goal, and location of mission, their application of these beliefs was shaped by their experiences. Theological analysis of contemporary Christian practice must therefore consider the cultural, sociological, and historical influences on the expression of foundational convictions.

OPPORTUNITIES FOR FURTHER RESEARCH

This research has developed a theory to explain the diverse patterns of mission involvement among conservative evangelical local churches in Australia. It concludes that a local church's relational networks have a profound effect on its pattern of mission engagement as they shape the missional beliefs, culture, and climate of practice. This theory is based on the analysis of conservative evangelical churches in NSW and the ACT. Further research to test this theory through a broad-based survey of diverse evangelical churches in the rest of the nation and overseas would be very fruitful. Furthermore, a similar examination of local churches in other traditions, particularly Pentecostal, Roman Catholic, and Eastern Orthodox, would further enrich the theory. These church traditions all have a significant history of involvement in mission activities within and beyond Australia and their experiences would provide a valuable point of comparison.

A second opportunity for research is in the development of tools to assess the climate for mission in local churches. This research has found organizational climate to be a valuable lens through which to view a local church's level of engagement with mission. By assessing the behaviors that church members see as normal and expected, a clearer and more comparative measure of local church activities would be attained. A tool like this could consider the various dimensions of involvement in local and distant mission through a survey of church members. By asking about the church's encouragement towards practices such as prayer for mission, sharing one's faith with others, and communicating with mission workers, the climate for mission could be quantified. Results would provide feedback to church leaders on areas of strength and weakness in their missions approach and could be used to benchmark across churches. Furthermore, it could be employed in action research to assess the effect of interventions related to mission engagement. Though there is significant complexity in developing a tool that is both valid and reliable it would facilitate a range of future research possibilities.[1]

PRACTICAL IMPLICATIONS

This research has explored the patterns of Sydney evangelical church involvement in mission through the application of a grounded theory approach. It has provided a clearer understanding of how churches are engaged in mission and has proposed a theory to explain the variation in local church participation in local and distant mission. This has been a primarily descriptive exercise that may not be entirely generalizable to other church traditions or places; however, there are several implications which should be considered by church and mission leaders who desire to see greater participation of local churches in global mission.

Firstly, the development of rich mutual relationships between church members and mission workers must be a priority. For church leaders this will mean creating opportunities for personal connection with mission workers at every stage of their service. This will happen more naturally if the workers come from within the church, but it will always require intentionality. In regular church gatherings and extra events, mission workers need time to relate to church members. Church members also need encouragement and support to communicate with mission workers and processes may help to facilitate this. Information from mission workers must not only be shared with church members but interacted with in meaningful ways. The increased accessibility of digital communication makes this relational connection easier. Mission workers and organizations also need to invest in the development of these connections. Distant mission workers must recognize that part of their ministry is to the churches that have sent them. A truly mutual partnership will see the mission worker sharing their experience and insights with local churches with the goal of developing mission participation. Opportunities for teaching and preaching should be embraced with honest and authentic communication to build relational connection. Those who lead mission organizations must also recognize the value of these connections and seek to maximize the time available for mission workers to do this. Investing resources into the development of these personal

---

1. Ehrhart et al., *Organizational Climate and Culture*, 77–78.

connections is likely to be of greater benefit than raising the profile of the organization as a whole. Providing training to mission workers in the effective use of digital media and secure communication platforms to develop and maintain relationships with their partner churches would be of great value. They may also provide resources to help churches develop internal processes that facilitate relational connections. By prioritizing rich mutual relational networks between churches and mission workers, current and future participation in mission will be strengthened.

Secondly, church leaders must seek to align the missional beliefs of their church with a unified participatory missiology. This means evaluating the church's approach to local and distant mission, and considering what people believe regarding their capacity and responsibility for global mission. If capacity is seen as a limit to mission involvement, an intentional emphasis to develop a theology of abundance, including a critique of market economy assumptions, may be needed. Exploration of the variety of ways in which people can participate in mission and the resources they have available will further address beliefs about capacity. Providing an accurate understanding of global realities will help to address any sense that there is limited need for global mission and will help people to appreciate their own responsibility beyond their local community. This is ideally brokered through personal engagement with people and contexts, rather than statistics. The attitude towards global mission must also be considered and the privilege of participating with God in his work emphasized.

Finally, organizational structures, practices, and processes can be used to facilitate local church engagement. Identifying leaders who will guide and stimulate involvement through appropriate internal church systems will help church members see participation in global mission as normal and expected behavior. Church practices, including the dissemination of information, collection of money, and facilitation of prayer, will all help to maintain member involvement, but only to the extent that they enhance the relational connection with distant mission workers. The social capital benefits that flow through these relationships must be harnessed to strengthen the local church culture of mission engagement locally and at a distance. This will not only benefit the local church, but also the mission workers they partner with and the global mission endeavor to every nation, tribe, and tongue.

Appendix 1

Survey Tool

SECTION 1—CHURCH DESCRIPTION

These are general questions to provide a broad picture of your church.

1. Which of the following adjectives would you use to describe your church? (You can select more than one)

    ☐ Evangelical

    ☐ Missional

    ☐ Charismatic

    ☐ Reformed

    ☐ Pentecostal

    ☐ Emerging, Emergent

2. How many adults would attend your church's services on a typical weekend?

    ☐ Less than 50

    ☐ 50–99

    ☐ 100–249

    ☐ 250–499

    ☐ More than 500

3. What is your church's approximate total annual income?

   ☐ Less than $150,000
   ☐ $150,000–$299,999
   ☐ $300,000–$499,999
   ☐ $500,000–$999,999
   ☐ More than $1,000,000
   ☐ Prefer not to say

SECTION 2 — LOCAL MISSION ACTIVITIES

The following questions relate to mission activities carried out within Australia, particularly in your local community. Please indicate below how often your church conducted any of the following mission activities within your local community, in the last 12 months.

4. Evangelistic church services or events (e.g., guest services, outreach men's event)

   ☐ Monthly or more often
   ☐ Every two or three months
   ☐ At least twice a year
   ☐ Once a year
   ☐ None

5. Evangelistic Bible studies or courses (e.g., Christianity Explored, Alpha course)

   ☐ Monthly or more often
   ☐ Every two or three months
   ☐ At least twice a year
   ☐ Once a year
   ☐ None

6. Street or shopping centre evangelism, door-knocking, or drop-in centres

   ☐ Monthly or more often
   ☐ Every two or three months
   ☐ At least twice a year
   ☐ Once a year
   ☐ None

7. Other visiting (e.g., prisons, hospitals, fringe attenders)

   ☐ Monthly or more often
   ☐ Every two or three months
   ☐ At least twice a year
   ☐ Once a year
   ☐ None

8. Other evangelistic or outreach activities not mentioned above

   ☐ Monthly or more often
   ☐ Every two or three months
   ☐ At least twice a year
   ☐ Once a year
   ☐ None

9. Apart from church staff, how many people does your church support practically, financially or through prayer to do mission work in your local community or elsewhere in Australia? (e.g., student ministry, school chaplaincy, prison ministries, etc.)

   _

   (Please answer with a number. If "none," please put "0")

10. How many organizations with a focus on mission work in your local community or elsewhere in Australia does your church support practically, financially, or through prayer? (i.e., apart from support for individuals)

(Please answer with a number. If "none," please put "0")

11. Apart from your church activities, approximately how much money does your church contribute to mission work within Australia each year?

    ☐ Less than $10,000
    ☐ $10,000–$29,999
    ☐ $30,000–$49,999
    ☐ $50,000–$99,999
    ☐ More than $100,000
    ☐ Prefer not to say

SECTION 3—MISSION ACTIVITIES OUTSIDE OF AUSTRALIA

12. Does your church have a particular focus on overseas mission in one or more of the following? (You can select more than one)

    ☐ A particular people group.
    ☐ A particular nation.
    ☐ A region of the world.
    ☐ A particular need or ministry (e.g., poverty alleviation, missionary aviation, theological education)
    ☐ None of the above.

Mission organizations often describe an individual, a couple OR a family serving overseas as one "missionary unit." Using this measure, how many "missionary units" does your church support in overseas mission?

13. Who are members of a mission agency/organization?

   _____
   (Please answer with a number. If "none," please put "0")

14. Who are not members of a mission agency/organization?

   _____
   (Please answer with a number. If "none," please put "0")

15. Over the past twelve months, has your church had a specific commitment to people serving in missions outside Australia? (You can select more than one)

   ☐ Yes, a personal relationship with individuals/groups

   ☐ Yes, by sending a person or group to visit them

   ☐ Yes, a regular financial commitment

   ☐ Yes, a regular prayer commitment

   ☐ Yes, another kind of link

   ☐ No links of this kind

16. Over the past twelve months, did your church have personal contact with the missionaries you support (e.g., by email, phone call, skype, letter, or in person)? If so, how often?

   ☐ Monthly or more often

   ☐ Every two or three months

   ☐ At least twice a year

   ☐ Once a year

   ☐ None

17. Over the past twelve months, were specific prayers for particular missionaries or mission organizations included in your church's services, small groups, prayer meetings etc.? If so, how often?

    ☐ Monthly or more often

    ☐ Every two or three months

    ☐ At least twice a year

    ☐ Once a year

    ☐ None

18. How many mission organizations that primarily send people or resources outside Australia does your church support practically, financially or through prayer? (i.e., apart from support for individuals)

    _____

    (Please answer with a number. If "none," please put "0")

In the past two years, has your church organized any mission trips (one week or longer), including trips jointly organized with another church or organization?

19. Mission trips to other parts of Australia

    _____

    (Please answer with a number. If "none," please put "0")

20. Mission trips outside of Australia

    _____

    (Please answer with a number. If "none," please put "0")

21. Approximately how much money does your church contribute towards missions outside Australia each year?

    ☐ Less than $10,000

    ☐ $10,000–$29,999

    ☐ $30,000–$49,999

    ☐ $50,000–$99,999

    ☐ More than $100,000

    ☐ Prefer not to say

22. Does your church have a written policy or strategy regarding your involvement in overseas mission?

    ☐ Yes

    ☐ No

23. In the last five years, how many missionary "units" from your church have been sent outside Australia for twelve months or more? (An individual missionary, or a couple serving as missionaries, or a family serving as missionaries are each considered as one "unit")

    (Please answer with a number. If "none," please put "0")

Appendix 2

Semi-structured Interview Guide

1. Approximately how long have you been a part of this church? And in what ways are you involved?
2. Different churches understand their purpose in different ways. What do you see as the purpose (or purposes) of your church?
3. How does involvement in mission relate to the purpose of the church?
4. Can you tell me about the ways your church is involved in mission (outreach) locally?
5. Can you tell me about the ways your church is involved in mission in other places/overseas?
6. What reasons do you hear at your church for why members should be involved in mission?
7. Can you tell me the stories of how your church came to support these missionaries / ministries?
8. Can you tell me about any missionaries or ministries that you used to support that you don't anymore? OR, Can you tell me about any ministries or missionaries that have been considered or recommended but that the church didn't decide to support?
9. Can you tell me about the ways that your church's involvement in mission is featured in Sunday Services?

10. Who are the main drivers of the church's mission activities? What do they do?
11. How are most typical church members/attenders (non-leaders) involved in mission in this church?
12. Do you think your church's level of involvement in mission too high, not high enough, or about right? Why do you feel that way?

Appendix 3

Qualitative Analysis Codes

Ecclesiology

- Church Culture
- Church Key People
- Church Nature
- Church Purpose
- Church Structure
- Congregational Membership

Missiology

- Agent
- Biblical References
- Location
- Motivation
- Nature
- Teaching on Mission

Practices and Processes:

- Distant Mission Practices and Processes
  - Church Systems
  - Finances

- Information
- Mobilisation
- Organizations
- Prayer
- Short-term Mission
- Support Capacity

- Local Mission Practices and Processes
  - Attractive
  - Outreach
  - Prayer
  - Serving Community
  - Training for Mission

Missionary Connections
- Details of Mission Work
- Impact on Church
- Personal Contact
- Relationship

Outside Cultural Influence

Partnership

Bibliography

Adler, Gary J., and Andrea L. Ruiz. "The Immigrant Effect: Short-Term Mission Travel as Transnational Civic Remittance." *Sociology of Religion* 79 (2018) 323–55. https://doi.org/10.1093/socrel/srx060/.
Allen, Roland. *Missionary Methods: St. Paul's or Our's?* Grand Rapids: Eerdmans, 1962.
———. *The Spontaneous Expansion of the Church: And the Causes Which Hinder It.* Grand Rapids: Eerdmans, 1962.
Ammerman, Nancy T. "Congregations: Local, Social, and Religious." In *The Oxford Handbook of the Sociology of Religion*, edited by Peter B. Clarke, 562–79. Oxford: Oxford University Press, 2011. https://doi.org/10.1093/oxfordhb/9780199588961.013.0032.
Arlund, Pam. "Acts 1:8 Sequentialism." In *Conversations on When Everything Is Missions: Recovering the Mission of the Church*, edited by Denny Spitters and Matthew Ellison, 51–56. Mumbai: Bottomline Media, 2020.
Arthur, Edwin David. *Mission Agencies in Crisis?* Oxford: Regnum, 2020.
Australian Bureau of Statistics. *2016 Census*. https://www.abs.gov.au/websitedbs/censushome.nsf/home/2016.
Banks, Robert J. *Paul's Idea of Community*. Rev. ed. Peabody, MA: Hendrickson, 1994.
Barram, Michael D. *Missional Economics: Biblical Justice and Christian Formation.* Grand Rapids: Eerdmans, 2018.
Barrett, David B., et al., eds. *World Christian Encyclopedia: A Comparative Survey of Churches and Religions in the Modern World.* Vol. 1. 2nd ed. Oxford: Oxford University Press, 2001.
Barth, Karl. *Church Dogmatics*. Edited by Thomas F. Torrance and Geoffrey W. Bromiley. 13 vols. Edinburgh: T. & T. Clark, 1956–75.
———. *God Here and Now*. Translated by Paul M. van Buren. London: Routledge, 2003.
Beals, Paul A. *A People for His Name: A Church-Based Missions Strategy*. Rev. ed. Pasadena, CA: William Carey Library, 1995.
Bebbington, D. W. *Evangelicalism in Modern Britain: A History from the 1730s to the 1980s.* London: Routledge, 1989.
Beirn, Steve, and George W. Murray. *Well Sent: Reimagining the Church's Missionary-Sending Process*. Fort Washington, PA: CLC, 2015.
Bellamy, John, et al. *Enriching Church Life: A Practical Guide for Local Churches*. Adelaide: NCLS, 2006.
Bender, Kimlyn J. "Barth on the Church." In *Wiley Blackwell Companion to Karl Barth*, edited by George Hunsinger and Keith L. Johnson, 242–53. Hoboken, NJ: Wiley, 2020.

Bertalanffy, Ludwig Von. "The History and Status of General Systems Theory." *Academy of Management Journal* 15 (1972) 407–26.
Beyerlein, Kraig, and John R. Hipp. "From Pews to Participation: The Effect of Congregation Activity and Context on Bridging Civic Engagement." *Social Problems* 53 (2006) 97–117. https://doi.org/10.1525/sp.2006.53.1.97/.
Birks, Melanie, and Jane Mills. *Grounded Theory: A Practical Guide*. 2nd ed. Los Angeles: Sage, 2015.
Blauw, Johannes. *The Missionary Nature of the Church: A Survey of the Biblical Theology of Mission*. Foundations of Christian Mission. London: Lutterworth, 1962.
Blomberg, Craig L. *Christians in an Age of Wealth: A Biblical Theology of Stewardship*. Biblical Theology for Life. Grand Rapids: Zondervan, 2013.
Bolt, Peter. "Following Jesus and Fishing for People: Evangelistic Mission in the Third Millennium." In *Ripe for Harvest: Christian Mission in the New Testament and Our World*, edited by Richard J. Gibson, 1–35. Carlisle, UK: Paternoster, 1998.
———. *Mission Minded*. Kingsford: St. Matthias, 1992.
Bolt, Peter, and Mark Thompson, eds. *Donald Robinson Selected Works*. Vol. 1, *Assembling God's People*. Camperdown: Australian Church Record, 2008.
———, eds. *Donald Robinson: Selected Works*. Vol. 2, *Preaching God's Word*. Camperdown: Australian Church Record, 2008.
Bonk, Jonathan J. *Missions and Money: Affluence as a Western Missionary Problem*. American Society of Missiology Series 15. Maryknoll, NY: Orbis, 1991.
Borthwick, Paul. *Western Christians in Global Mission: What's the Role of the North American Church?* Downers Grove, IL: InterVarsity Press, 2012.
Bosch, David Jacobus. *Transforming Mission: Paradigm Shifts in Theology of Mission*. American Society of Missiology Series 16. Maryknoll, NY: Orbis, 1991.
Bourdieu, P. "The Forms of Capital." In *Handbook of Theory and Research for the Sociology of Education*, edited by J. Richardson, 241–58. New York: Greenwood, 1986.
Bradley, Zach. *The Sending Church Defined*. Knoxville: Upstream Collective, 2015.
Braga, Stuart. *A Century Preaching Christ: Katoomba Christian Convention, 1903–2003*. Sydney: Katoomba Christian Convention, 2003.
Brammall, Anthony C. *Out of Darkness: 100 Years of Sydney Missionary and Bible College*. Croydon: SMBC, 2016.
Brown, C. M. "Friendship Is Forever: Congregation-to-Congregation Relationships." In *Effective Engagement in Short-Term Missions: Doing It Right!*, edited by Robert J. Priest, 209–37. Pasadena, CA: William Carey Library, 2008.
Brueggemann, Walter. "The Liturgy of Abundance, the Myth of Scarcity." *Christian Century* 116 (1999) 342–47.
Bryant, Antony. *Grounded Theory and Grounded Theorizing: Pragmatism in Research Practice*. New York: Oxford University Press, 2017.
Bryant, Antony, and Kathy Charmaz. *The Sage Handbook of Grounded Theory*. London: Sage, 2007. https://doi.org/10.4135/9781848607941.
Burt, Ronald S. "The Network Structure of Social Capital." *Research in Organizational Behavior* 22 (2000) 345–423.
Bush, Luis. "In Pursuit of True Christian Partnership: A Biblical Basis from Philippians." In *Partners in the Gospel: The Strategic Role of Partnership in World Evangelization*, edited by James H. Kraakevik and Dotsey Welliver, 3–15. Wheaton, IL: Billy Graham Center, Wheaton College, 1991.

Cameron, Helen. "Are Congregations Associations? The Contribution of Organizational Studies to Congregational Studies." In *Congregational Studies in the UK: Christianity in a Post-Christian Context*, edited by Mathew Guest et al., 139–51. Burlington, VT: Ashgate, 2004.

Cameron, Helen, and Catherine Duce. *Researching Practice in Mission and Ministry: A Companion*. London: SCM, 2013.

Cameron, Helen, et al. *Studying Local Churches: A Handbook*. London: SCM, 2005.

Cameron, Marcia Helen. *An Enigmatic Life: David Broughton Knox: Father of Contemporary Sydney Anglicanism*. Brunswick East: Acorn, 2006.

———. *Phenomenal Sydney: Anglicans in a Time of Change, 1945–2013*. Eugene, OR: Wipf & Stock, 2016.

Camp, Bruce K. "Major Paradigm Shifts in World Evangelization." *International Journal of Frontier Missions* 11 (1994) 133–38.

———. "A Theological Examination of the Two-Structure Theory." *Missiology: An International Review* 23 (1995) 197–209.

Carey, William. *An Enquiry into the Obligations of Christians to Use Means for the Conversion of the Heathens. In Which the Religious State of the Different Nations of the World, the Success of Former Undertakings, and the Practicability of Further Undertakings, Are Considered*. Leicester, UK: Ann Ireland, 1792.

Carne, Steven Arthur. "Koinōnia for the Nations: A Biblical Model of Church-Missionary Partnership." *Global Missiology* 4 (2012). http://ojs.globalmissiology.org/index.php/english/article/view/1033.

Chapman, John. *Know and Tell the Gospel*. 2nd ed. Kingsford: Matthias Media, 1998.

———. *Setting Hearts on Fire: A Guide to Giving Evangelistic Talks*. Kingsford: Matthias Media, 1999.

Charmaz, Kathy. *Constructing Grounded Theory*. 2nd ed. London: Sage, 2014.

Chester, Tim. "Missional Church and Global Mission." *Tim Chester* (blog), November 10, 2009. https://timchester.wordpress.com/2009/11/10/missional-church-and-global-mission/.

———. "Social Involvement and Evangelism (Part I): Two Strong Cases." *The Briefing*, January 1, 2005. http://matthiasmedia.com/briefing/2005/01/social-involvement-and-evangelism-part-i-two-strong-cases/.

Chester, Tim, and Steve Timmis. *Total Church: A Radical Reshaping around Gospel and Community*. Wheaton, IL: Crossway, 2008.

Chester, Tim, and Tony Payne. "Social Involvement and Evangelism (Part II): How They Relate." *The Briefing*, February 1, 2005. http://matthiasmedia.com/briefing/2005/02/social-involvement-and-evangelism-part-ii-how-they-relate/.

Chilton, Hugh. "Evangelicals and the End of Christian Australia: Nation and Religion in the Public Square 1959–1979." PhD diss., University of Sydney, 2014.

Claridge, Tristan. "Dimensions of Social Capital—Structural, Cognitive, and Relational." *Social Capital Research* (blog), January 20, 2018. https://www.socialcapitalresearch.com/literature/theory/dimensions/.

Clark, Margaret S., and Judson R. Mills. "A Theory of Communal (and Exchange) Relationships." In *Handbook of Theories of Social Psychology*, edited by P. A. Van Lange et al., 2:232–50. London: Sage, 2012.

Clarke, Adele E. "Situating Grounded Theory and Situational Analysis in Interpretive Qualitative Inquiry." In *The Sage Handbook of Current Developments in Grounded*

Theory, edited by Antony Bryant and Kathy Charmaz, 3–48. London: Sage, 2019. https://doi.org/10.4135/9781526485656.n3.

Claydon, David, ed. *A New Vision, a New Heart, a Renewed Call: Lausanne Occasional Papers from the 2004 Forum on World Evangelization in Pattaya, Thailand*. Vol. 2. Pasadena, CA: William Carey Library, 2004.

CMS Australia. "History." https://www.cms.org.au/about-us/history/.

Cole, Graham. "The Doctrine of the Church: Towards Conceptual Clarification." In *Church, Worship, and the Local Congregation*, edited by B. G. Webb, 3–17. Homebush West: Lancer, 1987.

Coleman, James S. *Foundations of Social Theory*. Cambridge, MA: Belknap, 1990.

———. "Social Capital in the Creation of Human Capital." *American Journal of Sociology* 94 (1988) S95–120.

Compassion. "About Us." https://www.compassion.com.au/about-us.

Corbin, Juliet, and Anselm Strauss. *Basics of Qualitative Research: Techniques and Procedures for Developing Grounded Theory*. 3rd ed. Thousand Oaks, CA: Sage, 2008. https://doi.org/10.4135/9781452230153.

Corwin, Gary. "MissionS: Why the 'S' Is Still Important." *Evangelical Missions Quarterly* 53 (2017) 4–5.

Costas, Orlando. *The Church and Its Mission: A Shattering Critique from the Third World*. Wheaton, IL: Tyndale House, 1974.

Creswell, John W. *Research Design: Qualitative, Quantitative, and Mixed Methods Approaches*. 4th ed. Los Angeles: Sage, 2014.

Crider, Caleb, et al. *Tradecraft: For the Church on Mission*. Portland: Urban Loft Publishers, 2013.

Cronshaw, Darren, and Stuart Devenish. "The Continuing Conversion of the Australian Church: A Missional Conversation with Darrell Guder." *Pacifica: Australasian Theological Studies* 27 (2014) 78–96.

Cronshaw, Darren, and Steve Taylor. "The Congregation in a Pluralist Society: Rereading Newbigin for Missional Churches Today." *Pacifica: Australasian Theological Studies* 27 (June 2014) 206–28.

Cropanzano, Russell, and Marie S. Mitchell. "Social Exchange Theory: An Interdisciplinary Review." *Journal of Management* 31 (2005) 874–900.

Cropanzano, Russell, et al. "Social Exchange Theory: A Critical Review with Theoretical Remedies." *Academy of Management Annals* 11 (2017) 479–516. https://doi.org/10.5465/annals.2015.0099/.

Crotty, Michael. *The Foundations of Social Research: Meaning and Perspective in the Research Process*. London: Sage, 1998.

Cupit, Tony, et al., eds. *From Five Barley Loaves: Australian Baptists in Global Mission, 1864–2010*. Northcote: Morning Star, 2014.

DeYoung, Kevin, and Greg Gilbert. *What Is the Mission of the Church? Making Sense of Social Justice, Shalom, and the Great Commission*. Wheaton, IL: Crossway, 2011.

Dickson, John. *The Best Kept Secret of Christian Mission: Promoting the Gospel with More Than Our Lips*. Grand Rapids: Zondervan, 2010.

———. *Promoting the Gospel: The Whole of Life for the Cause of Christ*. Rev. ed. Sydney South: Aquila, 2005.

Dickson, John P. *Mission-Commitment in Ancient Judaism and in the Pauline Communities: The Shape, Extent and Background of Early Christian Mission*. Tübingen: Mohr Siebeck, 2003.

Dipple, Bruce. *Becoming Global: Integrating Global Mission and Your Local Church: A Practical Approach*. Croydon: Sydney Missionary and Bible College, 2011.

Donaldson, James, ed. "Constitutions of the Holy Apostles." In *Ante-Nicene Fathers: The Writings of the Fathers Down to A.D. 325*. Vol. 7, *Fathers of the Third and Fourth Centuries*, edited by Alexander Roberts et al., 385–508. Peabody, MA: Hendrickson, 1994.

Dowsett, Rose. "The Lausanne Movement and the World Evangelical Alliance." In *The Lausanne Movement: A Range of Perspectives*, edited by Lars Dahle et al., 399–410. Oxford: Regnum, 2014.

Doyle, Robert. "A Response to Graham Cole's Paper." In *Church, Worship, and the Local Congregation*, 19–25. Homebush West: Lancer, 1987.

Driver, John. *Images of the Church in Mission*. Scottdale, PA: Herald, 1997.

Dulles, Avery. *Models of the Church*. New York: Image, 2002.

Dunaetz, David R. "A Missionary's Relationship to Sending Churches. Communal and Exchange Relationships." In *Churches on Mission: God's Grace Abounding to the Nations*, edited by Geoffrey Hartt et al., 303–23. Pasadena, CA: William Carey Library, 2017.

Ehrhart, Mark G., et al. *Organizational Climate and Culture: An Introduction to Theory, Research, and Practice*. New York: Routledge, 2013. https://doi.org/10.4324/9781315857664/.

Ekström, Bertil, ed. *The Church in Mission: Foundations and Global Case Studies*. Pasadena, CA: William Carey Library, 2016.

Emerson, Richard M. "Social Exchange Theory." *Annual Review of Sociology* 2 (1976) 335–62.

Engel, James F., and William A. Dyrness. *Changing the Mind of Missions: Where Have We Gone Wrong?* Downers Grove, IL: InterVarsity Press, 2000.

Engen, Charles van. *God's Missionary People: Rethinking the Purpose of the Local Church*. Grand Rapids: Baker, 1991.

———. "'Mission' Defined and Described." In *Missionshift: Global Mission Issues in the Third Millennium*, edited by David J. Hesselgrave and Ed Stetzer, 7–29. Nashville: B&H Academic, 2010.

———. *Mission on the Way: Issues in Mission Theology*. Grand Rapids: Baker, 1996.

Engler, Steven. "Grounded Theory." In *The Routledge Handbook of Research Methods in the Study of Religion*, edited by Michael Stausberg and Steven Engler, 256–74. Routledge Handbooks in Religion. New York: Routledge, 2014.

Escobar, Samuel. "A Movement Divided: Three Approaches to World Evangelization Stand in Tension with One Another." *Transformation: An International Journal of Holistic Mission Studies* 8 (1991) 7–13.

Fetters, Michael D., et al. "Achieving Integration in Mixed Methods Designs- Principles and Practices." *Health Services Research* 48 (2013) 2134–56. https://doi.org/10.1111/1475-6773.12117/.

Flemming, Dean. *Recovering the Full Mission of God: A Biblical Perspective on Being, Doing, and Telling*. Downers Grove, IL: IVP Academic, 2013.

Flett, John G. *The Witness of God: The Trinity, Missio Dei, Karl Barth, and the Nature of Christian Community*. Grand Rapids: Eerdmans, 2010.

Foley, Michael W., and Dean R. Hoge. *Religion and the New Immigrants*. Oxford: Oxford University Press, 2007.

Forsyth, Robert. "Promoting the Gospel." *Sydney Anglicans* (blog), November 9, 2005. https://sydneyanglicans.net/news/promoting_the_gospel/.

Franklin, Kirk J., and Cornelius J. P. Niemandt. "Funding God's Mission: Towards a Missiology of Generosity." *Missionalia* 43 (2015) 384–409.

Frost, Michael, and Alan Hirsch. *The Shaping of Things to Come: Innovation and Mission for the 21st-Century Church*. Rev. ed. Grand Rapids: Baker, 2013.

Fulkerson, Gregory M., and Gretchen H. Thompson. "The Evolution of a Contested Concept: A Meta-Analysis of Social Capital Definitions and Trends (1988—2006)." *Sociological Inquiry* 78 (2008) 536–57.

Fuller, James Robert. "Evaluating the Functioning of a Local Congregation through an Open Systems Approach." PhD diss., Southern Baptist Theological Seminary, 1987.

Gagné, Marylène, and Edward L. Deci. "Self-Determination Theory and Work Motivation." *Journal of Organizational Behavior* 26 (2005) 331–62.

Geys, Benny, and Zuzana Murdoch. "Measuring the 'Bridging' versus 'Bonding' Nature of Social Networks: A Proposal for Integrating Existing Measures." *Sociology* 44 (2010) 523–40.

Giles, Kevin. *What on Earth Is the Church? An Exploration in New Testament Theology*. North Blackburn: Dove, 1995.

Glaser, Barney G. *Basics of Grounded Theory Analysis: Emergence vs. Forcing*. Mill Valley, CA: Sociology, 1992.

———. *Theoretical Sensitivity: Advances in the Methodology of Grounded Theory*. Mill Valley, CA: Sociology, 1978.

Glaser, Barney G., and Anselm L. Strauss. *The Discovery of Grounded Theory: Strategies for Qualitative Research*. London: Routledge, 2017.

Goheen, Michael W. "'As the Father Has Sent Me, I Am Sending You': J. E. Lesslie Newbigin's Missionary Ecclesiology." PhD diss., University of Utrecht, 2000.

———. *Introducing Christian Mission Today: Scripture, History, and Issues*. Downers Grove, IL: IVP Academic, 2014.

———. "Liberating the Gospel from Its Modern Cage: An Interpretation of Lesslie Newbigin's Gospel and Modern Culture Project." *Missionalia* 30 (2002) 360–75.

———. *A Light to the Nations: The Missional Church and the Biblical Story*. Grand Rapids: Baker Academic, 2011.

Granovetter, Mark S. "The Strength of Weak Ties." *American Journal of Sociology* 78 (1973) 1360–80.

Greear, J. D. *Gaining by Losing: Why the Future Belongs to Churches That Send*. Grand Rapids: Zondervan, 2015.

Griffiths, Michael. *A Task Unfinished: How to Recruit, Support, and Pray for Missionaries and Christian Workers in a Constantly Changing World*. Crowborough: MARC, 1996.

Groza, Andrew A. "The Seldom Acknowledged Difficulties of Leading Missional Churches: Challenges Faced by Those Who Seek to Explore Different Forms of Being and Doing Church." *Ecclesial Practices* 6 (2019) 163–81.

Guder, Darrell L., ed. *Missional Church: A Vision for the Sending of the Church in North America*. Grand Rapids: Eerdmans, 1998.

Guetterman, Timothy C., et al. "Contemporary Approaches to Mixed Methods-Grounded Theory Research: A Field-Based Analysis." *Journal of Mixed Methods Research* 13 (2019) 179–95. https://doi.org/10.1177/1558689817710877/.

Guiana, Alan. "Letter from the West Indies." *Theology* 59 (1956) 240–43.
Halcrow, Jeremy. "Sydney Churches Accelerate Saddleback-Style." *Sydney Anglicans* (blog), September 2, 2005. https://sydneyanglicans.net/blogs/sydney_churches_accelerate_ saddleback_style/.
Hanifan, L. J. "The Rural School Community Center." *Annals of the American Academy of Political and Social Science* 67 (1916) 130–38.
Harris, Margaret. *Organising God's Work: Challenges for Churches and Synagogues*. London: Palgrave Macmillan, 1998.
Hartt, Geoffrey, et al., eds. *Churches on Mission: God's Grace Abounding to the Nations*. Pasadena, CA: William Carey Library, 2017.
Hibbert, Richard, et al. "The Journey towards Long-Term Missionary Service: How Australian Missionaries Are Being Called and Choose Mission Agencies." *Missiology: An International Review* 43 (2015) 469–82.
Hiebert, Paul G. *Transforming Worldviews: An Anthropological Understanding of How People Change*. Grand Rapids: Baker Academic, 2008.
Hiemstra, Rick. "Canadian Evangelicals and Long-Term, Career Missions: Calling, Sending, and Training." Canadian Evangelical Missions Engagement Study (CEMES). Toronto: Faith Today, 2017. https://www.evangelicalfellowship.ca/Communications/ Research/Canadian-Evangelical-Missions-Engagement-Study/.
———. "Canadian Evangelicals and Mission Priorities." Canadian Evangelical Missions Engagement Study (CEMES). Toronto: Faith Today, 2017. https://www.evangelicalfellowship.ca/Communications/Research/Canadian-Evangelical-Missions-Engagement-Study/.
———. "Canadian Evangelicals and Missions Promotion in the Local Church." Canadian Evangelical Missions Engagement Study (CEMES). Toronto: Faith Today, 2017. https://www.evangelicalfellowship.ca/Communications/Research/Canadian-Evangelical-Missions-Engagement-Study/.
———. "Canadian Evangelicals and Short-Term Missions." Canadian Evangelical Missions Engagement Study (CEMES). Toronto: Faith Today, 2017. https://www.evangelicalfellowship.ca/Communications/Research/Canadian-Evangelical-Missions-Engagement-Study/.
———. "Canadian Evangelical Missions Engagement Methodology." Canadian Evangelical Missions Engagement Study (CEMES). Toronto: Faith Today, 2017. https://www.evangelicalfellowship.ca/Communications/Research/Canadian-Evangelical-Missions-Engagement-Study/.
Hillsong Church Australia. *Annual Report 2015*. Castle Hill, NSW, 2015. https://d9nqqwcssctr8.cloudfront.net/wp-content/uploads/2016/11/01062301/Hillsong-Annual-Report-2015-WEB-V3.pdf.
Hoover, Sharon R. *Mapping Church Missions: A Compass for Ministry Strategy*. Downers Grove, IL: InterVarsity Press, 2018.
Hopewell, James F. *Congregation: Stories and Structures*. Philadelphia: Fortress, 1987.
Horner, David. *When Missions Shapes the Mission*. Nashville: B&H, 2011.
Horton, Dennis. "Long-Term Impact through Short-Term Missions: Key Components for Meaningful and Effective Crosscultural Partnerships." *Journal of the Evangelical Missiological Society* 1 (2021) 17–28.
Hunt, Stephen. *The Alpha Enterprise: Evangelism in a Post-Christian Era*. Aldershot, UK: Ashgate, 2004.

Hunter, Danny. "'Short Time, or Long': Best Practices to Turn Short-Term Missions into Long-Term Partnerships." *Journal of the Evangelical Missiological Society* 1 (2021) 1–16.
Hutchinson, Mark. *Iron in Our Blood: A History of the Presbyterian Church in NSW, 1788–2001*. Sydney: Ferguson Publications and the Centre for the Study of Australian Christianity, 2001.
Inkson, Kerr. "Are Humans Resources?" *Career Development International* 13 (2008) 270–79.
Jensen, Michael P. *Sydney Anglicanism: An Apology*. Eugene, OR: Wipf & Stock, 2012.
Jensen, Peter. "2001 Presidential Address." Delivered at Sydney Anglican Diocese Synod, Sydney, October 26, 2001. https://www.sds.asn.au/presidential-address-2001-0.
———. "The Architecture of a Missionary Church." In *Exploring the Missionary Church*, edited by B. G. Webb, 105–24. Homebush West: Lancer, 1993.
Jensen, Phillip. "What Is Church For?" *The Briefing*, December 12, 2011. https://matthiasmedia.com/briefing/2011/12/what-is-church-for/.
Johnson, Andy. *Missions: How the Local Church Goes Global*. Wheaton, IL: Crossway, 2017.
Johnson, R. Burke, et al. "Grounded Theory in Practice: Is It Inherently a Mixed Method?" *Research in the Schools* 17 (2010) 65–78.
Johnson, Todd M., and Gina A. Zurlo. *World Christian Encyclopedia*. 3rd ed. Edinburgh: Edinburgh University Press, 2020.
Judd, Stephen, and K. J. Cable. *Sydney Anglicans: A History of the Diocese*. Sydney: Anglican Information Office, 2000.
Kärkkäinen, Veli-Matti. *Introduction to Ecclesiology: Ecumenical, Historical, and Global Perspectives*. Downers Grove, IL: InterVarsity, 2002.
Kellahan, Michael. "Outsourcing Church: There Is a Cost." *Mission-Minded Church* (blog), March 24, 2009. https://sydneyanglicans.net/news/outsourcing_church_there_is_a_cost/.
Keller, Timothy J. *Center Church: Doing Balanced, Gospel-Centered Ministry in Your City*. Grand Rapids: Zondervan, 2012.
Kim, Kirsteen. *Joining in with the Spirit: Connecting World Church and Local Mission*. London: SCM, 2012.
Kim, Sebastian, and Kirsteen Kim. "Korean Missions: Joy over Obligation." *Missiology: An International Review* 48 (2020) 279–88.
Klink, Edward, and Darian Lockett. *Understanding Biblical Theology*. Grand Rapids: Zondervan, 2012.
Knox, D. Broughton. "The Biblical Concept of Fellowship." In *Church, Worship, and the Local Congregation*, edited by B. G. Webb, 59–82. Homebush West: Lancer, 1987.
———. "The Church, the Churches, and the Denominations of the Churches." *Reformed Theological Review* 48 (1989) 15–25.
———. "De-mythologizing the Church." In *Selected Works*. Vol. 2, *Church and Ministry*, edited by Kirsten Birkett, 23–32. Kingsford: Matthias Media, 2003.
———. "World Evangelism." In *Selected Works*. Vol. 2, *Church and Ministry*, edited by Kirsten Birkett, 225–32. Kingsford: Matthias Media, 2003.
Knox, D. Broughton, and Donald Robinson. "The Church Is a Missionary Society." *Australian Church Record* 22 (1957) 2.

Korcho, Mehari. "The Case for Missions in Ethiopian Diaspora Churches of America." In *Churches on Mission: God's Grace Abounding to the Nations*, edited by Geoffrey Hartt et al., 233–54. Pasadena, CA: William Carey Library, 2017.

Köstenberger, Andreas J., and Peter Thomas O'Brien. *Salvation to the Ends of the Earth: A Biblical Theology of Mission*. New Studies in Biblical Theology 11. Leicester, UK: Apollos, 2001.

Kuhn, Chase R. *The Ecclesiology of Donald Robinson and D. Broughton Knox: Exposition, Analysis, and Theological Evaluation*. Eugene, OR: Wipf & Stock, 2017.

Kuwana, Patrick. "Freedom to Live the Generous Life as God's Stewards." In *Christ-Centered Generosity: Global Perspectives on the Biblical Call to a Generous Life*, edited by R. Scott Rodin, Part IV. Colbert: Kingdom Life, 2015. Kindle.

Kwon, Seok-Woo, and Paul S. Adler. "Social Capital: Maturation of a Field of Research." *Academy of Management Review* 39 (2014) 412–22.

Kysar, Robert. *Stumbling in the Light: New Testament Images for a Changing Church*. St. Louis: Chalice, 1999.

Lausanne Movement. "The Cape Town Commitment." https://lausanne.org/statement/ctcommitment.

———. "The Lausanne Covenant." https://lausanne.org/statement/lausanne-covenant.

———. "The Local Church in Mission: Lausanne Occasional Paper 39." https://lausanne.org/occasional-paper/local-church-mission-lop-39.

———. "The Manila Manifesto." https://lausanne.org/statement/the-manila-manifesto.

Law, John. *After Method: Mess in Social Science Research*. London: Routledge, 2004.

Leffel, Gregory P. *Faith Seeking Action: Mission, Social Movements, and the Church in Motion*. Lanham, MD: Scarecrow, 2007.

Leonard, Rosemary, and John Bellamy. "Dimensions of Bonding Social Capital in Christian Congregations across Australia." *Voluntas: International Journal of Voluntary and Nonprofit Organizations* 26 (2015) 1046–65. https://doi.org/10.1007/s11266-015-9582-2/.

Liew Weng Cheung, Ivan. "Partnerships between Local Churches and Missions Agencies: Optimizing Missionary Mobilization and Member Care." DMin diss., Asbury Theological Seminary, 2013.

Lord, Andrew. *Network Church: A Pentecostal Ecclesiology Shaped by Mission*. Global Pentecostal and Charismatic Studies 11. Leiden: Brill, 2012.

Loy, David R. "The Religion of the Market." *Journal of the American Academy of Religion* 65 (1997) 275–90.

Luhmann, Niklas. *Introduction to Systems Theory*. Edited by Dirk Baecker. Translated by Peter Gilgen. Cambridge, UK: Polity, 2013.

Lynch, Mikey. "Dissecting the '5Ms'—Part 1: Portfolios." *Christian Reflections* (blog), December 4, 2013. https://genevapush.com/blogs/xian_reflections/dissecting-the-5ms-part-5-a-discipleship-pathway/.

Lyons, Brent J., and Brent A. Scott. "Integrating Social Exchange and Affective Explanations for the Receipt of Help and Harm: A Social Network Approach." *Organizational Behavior and Human Decision Processes* 117 (2012) 66–79. https://doi.org/10.1016/j.obhdp.2011.10.002/.

Mandryk, Jason. *Operation World*. 7th ed. Colorado Springs, CO: Biblica, 2010.

Manley, Ken R. "Conclusion: From Missionary Society to Mission in Partnership." In *From Five Barley Loaves: Australian Baptists in Global Mission, 1864–2010*, edited by Tony Cupit et al., 593–98. Northcote: Morning Star, 2014.

———. "Mission Policy and Leadership at Home, 1913–1957." In *From Five Barley Loaves: Australian Baptists in Global Mission, 1864–2010*, edited by Tony Cupit et al., 179–94. Northcote: Morning Star, 2014.

———. "Mission Policy and Leadership at Home, 1983–2010." In *From Five Barley Loaves: Australian Baptists in Global Mission, 1864–2010*, edited by Tony Cupit et al., 559–92. Northcote: Morning Star, 2014.

Marshall, Colin, and Tony Payne. *The Trellis and the Vine*. Kingsford: Matthias Media, 2009.

———. *The Vine Project: Shaping Your Ministry Culture around Disciple-Making*. Kingsford: Matthias Media, 2016.

Martin, Joanne. *Organizational Culture: Mapping the Terrain*. Thousand Oaks, CA: Sage, 2002.

Mascord, K. A. "Equipping the Local Church for Mission." In *Exploring the Missionary Church*, edited by B. G. Webb, 125–50. Homebush West: Lancer, 1993.

Matenga, Jay, and Malcolm Gold. *Mission in Motion: Speaking Frankly about Mobilization*. Globalization of Mission. Pasadena, CA: William Carey Library, 2016.

McGavran, Donald A. *The Bridges of God: A Study in the Strategy of Missions*. Eugene, OR: Wipf & Stock, 2005.

———. *Understanding Church Growth*. Grand Rapids: Eerdmans, 1970.

———. *Understanding Church Growth*. 2nd ed. Grand Rapids: Eerdmans, 1980.

McGavran, Donald A., and Win Arn. *How to Grow a Church*. Glendale, CA: Regal, 1973.

McGavran, Donald A., and C. Peter Wagner. *How Churches Grow: The New Frontiers of Mission*. New York: Friendship, 1966.

———. *Understanding Church Growth*. 3rd ed. Grand Rapids: Eerdmans, 1990.

Meeker, B. F. "Decisions and Exchange." *American Sociological Review* 36 (1971) 485–95.

Metcalf, Samuel F. "When Local Churches Act Like Agencies." *Evangelical Missions Quarterly* 29 (1993) 142–49.

Minear, Paul S. *Images of the Church in the New Testament*. Philadelphia: Westminster, 1960.

Missions Interlink. "The Croydon Declaration: Mission Leaders Express Regret." The Missions Commission of the Australian Evangelical Alliance Inc, August 2005.

Moltmann, Jurgen. *The Church in the Power of the Spirit: A Contribution to Messianic Ecclesiology*. London: SCM, 1977.

Morgan, Gareth. *Images of Organization*. San Francisco: Berrett-Koehler, 1998.

Morgan, J. Rupert. "Global Trends and the North American Church in Mission: Discovering the Church's Role in the Twenty-First Century." *International Bulletin of Mission Research* 40 (2016) 325–38.

Mott, John R. *The Decisive Hour of Christian Missions*. London: Church Missionary Society, 1910.

Moyes, Gordon. *How to Grow an Australian Church: A Practical Guide for Church Growth*. Glen Iris: Vital, 1975.

Murray, Andrew. *The Key to the Missionary Problem*. London: Nisbet, 1902.

Murray, Kevin. "Overseas Mission: Crisis and Opportunities." In *Burning or Bushed: The Presbyterian Church of Australia 40 Years On*, edited by Paul F. Cooper and David A. Burke, 244–57. Stanhope Gardens: Eider, 2017.

Nahapiet, Janine, and Sumantra Ghoshal. "Social Capital, Intellectual Capital, and the Organizational Advantage." *Academy of Management Review* 23 (1998) 242–66.
National Health and Medical Research Council. *National Statement on Ethical Conduct in Human Research 2007 (Updated 2018)*. Canberra: NHMRC, 2018. https://www.nhmrc.gov.au/guidelines/publications/e72
NCLS Research. *2016 NCLS: Leader Survey (LS1)*. Sydney: NCLS Research, 2016.
———. *2016 NCLS: Leader Survey (LS2)*. Sydney: NCLS Research, 2016.
———. *2016 NCLS: Operations Survey*. Sydney: NCLS Research, 2016.
Neill, Stephen. *Creative Tension*. London: Edinburgh House, 1959.
———. *A History of Christian Missions*. Harmondsworth: Penguin, 1964.
Newbigin, J. E. Lesslie. "Cross-Currents in Ecumenical and Evangelical Understandings of Mission." *International Bulletin of Missionary Research* 6 (1982) 146–51. https://doi.org/10.1177/239693938200600401/.
———. *Foolishness to the Greeks: The Gospel and Western Culture*. Grand Rapids: Eerdmans, 1986.
———. *The Gospel in a Pluralist Society*. Grand Rapids: Eerdmans, 1989.
———. "Mission and Missions." *Christianity Today*, August 1, 1960.
———. *One Body, One Gospel, One World: The Christian Mission Today*. London: International Missionary Council, 1958. https://newbiginresources.org/1958-one-body-one-gospel-one-world-the-christian-mission-today/.
———. *The Open Secret: An Introduction to the Theology of Mission*. Rev. ed. Grand Rapids: Eerdmans, 1995.
Noble, Richard A. *On Mission Together: Integrating Missions into the Local Church*. Beaver Falls, PA: Falls City, 2019.
Noll, Mark A., et al, eds. *Evangelicals: Who They Have Been, Are Now, and Could Be*. Grand Rapids: Eerdmans, 2019.
O'Brien, P. T. "The Church as a Heavenly and Eschatological Entity." In *The Church in the Bible and the World: An International Study*, edited by D. A. Carson, 88–119. Exeter, UK: Paternoster, 1987.
———. "The Fellowship Theme in Philippians." *Reformed Theological Review* 37 (1978) 9–18.
OMF. "6 Ways to Reach God's World." https://omf.org/video/6ways-overview/.
Osmer, Richard Robert. *Practical Theology: An Introduction*. Grand Rapids: Eerdmans, 2008.
Ostroff, Cheri, et al. "Organizational Culture and Climate." In *Handbook of Psychology: Industrial and Organizational Psychology*, edited by Neal W. Schmitt and Scott Highhouse, 12:643–76. 2nd ed. Hoboken, NJ: Wiley, 2012.
Ott, Craig. *The Church on Mission: A Biblical Vision for Transformation among All People*. Grand Rapids: Baker Academic, 2019.
———. *The Mission of the Church: Five Views in Conversation*. Grand Rapids: Baker Academic, 2016.
Parsons, Greg H. *Ralph D. Winter: Early Life and Core Missiology*. Pasadena, CA: William Carey International University Press, 2012.
Paterson, Cecily. *Never Alone: The Remarkable Story of David and Robyn Claydon*. Adelaide: SPCK-Australia, 2006.
Payne, Tony, et al. "Talking about Total Church (Part 1)." *The Briefing*, May 1, 2008. https://matthiasmedia.com/briefing/2008/05/talking-about-total-church-part-1/.

Pell, Edward Leigh. *Dwight L. Moody: His Life, His Work, His Words*. Richmond, VA: Johnson, 1900.

Pentecost, George F. "The Pastor in Relation to the Foreign Field." In *Ecumenical Missionary Conference, New York 1900: Report of the Ecumenical Conference on Foreign Missions, Held in Carnegie Hall and Neighboring Churches, April 21 to May 1*, edited by Edwin M. Bliss et al., 1:125–30. New York: American Tract Society, 1900.

Perkins, Gavin. "The Danger of Living the Gospel without Speaking the Gospel." *The Briefing*, July 17, 2008. http://thebriefing.com.au/2008/07/the-danger-of-living-the-gospel-without-speaking-the-gospel/.

Peterson, David. *Engaging with God: A Biblical Theology of Worship*. Downers Grove, IL: InterVarsity Press, 2002.

Pettigrew, Andrew M. "On Studying Organizational Cultures." *Administrative Science Quarterly* 24 (1979) 570–81.

Piggin, Stuart. "Australian Anglicanism in a World-Wide Context." In *Anglicanism in Australia: A History*, edited by Bruce Kaye, 200–222. Carlton South: Melbourne University Press, 2002.

———. "Evangelical Christianity in Australia." In *The Encyclopedia of Religion in Australia*, edited by James Jupp, 317–22. Port Melbourne: Cambridge University Press, 2009.

———. *Spirit, Word, and World: Evangelical Christianity in Australia*. Brunswick East: Acorn, 2012.

Piggin, Stuart, and Robert D. Linder. *Attending to the National Soul: Evangelical Christians in Australian History, 1914–2014*. Clayton: Monash University Publishing, 2020.

———. *The Fountain of Public Prosperity: Evangelical Christians in Australian History, 1740–1914*. Clayton: Monash University Publishing, 2018.

Pirolo, Neal. *Serving as Senders*. San Diego: Emmaus Road International, 1991.

———. *Serving as Senders Today*. San Diego: Emmaus Road International, 2012.

Plueddemann, James E. *Leading across Cultures: Effective Ministry and Mission in the Global Church*. Downers Grove, IL: IVP Academic, 2009.

Polkinghorne, Donald E. "Validity Issues in Narrative Research." *Qualitative Inquiry* 13 (2007) 471–86. https://doi.org/10.1177/1077800406297670/.

Powell, R., et al. *Research Profile 1807: Evangelical Churches Mission Support in Selected Denominations*. Sydney: NCLS Research, 2018. https://smbc.edu.au/ncls-profile-ts.

Powell, Ruth. "Part 1: Church Attendance Has Begun to Plateau." *YouTube*, February 11, 2020. https://www.youtube.com/watch?v=x8tUqu6M-ig/.

Powell, Ruth, and Mirriam Pepper. "Local Churches and Innovativeness: An Empirical Study of 2800 Australian Churches." In *Research in the Social Scientific Study of Religion*, edited by Andrew Village and Ralph W. Hoods, 29:278–301. Leiden: Brill, 2018.

———. "Local Churches in Australia: Research Findings from NCLS Research." Presented at the 2016 NCLS Church Life Pack Seminar, March 2017.

Priest, Robert J. "Introduction." In *Effective Engagement in Short-Term Missions: Doing It Right!*, edited by Robert J. Priest, i–ix. Pasadena, CA: William Carey Library, 2008.

Priest, Robert J., et al. "US Megachurches and New Patterns of Global Mission." *International Bulletin of Missionary Research* 34 (2010) 97–104.

Putnam, Robert D. *Bowling Alone: The Collapse and Revival of American Community*. New York: Simon & Schuster, 2000.

Putnam, Robert D., and David E. Campbell. *American Grace: How Religion Divides and Unites Us*. New York: Simon & Schuster, 2010.

Raiter, Michael. "'Sent for This Purpose': 'Mission' and 'Missiology' and Their Search for Meaning." In *Ripe for Harvest: Christian Mission in the New Testament and Our World*, edited by Richard J. Gibson, 106–49. Carlisle: Paternoster, 1998.

———. "Social Involvement and Evangelism (Part III): Some Final Reflections." *The Briefing*, February 1, 2005. http://matthiasmedia.com/briefing/2005/02/social-involvement-and-evangelism-part-iii-some-final-reflections/.

Reach Australia. "About Us." https://reachaustralia.com.au/about-us/.

Reese, Robert. "John Gatu and the Moratorium on Missionaries." *Missiology: An International Review* 42 (2014) 245–56.

Reisacher, Evelyne A. *Joyful Witness in the Muslim World: Sharing the Gospel in Everyday Encounters*. Grand Rapids: Baker Academic, 2016.

Robinson, Donald. "Church." In *New Bible Dictionary*, edited by J. D. Douglas, 1:222–29. Downers Grove, IL: InterVarsity, 1962.

———. "The Church of God: Its Form and Unity." In *Donald Robinson Selected Works*. Vol. 1, *Assembling God's People*, edited by Peter Bolt and Mark Thompson, 230–53. Camperdown: Australian Church Record, 2008.

———. "'The Church' Revisited: An Autobiographical Fragment." *The Reformed Theological Review* 48 (1989) 4–14.

———. "The Doctrine of the Church and Its Implications for Evangelism." In *Donald Robinson Selected Works*. Vol. 2, *Preaching God's Word*, edited by Peter Bolt and Mark Thompson, 103–13. Camperdown: Australian Church Record, 2008.

———. "Liturgical Patterns of Worship." In *Donald Robinson Selected Works*. Vol. 1, *Assembling God's People*, edited by Peter Bolt and Mark Thompson, 318–36. Camperdown: Australian Church Record, 2008.

———. "WCC Assembly." *Australian Church Record*, July 22, 1954.

Rodin, R. Scott. "A Vision for the Generous Life." In *Christ-Centered Generosity: Global Perspectives on the Biblical Call to a Generous Life*, edited by R. Scott Rodin, Part I. Colbert: Kingdom Life, 2015. Kindle.

Sampley, J. Paul. *Pauline Partnership in Christ: Christian Community and Commitment in Light of Roman Law*. Philadelphia: Fortress, 1980.

Saukani, Nasir, and Noor Azina Ismail. "Identifying the Components of Social Capital by Categorical Principal Component Analysis (CATPCA)." *Social Indicators Research* 141 (2019) 631–55. https://doi.org/10.1007/s11205-018-1842-2/.

Schein, Edgar H. *Organizational Culture and Leadership*. 4th ed. The Jossey-Bass Business & Management Series 2. San Francisco: Jossey-Bass, 2010.

Schnabel, Eckhard J. *Early Christian Mission: Paul and the Early Church*. Downers Grove, IL: InterVarsity, 2004.

Schneider, Jo Anne. "Organizational Social Capital and Nonprofits." *Nonprofit and Voluntary Sector Quarterly* 38 (2009) 643–62. https://doi.org/10.1177/0899764 009333956/.

Schwadel, Philip, et al. "Social Networks and Civic Participation and Efficacy in Two Evangelical Protestant Churches." *Review of Religious Research* 58 (2016) 305–17. https://doi.org/10.1007/s13644-015-0237-y/.

Sexton, J. S. *Four Views on the Church's Mission*. Counterpoints. Bible & Theology. Grand Rapids: Zondervan, 2017.

Shaw, Mark. "Robert Wuthnow and World Christianity: A Response to Boundless Faith." *International Bulletin of Missionary Research* 36 (2012) 179–84.

Shiner, Rory J. W. "Reading the New Testament in Australia: An Historical Account of the Origins, Development, and Influence of D. W. B. Robinson's Biblical Scholarship." PhD diss., Macquarie University, 2017.

Silberman, Tim. "Un-Missional Church? Knox-Robinson Ecclesiology and the Mission of the Local Church." *Colloquium: The Australian and New Zealand Theological Review* 51 (2019) 61–76.

Skreslet, Stanley H. *Picturing Christian Witness: New Testament Images of Disciples in Mission*. Grand Rapids: Eerdmans, 2006.

Spitters, Denny, and Matthew Ellison, eds. *Conversations on When Everything Is Missions: Recovering the Mission of the Church*. Mumbai: Bottomline Media, 2020.

———, eds. *When Everything Is Missions*. Mumbai: Bottomline Media, 2017.

Stackhouse, John G., ed. *Evangelical Ecclesiology: Reality or Illusion?* Grand Rapids: Baker Academic, 2003.

———. "Evangelicalism and Restorational Ecclesiologies." In *T. & T. Clark Handbook of Ecclesiology*, edited by Kimlyn J. Bender and D. Stephen Long, 259–73. London: Bloomsbury, 2020.

Stanley, Brian. *The Global Diffusion of Evangelicalism: The Age of Billy Graham and John Scott*. Downers Grove, IL: InterVarsity, 2013.

Sterland, S. *Support for People in Developing Countries by Australian Churches*. NCLS Research Fact Sheet 14026. Adelaide: Mirrabooka, 2014.

Sterland, S., and N. Hancock. *Australian Church Attenders on Overseas Mission Trips 2015–2016*. NCLS Research Fact Sheet 17010. Sydney: NCLS Research, 2017.

———. *Mission Trips Organised by Australian Churches 2015–2016*. NCLS Research Fact Sheet 17008. Sydney: NCLS Research, 2017.

———. *Support for Overseas Workers by Australian Protestant Churches in 2016*. NCLS Research Fact Sheet 17009. Sydney: NCLS Research, 2017.

———. *Support for People in Developing Countries by Australian Churches in 2016*. NCLS Research Fact Sheet 17007. Sydney: NCLS Research, 2017.

Stetzer, Ed. "Five Reasons Missional Churches Don't Do Global Missions—and How to Fix It." *Christianity Today*, September 24, 2009. http://www.christianitytoday.com/edstetzer/2009/september/five-reasons-missional-churches-dont-do-global-missions.html/.

———. "Missional and Missions." In *Conversations on When Everything Is Missions: Recovering the Mission of the Church*, edited by Denny Spitters and Matthew Ellison, 37–50. Mumbai: Bottomline Media, 2020.

Stott, John. *Christian Mission in the Modern World*. Downers Grove, IL: InterVarsity, 1975.

Strauss, Anselm L., and Juliet M. Corbin. *Basics of Qualitative Research: Grounded Theory Procedures and Techniques*. Newbury Park, CA: Sage, 1990.

Stroope, Michael W. *Transcending Mission: The Eclipse of a Modern Tradition*. Downers Grove, IL: IVP Academic, 2017.

Swinton, John, and Harriet Mowatt. *Practical Theology and Qualitative Research*. 2nd ed. London: SCM, 2016.

Sydney Diocesan Doctrine Commission. *A Theology of Christian Assembly*. Sydney: Anglican Diocese of Sydney, 2008.

Syn, M. W. "An Extended Model for Partnership between Mission Agencies and Churches in Singapore." DMin diss., Biola University, 2016.

———. *On Being the Antioch of Asia: Global Missions and Missions Partnership through Asian Lenses*. Singapore: Genesis, 2017.

Szreter, S., and Michael Woolcock. "Health by Association? Social Capital, Social Theory, and the Political Economy of Public Health." *International Journal of Epidemiology* 33 (2004) 650–67.

Taylor, William David, ed. *Global Missiology for the 21st Century: The Iguassu Dialogue*. Grand Rapids: Baker Academic, 2000.

Telford, Tom, and Lois Shaw. *Today's All-Star Missions Churches: Strategies to Help Your Church Get into the Game*. Grand Rapids: Baker, 2001.

Tennent, Timothy C. *Invitation to World Missions: A Trinitarian Missiology for the Twenty-First Century*. Grand Rapids: Kregel, 2010.

Tertullian. "On Idolatry." In *Ante-Nicene Fathers: The Writings of the Fathers Down to A.D. 325*. Vol. 3, *Latin Christianity: Its Founder, Tertullian*, edited by Alexander Roberts, et al., 61–77. Peabody, MA: Hendrickson, 1994.

Thomas, M. M. "Salvation and Humanization: A Crucial Issue in the Theology of Mission for India." *International Review of Mission* 60 (1971) 25–38.

Thompson, Mark. "Church, Mission, Evangelism, and Programs." *Theological Theology* (blog), April 14, 2010. http://markdthompson.blogspot.com/2010/04/church-mission-evangelism-and-programs.html/.

———. "Does the Local Church Have a Mission?" In *Exploring the Missionary Church*, edited by B. G. Webb, 1–26. Homebush West: Lancer, 1993.

Thrasher, William D. "Joy." In *Evangelical Dictionary of World Missions*, edited by A. Scott Moreau et al., 527. Grand Rapids: Baker, 2000.

Tidball, Derek J. *Who Are the Evangelicals? Tracing the Roots of Today's Movement*. London: Pickering, 1994.

Tongoi, Dennis. "Living Generously in an African Culture." In *Christ-Centered Generosity: Global Perspectives on the Biblical Call to a Generous Life*, edited by R. Scott Rodin, Part III. Colbert: Kingdom Life, 2015. Kindle.

Trinity Church Missionary Care Team, and David J. Wilson. *Mind the Gaps: Engaging the Church in Missionary Care*. New Kensington: Whitaker House, 2015.

Van Gelder, Craig, and Dwight J. Zscheile. *The Missional Church in Perspective: Mapping Trends and Shaping the Conversation*. The Missional Network Series. Grand Rapids: Baker Academic, 2011.

VanHuis, Michael. *2016 Mission CEO and Church Mission Leader Survey: Traversing the Global Landscape*. Wheaton, IL: Missio Nexus, 2016.

———. *Church Missions Leader Survey: Report and Analysis 2019*. Wheaton, IL: Missio Nexus, 2019.

Vatican II. "Ad Gentes: Decree on the Missionary Activity of the Church." In *Vatican Council II: The Conciliar and Post Conciliar Documents*, edited by Austin Flannery, 813–56. Northport: Costello, 1975.

Ver Beek, Kurt Alan. "Lessons from the Sapling: Review of Quantitative Research on Short-Term Missions." In *Effective Engagement in Short-Term Missions: Doing It Right!*, edited by Robert J. Priest, 475–97. Pasadena, CA: William Carey Library, 2008.

Vermeer, Paul, and Peer Scheepers. "Bonding or Bridging? Volunteering among the Members of Six Thriving Evangelical Congregations in the Netherlands." *Voluntas: International Journal of Voluntary and Nonprofit Organizations* 30 (2019) 962–75. https://doi.org/10.1007/s11266-019-00160-1/.

Verster, Pieter, and Frans Hancke. "Common 'Critical Success Factors' That Determine the Mission Impact of the Local Church: Results from an Analytical Study." *Missionalia* 32 (2004) 102–20.
Vicedom, Georg F. *The Mission of God: An Introduction to a Theology of Mission.* Translated by Gilbert A. Thiele and Dennis Hilgendorf. Saint Louis: Concordia, 1965.
Visser't Hooft, W. A. *The Genesis and Formation of the World Council of Churches.* Geneva: World Council of Churches, 1982.
Volf, Miroslav. "Being as God Is: Trinity and Generosity." In *God's Life in Trinity*, edited by Miroslav Volf and Michael Welker, 3–12. Minneapolis: Fortress, 2006.
Wagner, C. Peter. "Church Growth Movement." In *Evangelical Dictionary of World Missions*, edited by A. Scott Moreau et al., 199–200. Grand Rapids: Baker, 2000.
———. "Colour the Moratorium Grey." *International Review of Mission* 64 (1975) 165–76.
———. *Leading Your Church to Growth.* Ventura, CA: Regal, 1984.
———. *Your Church Can Grow.* Rev. ed. Ventura, CA: Regal, 1984.
———. *Your Spiritual Gifts Can Help Grow Your Church.* Glendale, CA: Regal, 1979.
Wainwright, Geoffrey. *Lesslie Newbigin: A Theological Life.* New York: Oxford University Press, 2000.
Walls, Andrew F. *The Missionary Movement in Christian History: Studies in the Transmission of Faith.* Maryknoll, NY: Orbis, 1996.
Ward, Pete. *Perspectives on Ecclesiology and Ethnography.* Grand Rapids: Eerdmans, 2012.
Warner, Rob. *Reinventing English Evangelicalism, 1966–2001.* Milton Keynes: Paternoster, 2007.
Warren, Rick. *The Purpose Driven Church: Growth without Compromising Your Message and Mission.* Grand Rapids: Zondervan, 1995.
Webb, Allan. *Your Church Can Make a World of Difference.* Epping: Hudson, 2005.
Webb, B. G., ed. *Church, Worship, and the Local Congregation.* Homebush West: Lancer, 1987.
———, ed. *Exploring the Missionary Church.* Homebush West: Lancer, 1993.
Weber, Max. *Protestant Work Ethic and the Spirit of Capitalism.* Translated by Talcott Parsons. New York: Start, 2013.
Williams, David Alun. "Relocating Holism: A Theology of Care for the Poor in Conversation with Sydney Anglicanism." DMiss diss., Fuller Theological Seminary, 2017.
Wilson, David J., and Lorene Wilson, eds. *Pipeline: Engaging the Church in Missionary Mobilization.* Littleton, CO: Carey, 2018.
Winter, Ralph D. "Churches Need Missions Because Modalities Need Sodalities." *Evangelical Missions Quarterly* 7 (1971) 195–200.
———. "Protestant Mission Societies: The American Experience." *Missiology: An International Review* 7 (1979) 139–78.
———. "Three Mission Eras: And the Loss and Recovery of Kingdom Mission, 1800–2000." In *Perspectives on the World Christian Movement: A Reader*, edited by Ralph D. Winter and Steven C. Hawthorne, 263–78. 4th ed. Pasadena, CA: William Carey Library, 2009.
———. "The Two Structures of God's Redemptive Mission." *Missiology: An International Review* 2 (1974) 121–39.

Woodhouse, John. "Evangelism and Social Responsibility." In *Christians in Society*, edited by B. G. Webb, 3–26. Homebush West: Lancer, 1988.

Woolcock, Michael, and Deepa Narayan. "Social Capital: Implications for Development Theory, Research, and Policy." *The World Bank Research Observer* 15 (2000) 225–49.

Wright, Christopher J. H. *The Mission of God: Unlocking the Bible's Grand Narrative*. Downers Grove, IL: InterVarsity, 2006.

———. *The Mission of God's People: A Biblical Theology of the Church's Mission*. Grand Rapids: Zondervan, 2010.

Wu, Jeanne. *Mission through Diaspora: The Case of the Chinese Church in the USA*. Carlisle: Langham Monographs, 2016.

Wuthnow, Robert. *All in Sync: How Music and Art Are Revitalizing American Religion*. Berkeley: University of California Press, 2003.

———. *Boundless Faith: The Global Outreach of American Churches*. Berkeley: University of California Press, 2009.

———. *Faith and Giving: From Christian Charity to Spiritual Practice*. The Center on Philanthropy at Indiana University, 2004. http://hdl.handle.net/1805/5898.

Yale Center for Faith & Culture. "Theology of Joy & the Good Life." https://faith.yale.edu/legacy-projects/theology-of-joy.

Young, F. Lionel. *World Christianity and the Unfinished Task: A Very Short Introduction*. Eugene, OR: Cascade, 2021.

Zehner, Edwin. "On the Rhetoric of Short-Term Mission Appeals, with Some Practical Suggestions for Team Leaders." In *Effective Engagement in Short-Term Missions: Doing It Right!*, edited by Robert J. Priest, 185–207. Pasadena, CA: William Carey Library, 2008.

Zohar, Dov, and David A. Hofmann. "Organizational Culture and Climate." In *The Oxford Handbook of Organizational Psychology*, edited by Steve W. J. Kozlowski, 1:633–66. New York: Oxford University Press, 2012.

Zurlo, Gina A., et al. "World Christianity and Mission 2020: Ongoing Shift to the Global South." *International Bulletin of Mission Research* 44 (2020) 8–19.

www.ingramcontent.com/pod-product-compliance
Lightning Source LLC
Chambersburg PA
CBHW061431300426
44114CB00014B/1634